I0901645

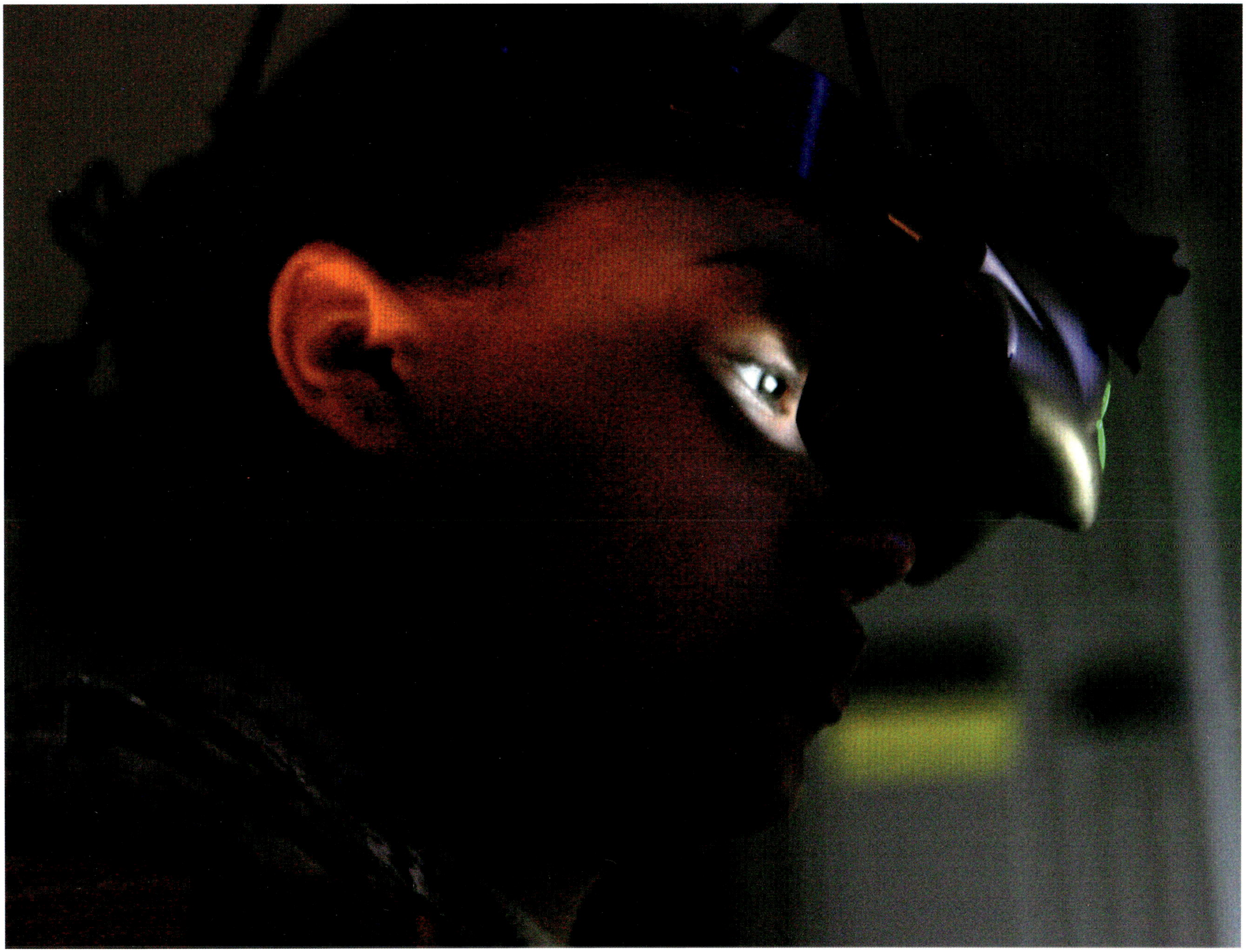

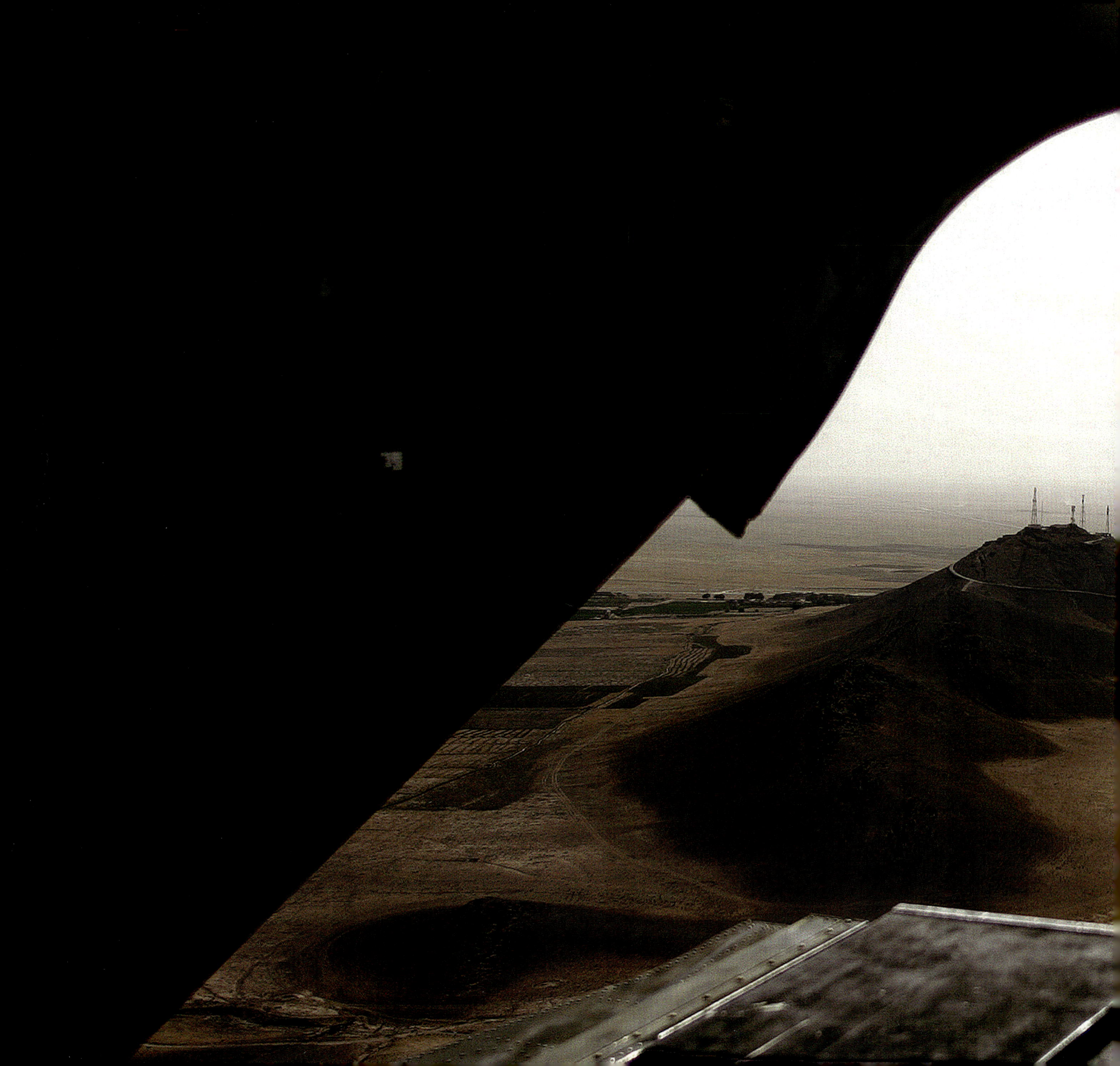

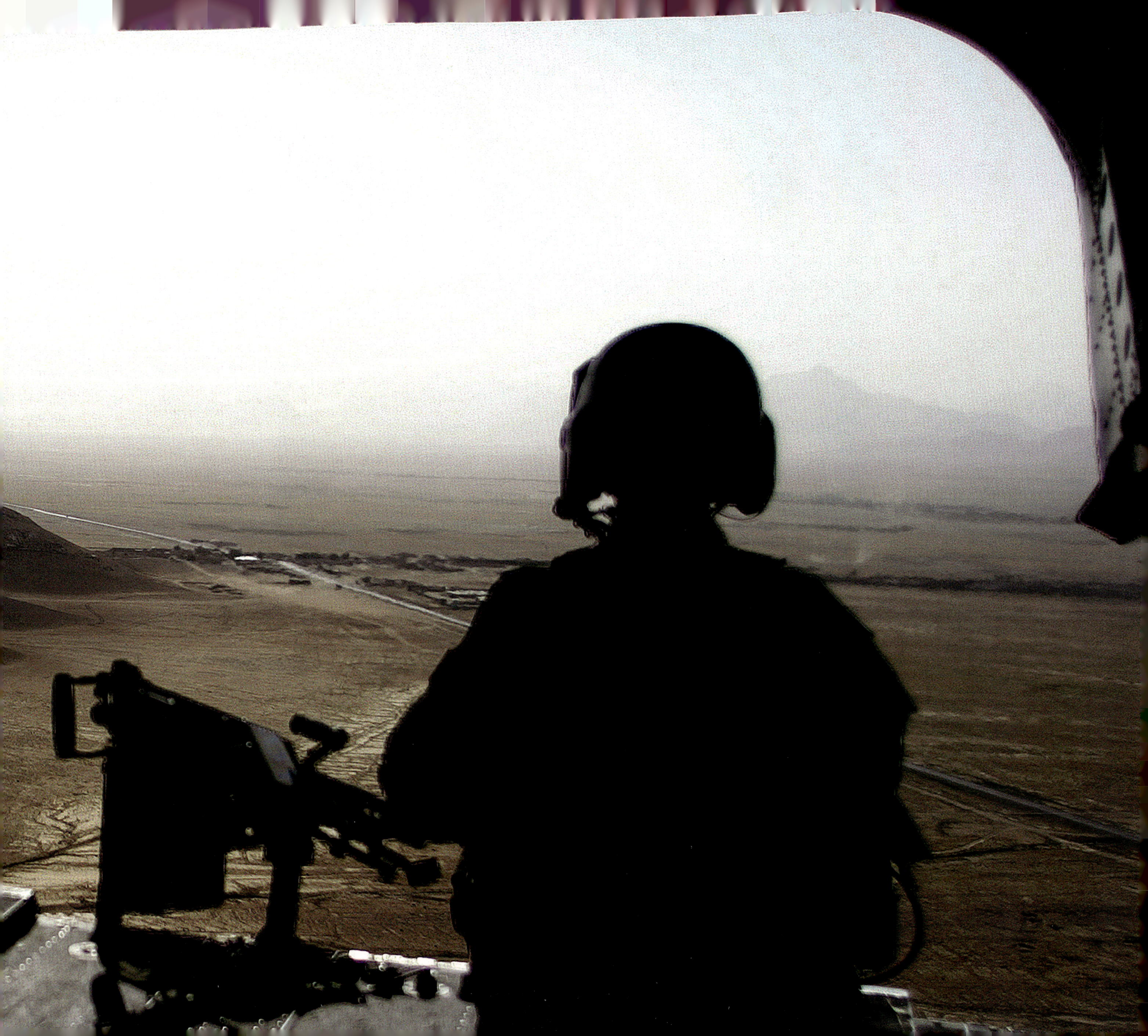

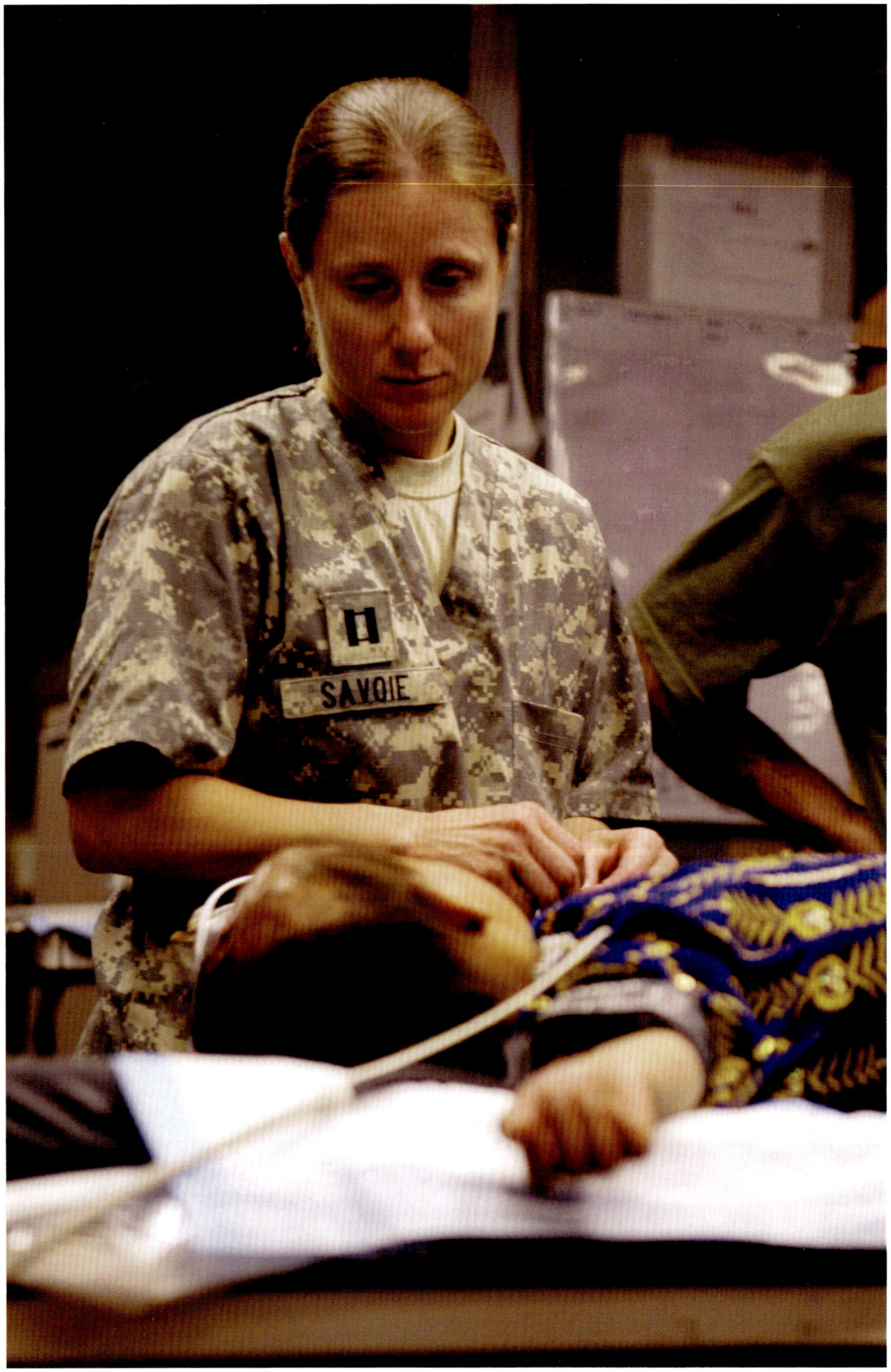
SAVOIE

America's Women Down Range

Steven Clevenger

MUSEUM OF NEW MEXICO PRESS
SANTA FE, NEW MEXICO

Dedicated to my mother Thelma
and my father Keith Clevenger
who did their part in fighting fascism,
a struggle that continues today.

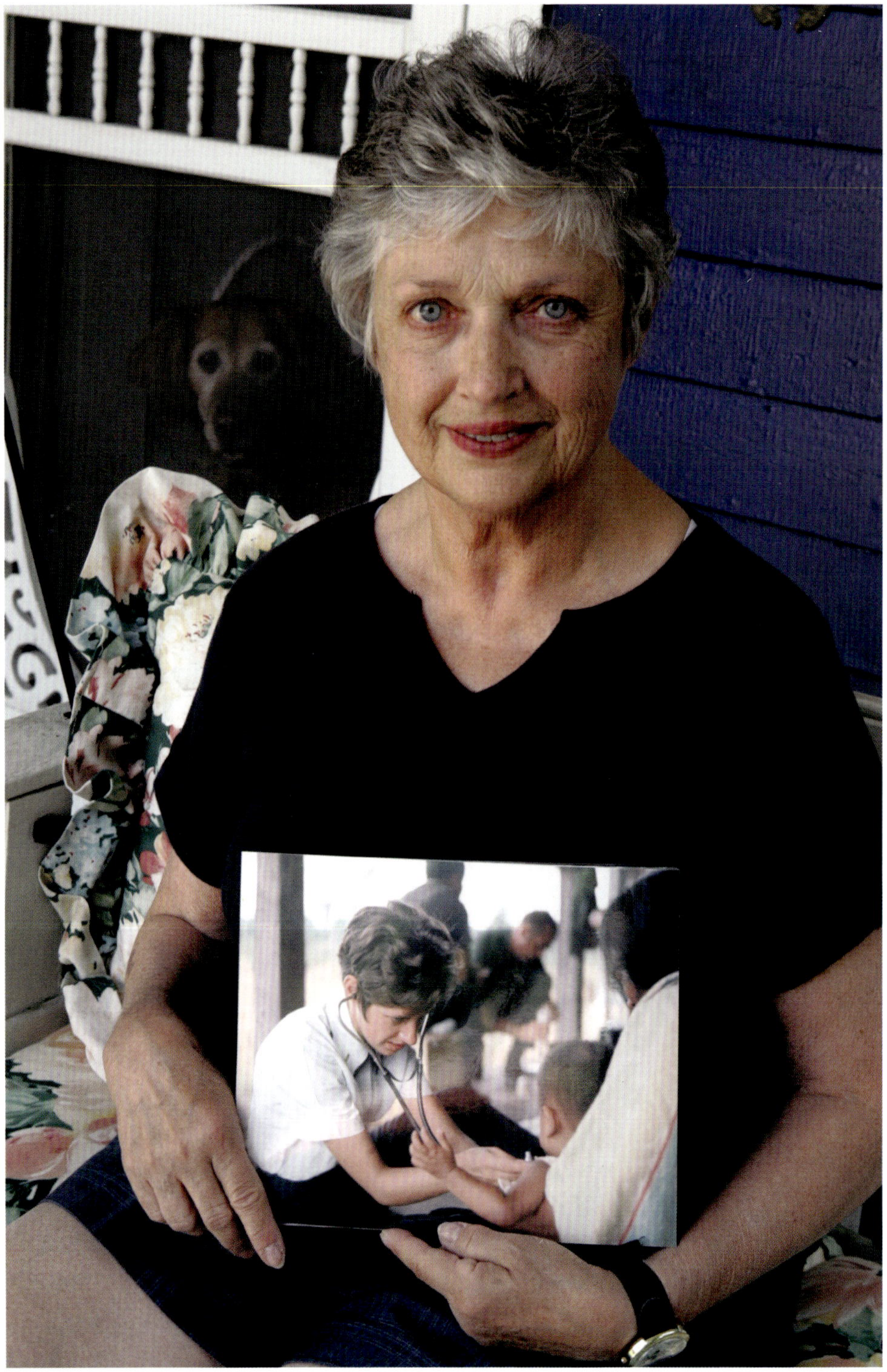

Barbara Mahoney sits on her front porch holding a photo of herself as a nurse in Thailand while treating a local youth. Mahoney served as a US Air Force nurse in a remote Thailand base during the Vietnam War. Her dog watches from inside the house.

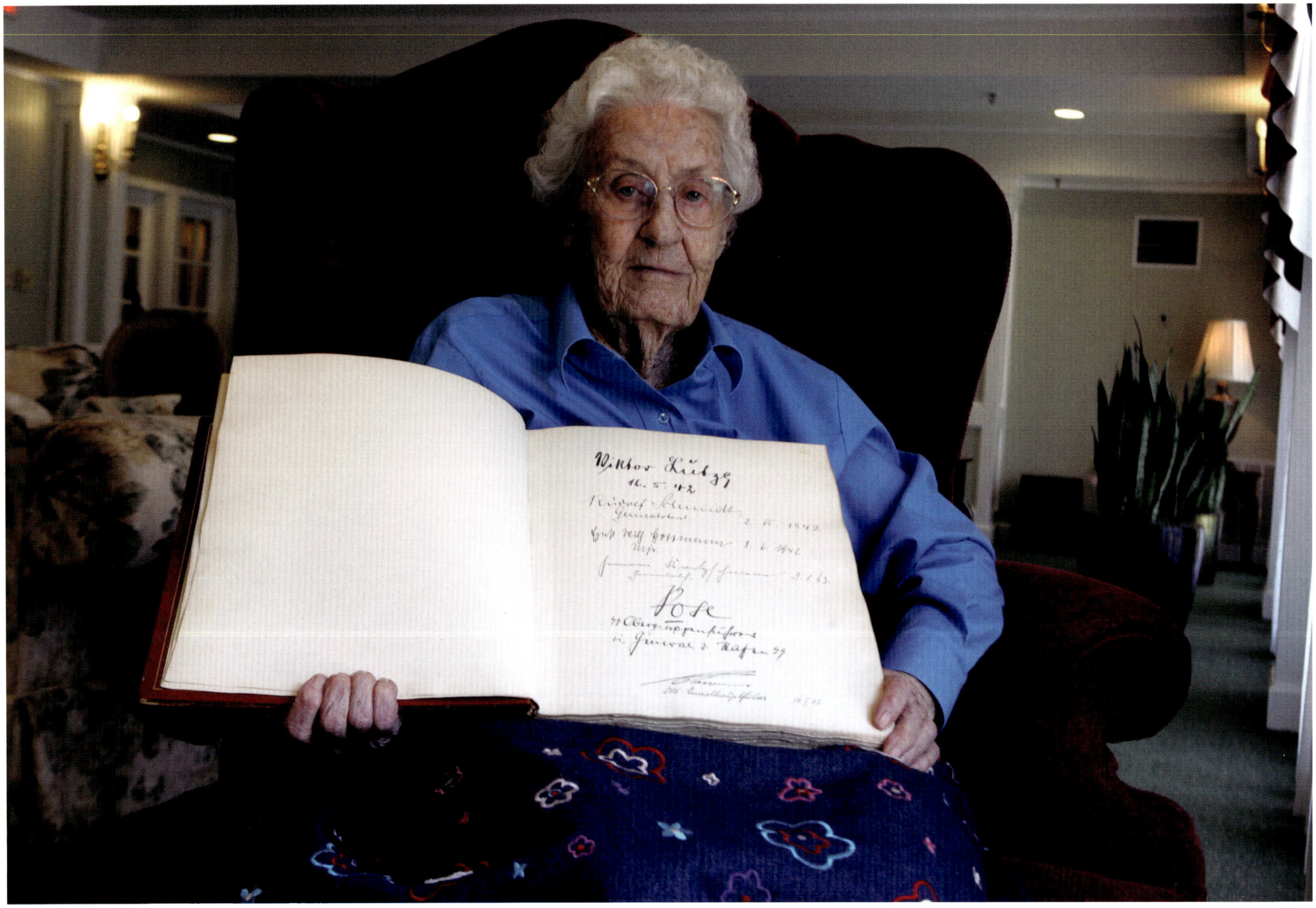

WWII Red Cross veteran Janet Blair holds a Nazi guest book. Entering a spa shortly after the staff had evacuated, she picked up the spa guest book intending to use it as a photo album. Later, she realized from the signatures in the book that the spa had served high-level Nazis.

Preface

by Steven Clevenger

Down range. In military slang, "down range" is a term for being deployed overseas, usually in a war zone. It can also refer to the direction of fire: away from the source and in the direction of the target.

Former US Army military police officer Roselle Graskey, one of the women interviewed in this book, defines "down range" as any area that may include someone who could hurt you. "When I'm down range, my head is on a swivel, and I maintain situational awareness," Graskey says. "Worked back when I was in the army, works still." Graskey deployed to Iraq in 1990 to guard Iraqi prisoners who had been captured during the Gulf War, a position not available to previous generations of women in the military.

In January 2013, Defense Secretary Leon E. Panetta lifted the ban on women in combat roles and gave the military three years to complete integration.[1] By August 2015, two women had completed the grueling Army Ranger School in Fort Benning, Georgia, leading to a decree from the Pentagon that all combat jobs were to be open to women.[2] The decision to open combat jobs to women is important not only because it expands the roles women can take in the military, but also because it creates opportunities for women to advance into the highest ranks of the military. Combat experience is considered critical to obtaining higher rankings.

The issue of females becoming integrated into combat units remains a controversial subject. Some argue that the presence of women is disruptive to unit cohesion. Male members could be overly protective of female members and, in doing so, endanger the mission. The presence of women could lead to sexual tension and harassment. The difference in a woman's upper-body strength compared to that of a man could slow down a unit in completing various tasks. Others argue that women bring skills and insights to the fight that men don't typically excel in or possess. For example, female members of the army and marines can interact with certain Muslim women in ways that may be impossible for males to do because of cultural traditions and practices.

Women have a long yet underappreciated history in the American military, having served in every conflict from the American Revolution to the current War on Terror. From their days as cooks and nurses to the combat roles they fulfill today, women continue to have a powerful and lasting impact within the military. The first women to serve in the military typically did so because their husbands were fighting in the American Revolution. These women were mostly cooks, nurses, and laundresses, and their supportive roles enabled combat soldiers to stay healthy on the front lines.

I became interested in pursuing this project on women in the military while working on my previous book, *America's First Warriors* (Museum of New Mexico Press, 2010), a study of Native American veterans. While embedded with a New Mexico National Guard unit in Iraq, I noticed the large numbers of women who had been deployed. Many of these women were filling combat positions. I felt that their stories should be told.

My method of developing the contents of the book involved "embeds" in both Iraq and Afghanistan. While there, I photographed active-duty women performing their jobs, and I photographed and interviewed women included in this book. In my search for veterans, I went to events in the United States where I knew female veterans would be in attendance, events such as the Department of Defense Warrior Games. I contacted individual veterans, both retired and active-duty, through organizations that serve veterans, including two different homeless outreach programs. Another organization, specializing in psychological counseling, also collaborated with me by providing me with the name of one of their clients after gaining her permission. Frankly, I avoided the US Department of Veterans Affairs, anticipating lots of paperwork and government reluctance to cooperate with me as a member of the press. I also felt that contacting smaller veteran outreach groups would provide greater access to veterans, and that one interviewed veteran would lead to the next.

An examination of the ongoing role of women in military history shows an increase in high-ranking positions held by females. As the evolution of women in the military continues, the United States is on track toward fully utilizing the power, intelligence, and influence of female military leaders.

NOTES

1. Elisabeth Bumiller and Thom Shanker, "Pentagon Is Set to Lift Combat Ban for Women," published January 23, 2013. https://www.nytimes.com/2013/01/24/us/pentagon-says-it-is-lifting-ban-on-women-in-combat.html

2. Joe Lacdan, "First enlisted female to graduate from Ranger School reflects on experience," published August 28, 2019. https://www.army.mil/article/226137/first_enlisted_female_to_graduate_from_ranger_school_reflects_on_experience

America's Women Down Range

Women in Service

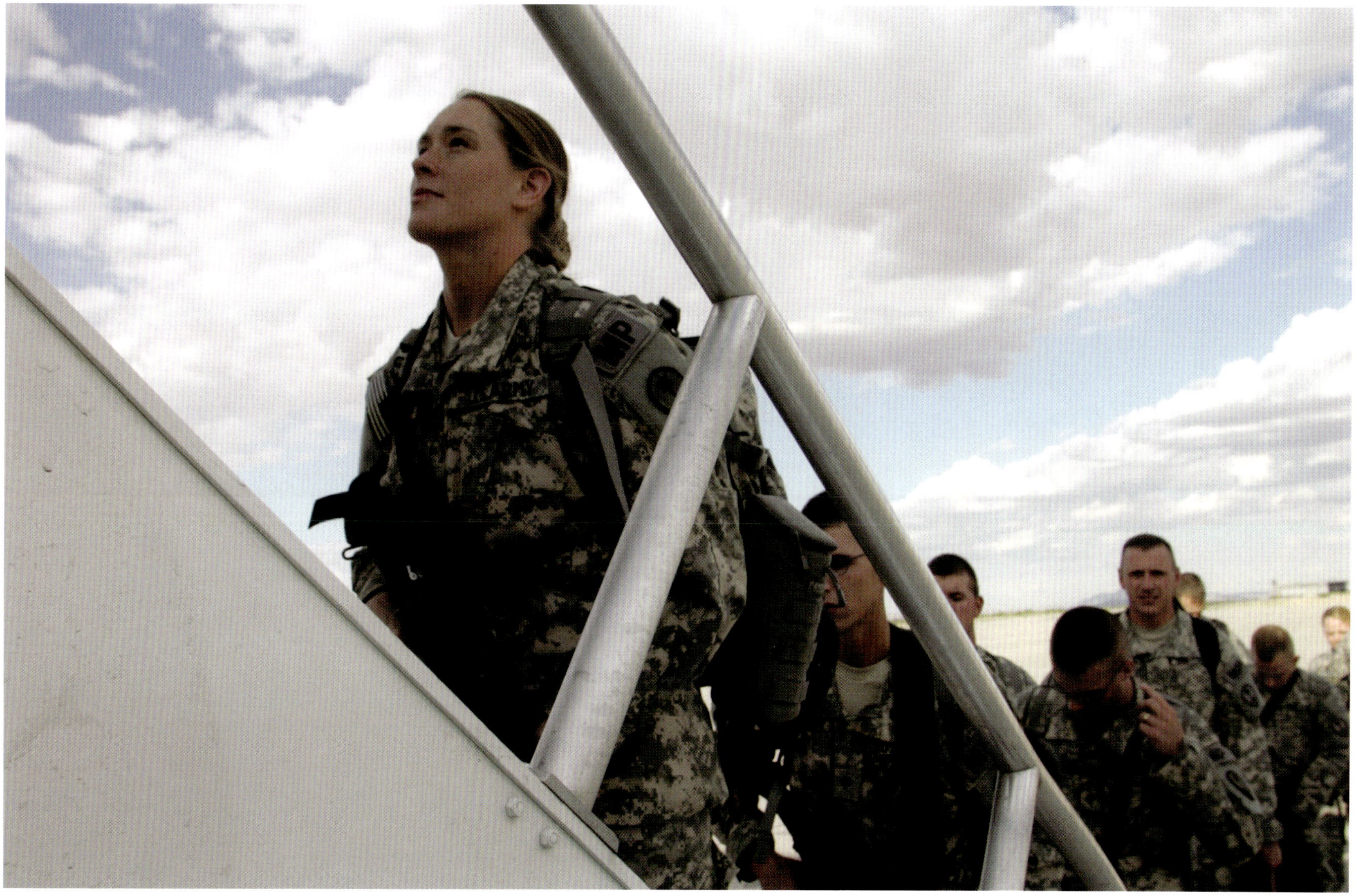

A female military police officer climbs the stairs to a charter aircraft located in El Paso for a flight to Afghanistan.

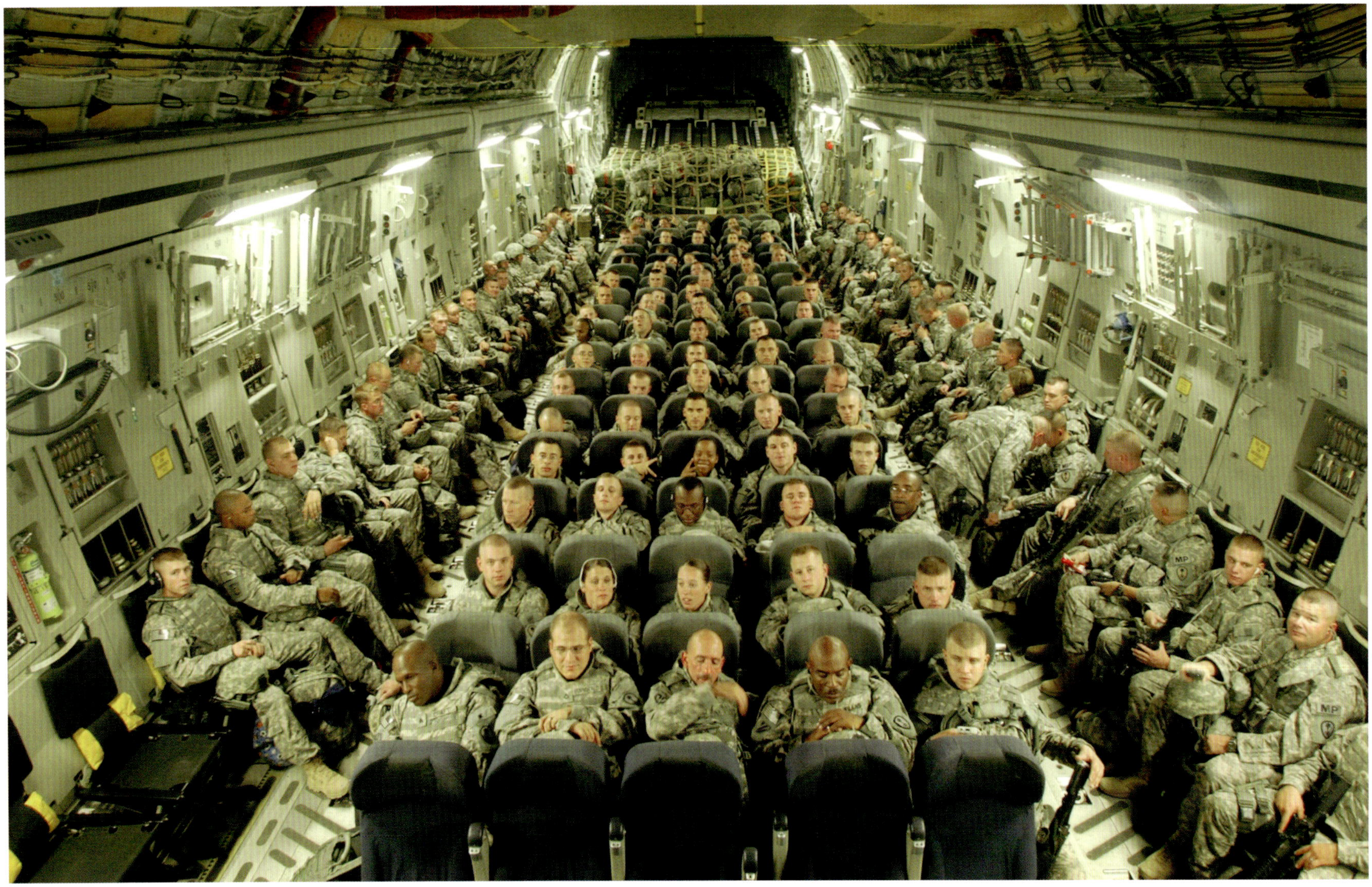

During their flight from Kyrgyzstan to Afghanistan, soldiers are wide awake.
In Kyrgyzstan, the troops were transferred from a civilian contract airliner to a military transport.

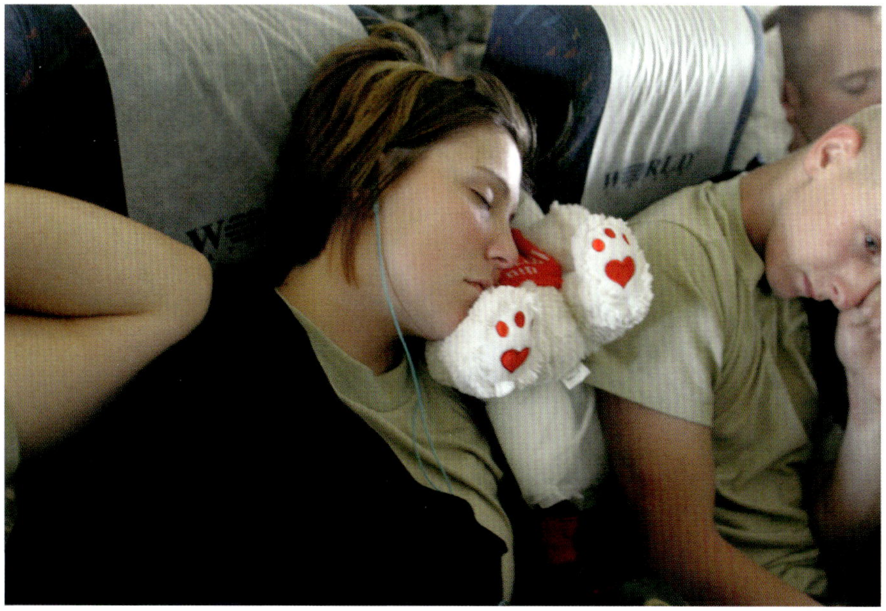

A female member of an MP company sleeps during the company's flight to Afghanistan, where they will be deployed for a year.

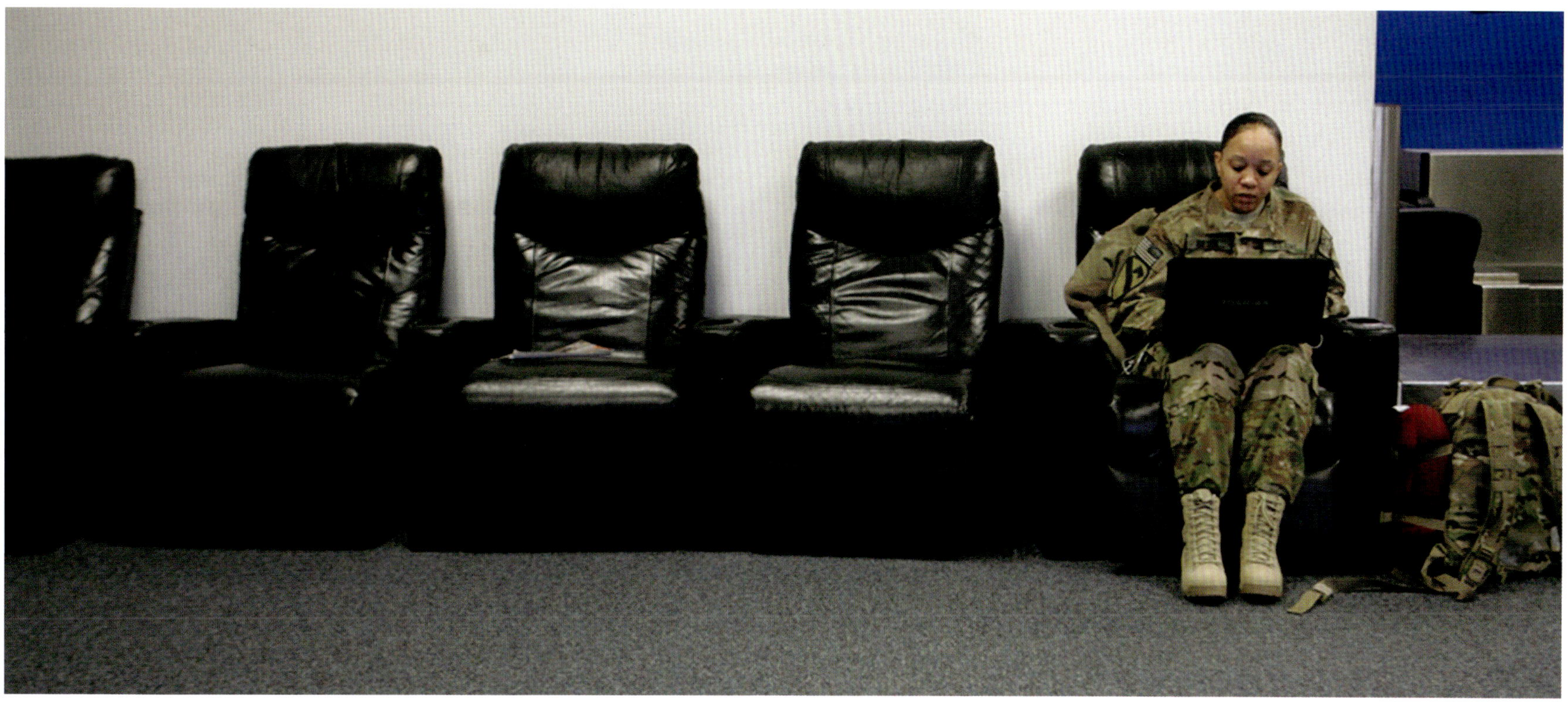

1SG Geter waits to check in at Dallas/Fort Worth International Airport for her return flight to Kuwait, where she had been deployed. Geter had been on a two-week rest and recreation leave. During her leave, she visited her two children in South Carolina.

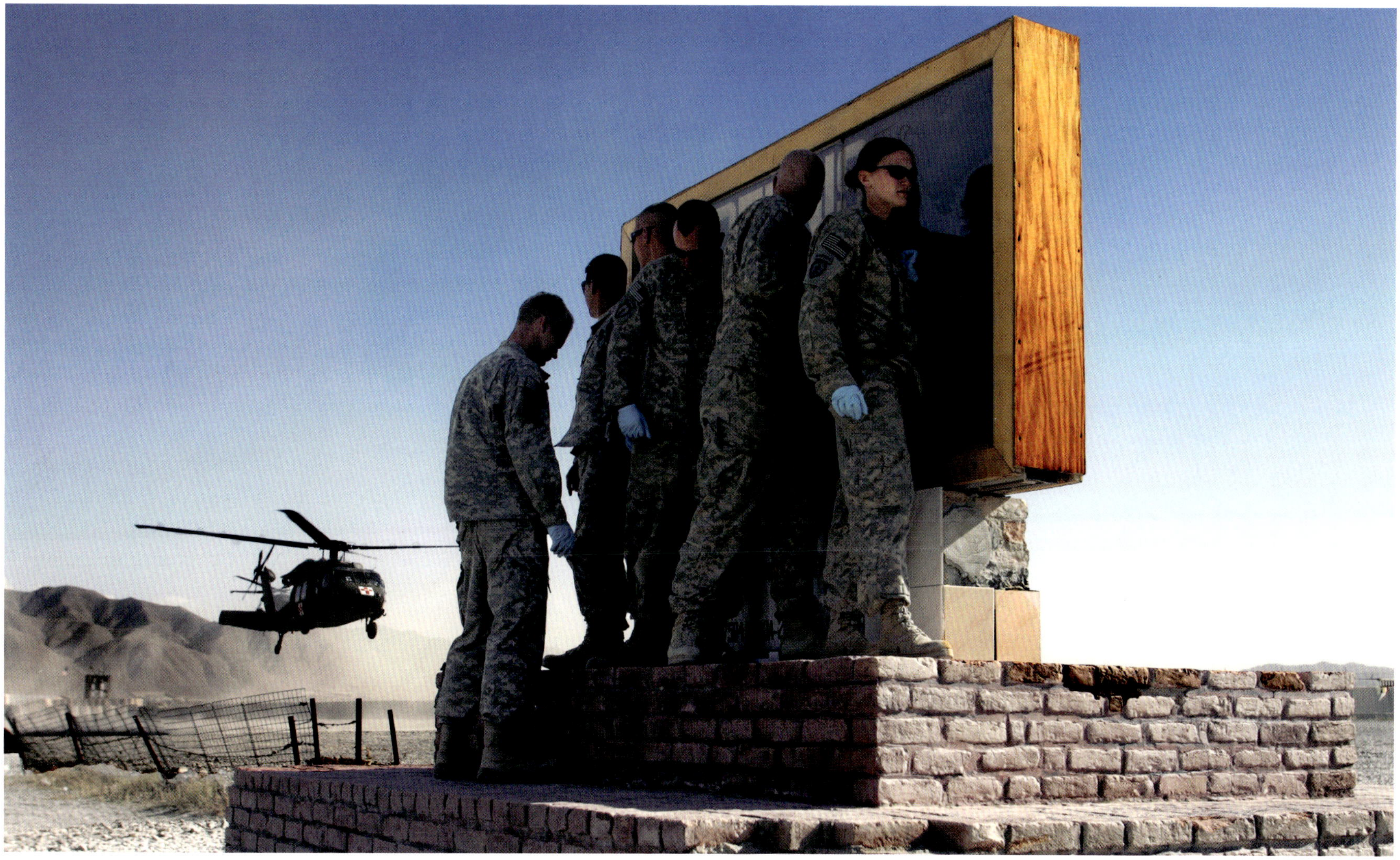

Flight line workers use a sign identifying Forward Operating Base Orgun-E [FOB O-E] to block the downwash of an approaching medevac helicopter. The chopper is carrying an injured Afghan who was treated at the base by a Forward Surgical Team [FST].

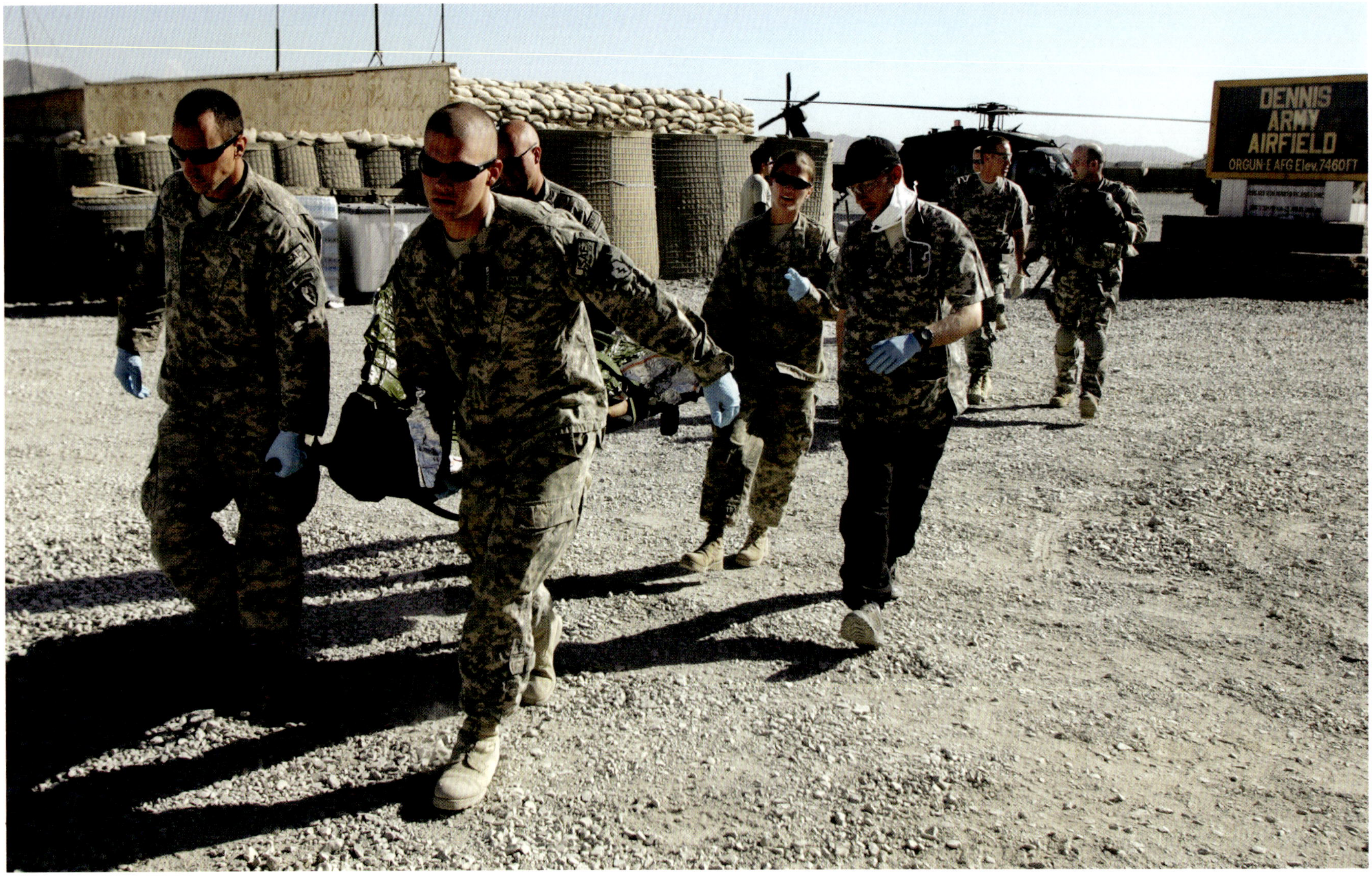

Ground crew along with an FST doctor transport a patient from a medevac helicopter to the base hospital on FOB O-E.

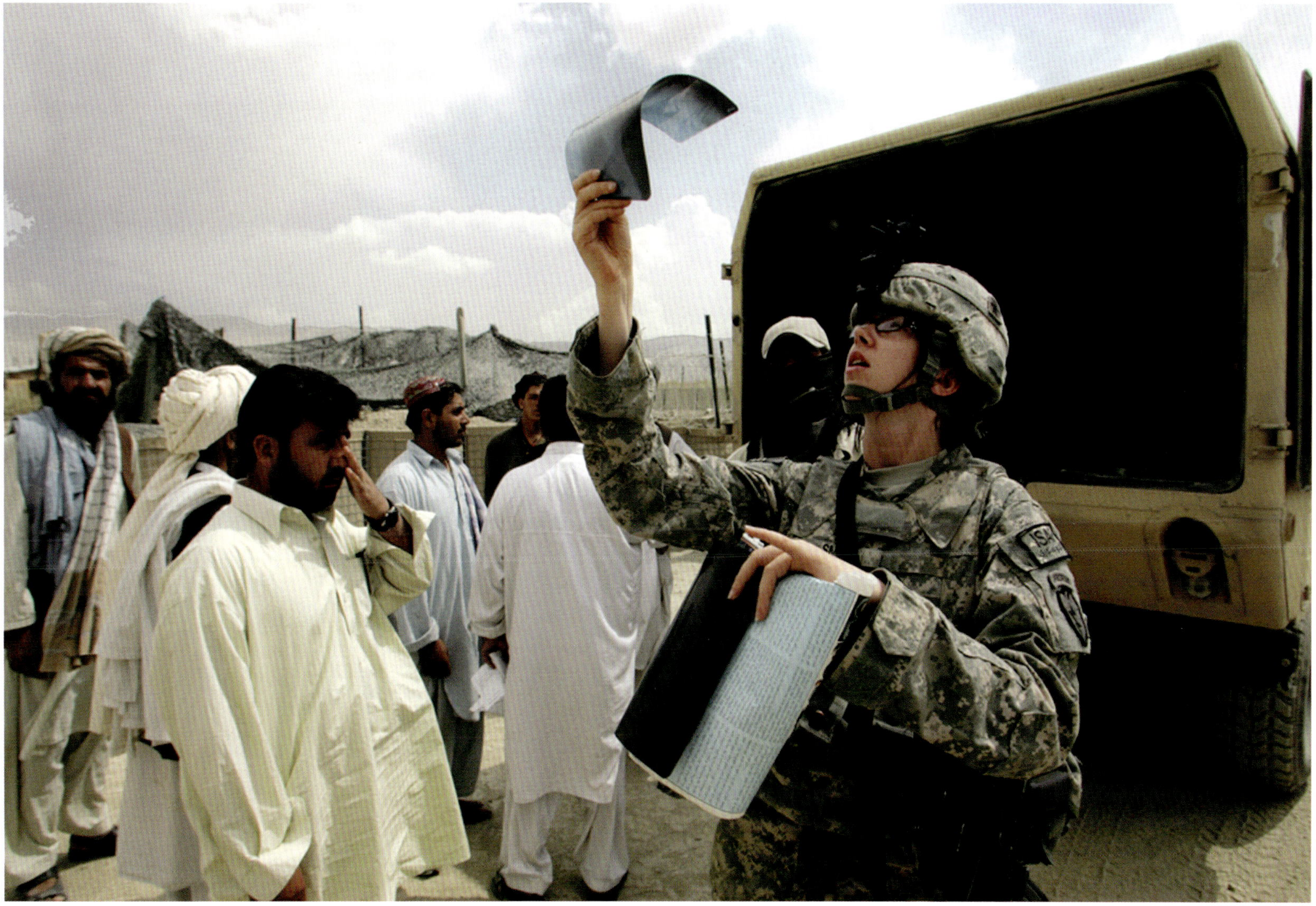

SPC Megan Smith, a medic with the 758th FST, examines an x-ray of an Afghan wanting to gain entrance to a weekly clinic held for residents of a nearby town. Afghans showed up at the front gate of the FOB O-E, where medics such as Smith gave them pre-examinations. The weekly clinic allowed them to receive treatment otherwise not available in their area.

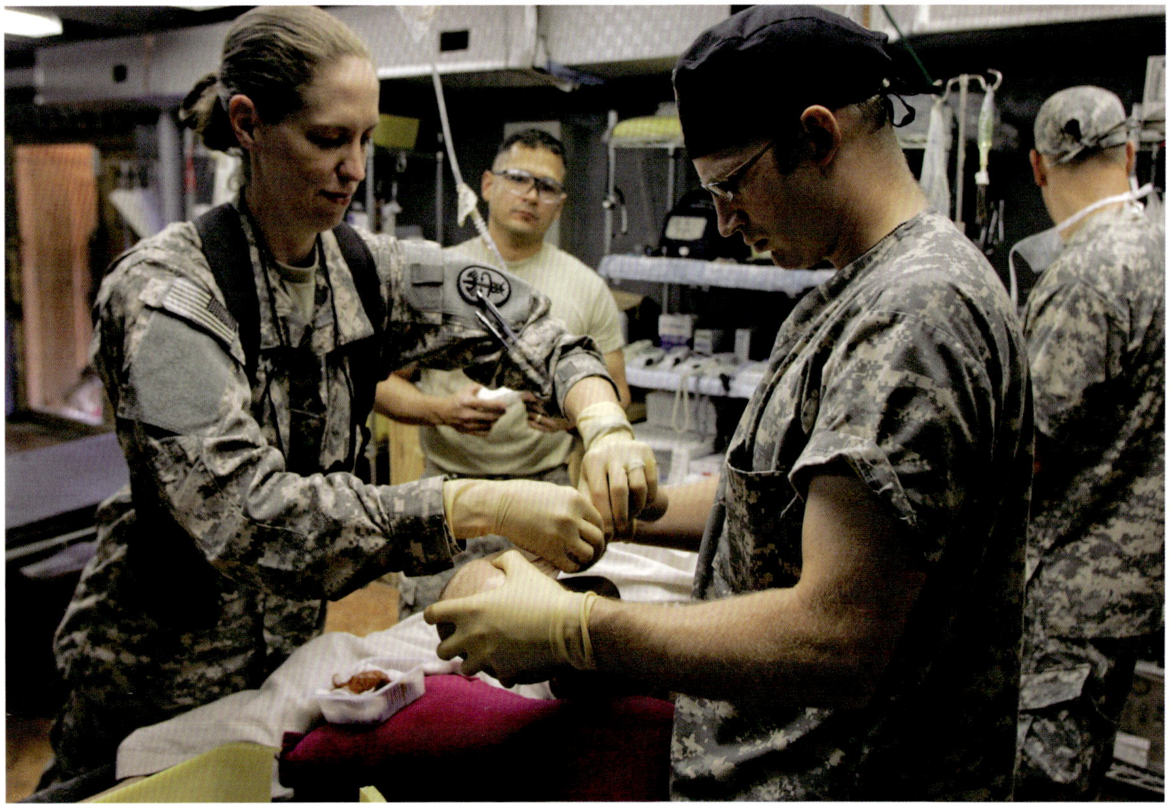

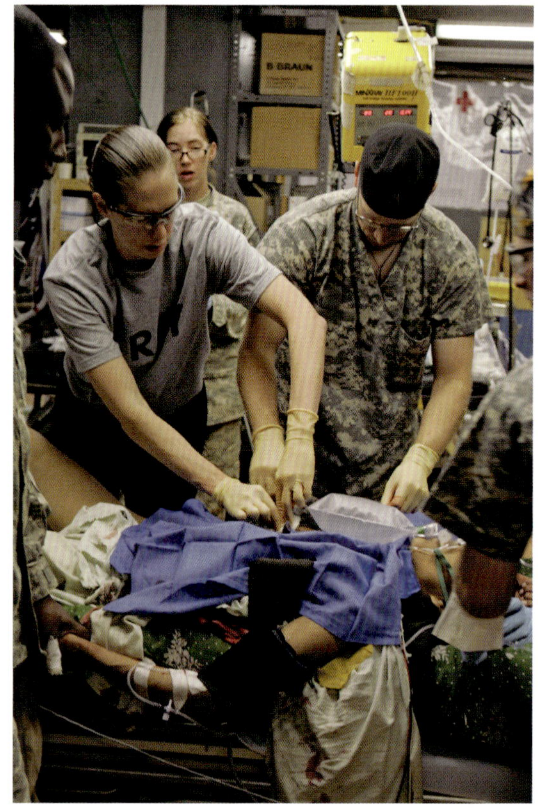

US Army doctor MAJ Randy Kjorstad performs an emergency operation on one of two Afghan boys who were wounded while playing with an old Russian land mine. The hospital is located on FOB O-E in eastern Afghanistan. Both boys survived.

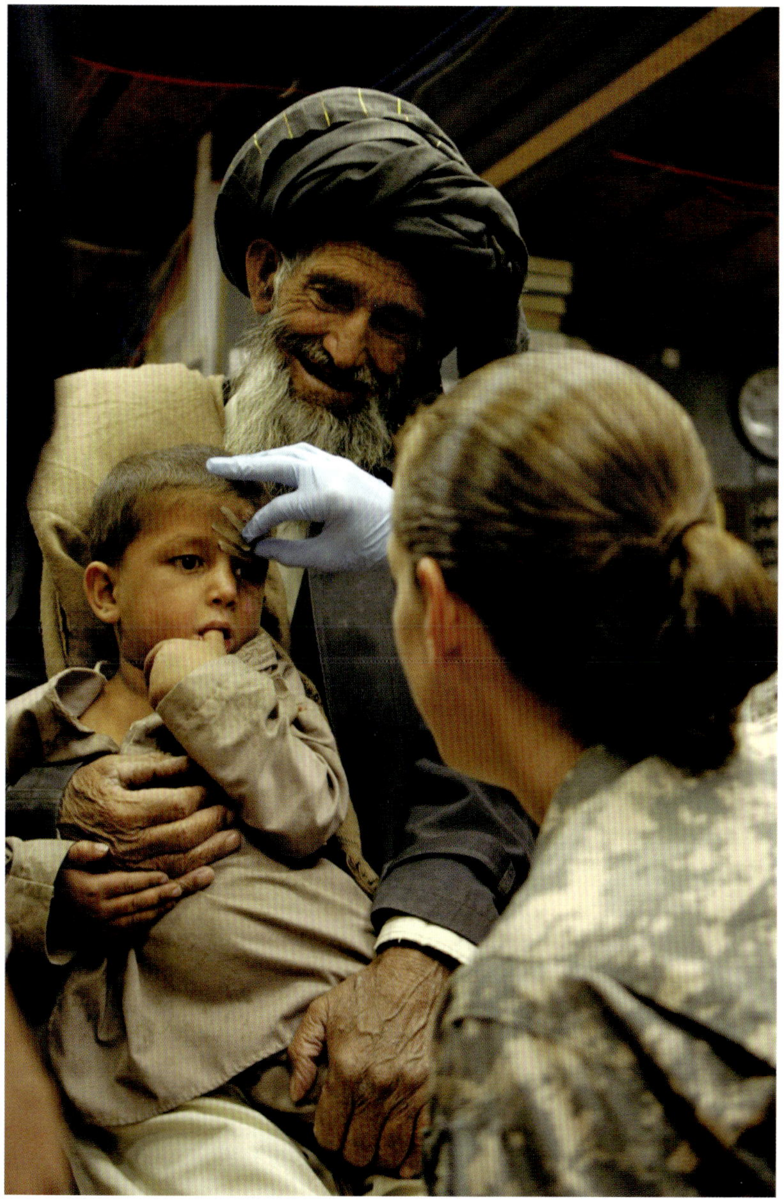

US Army doctor MAJ Randy Kjorstad examines the injured child of the Afghan man holding him. At the FOB O-E hospital, local Afghan civilians, some even with severe injuries, were allowed access to the care offered by the staff.

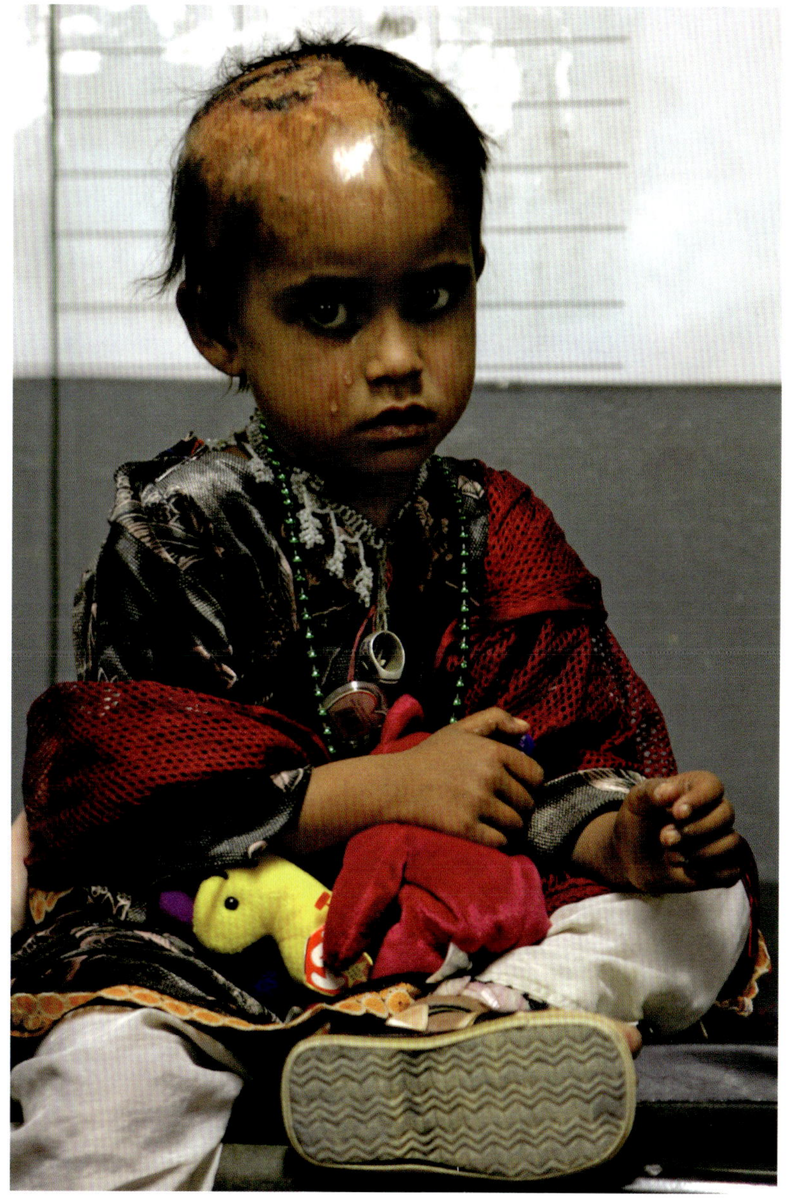

After initial treatment for a burn to her head and a follow-up skin graft, a young Afghan girl cries during her final treatment. Children seen at the clinic were given toys to help distract them from painful treatments.

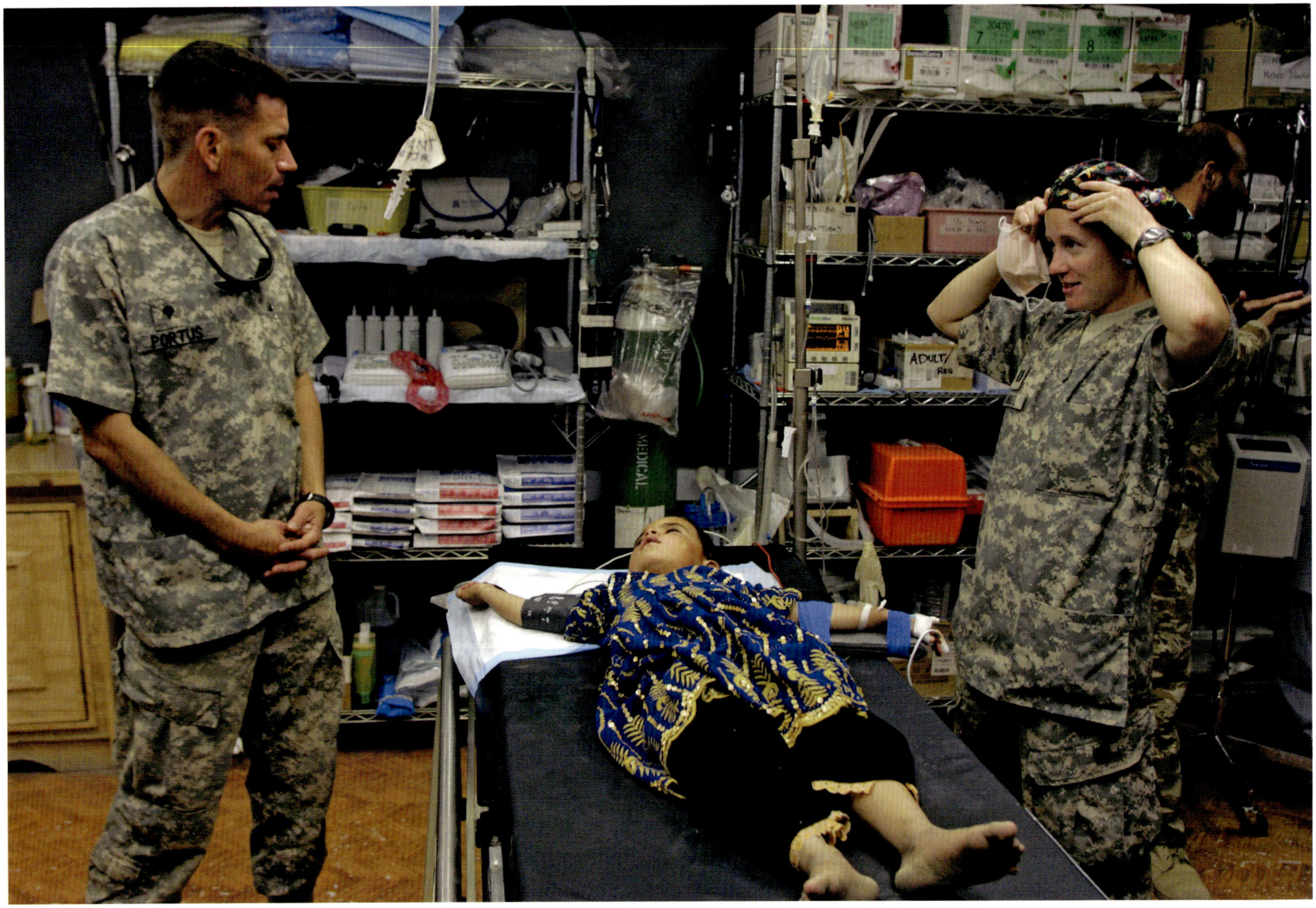

Captain and member of the FST Ann Savoie, right, prepares an injured Afghan child for surgery with help from her colleague. The child had been injured when a pot of boiling water fell off a stove onto her head. The child underwent several skin transplants at FOB O-E.

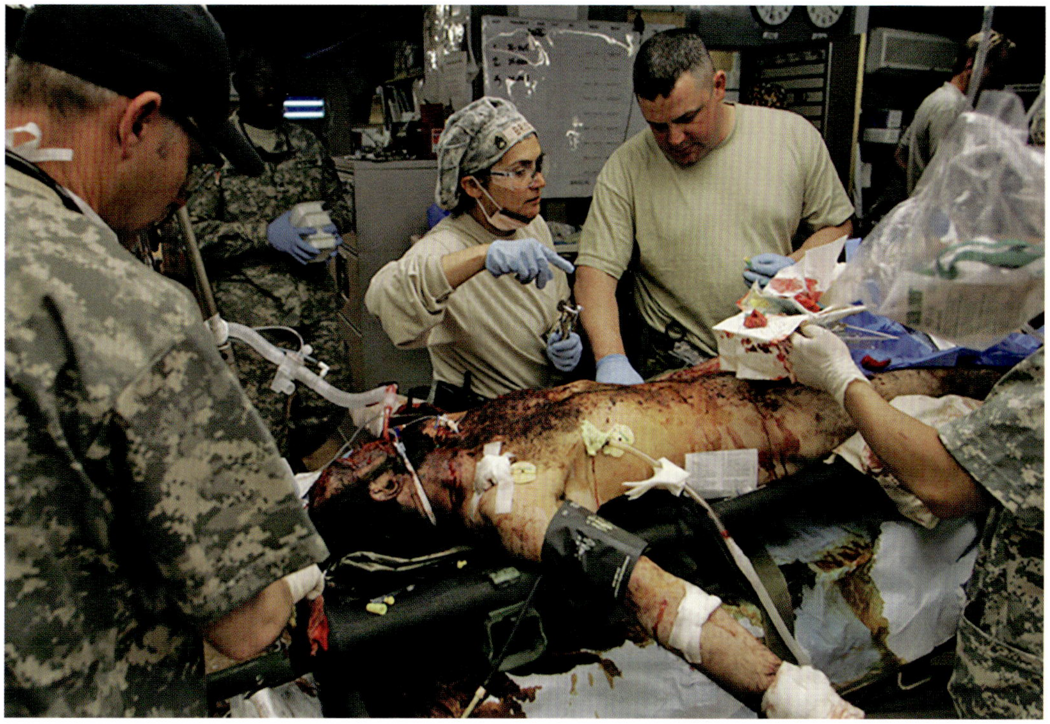

The Afghan National Police officer's body goes through the initial process of being cleaned up before being turned over to his comrades for burial. SSG Christine Bristol instructs SG Jason Abercrombie on what needs to be done; bandages, tubes, and other items used during his treatment were removed. The officer and his colleague were hit by an IED and flown to FOB O-E for treatment.

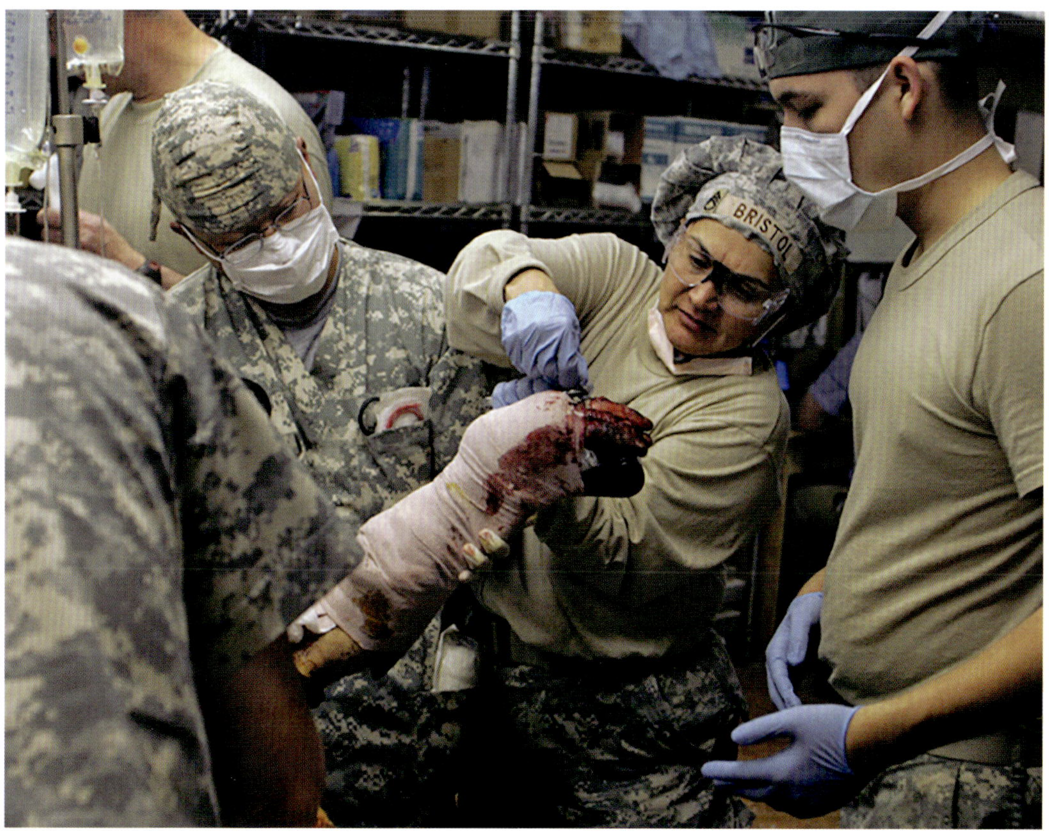

SSG Christine Bristol cuts the ring off of an Afghan National Police officer. The officer, who died as a result of his injuries, was wounded by an IED and flown from the site of the explosion to receive treatment at FOB O-E.

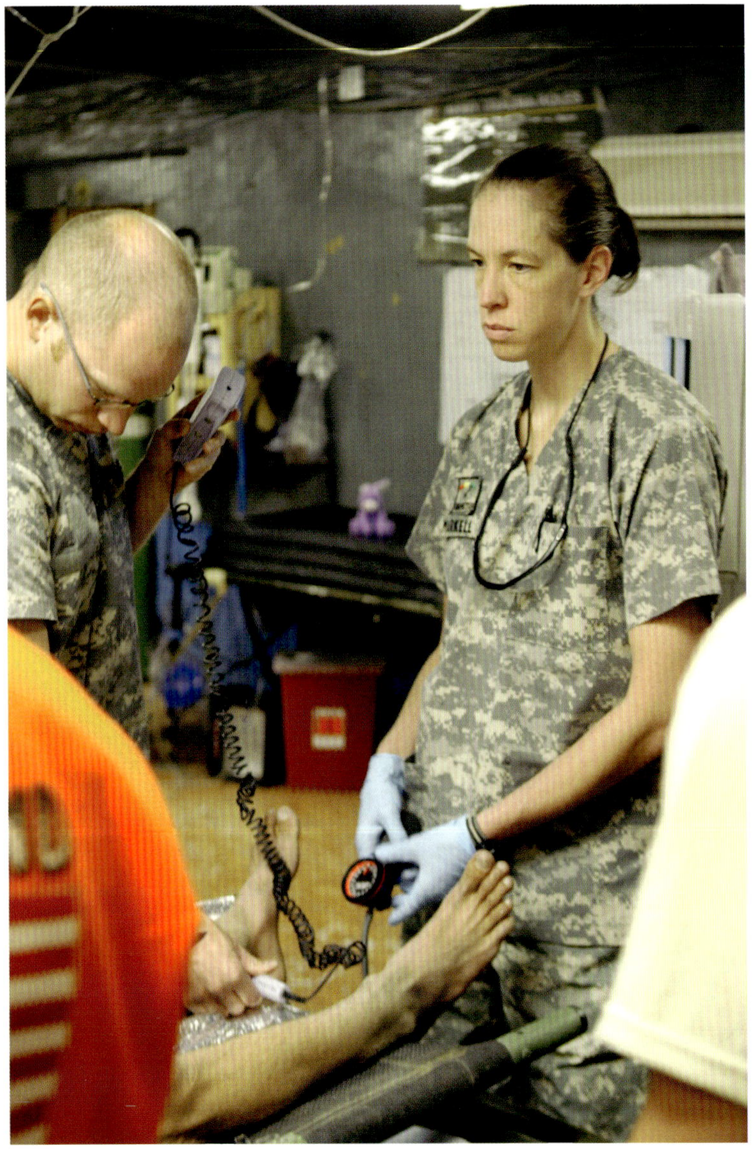

US Army doctor MAJ Randy Kjorstad shows signs of fatigue as she provides medical care to a patient.

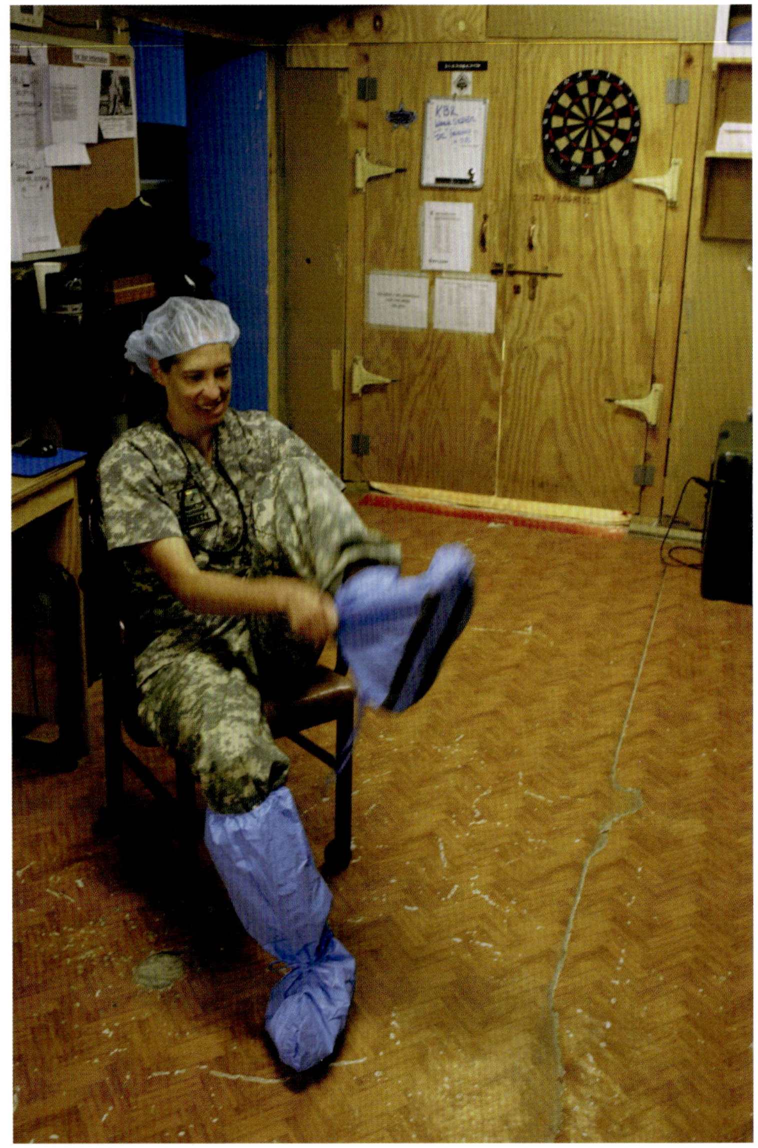

MAJ Randy Kjorstad prepares for surgery. The child underwent several skin transplants at FOB O-E.

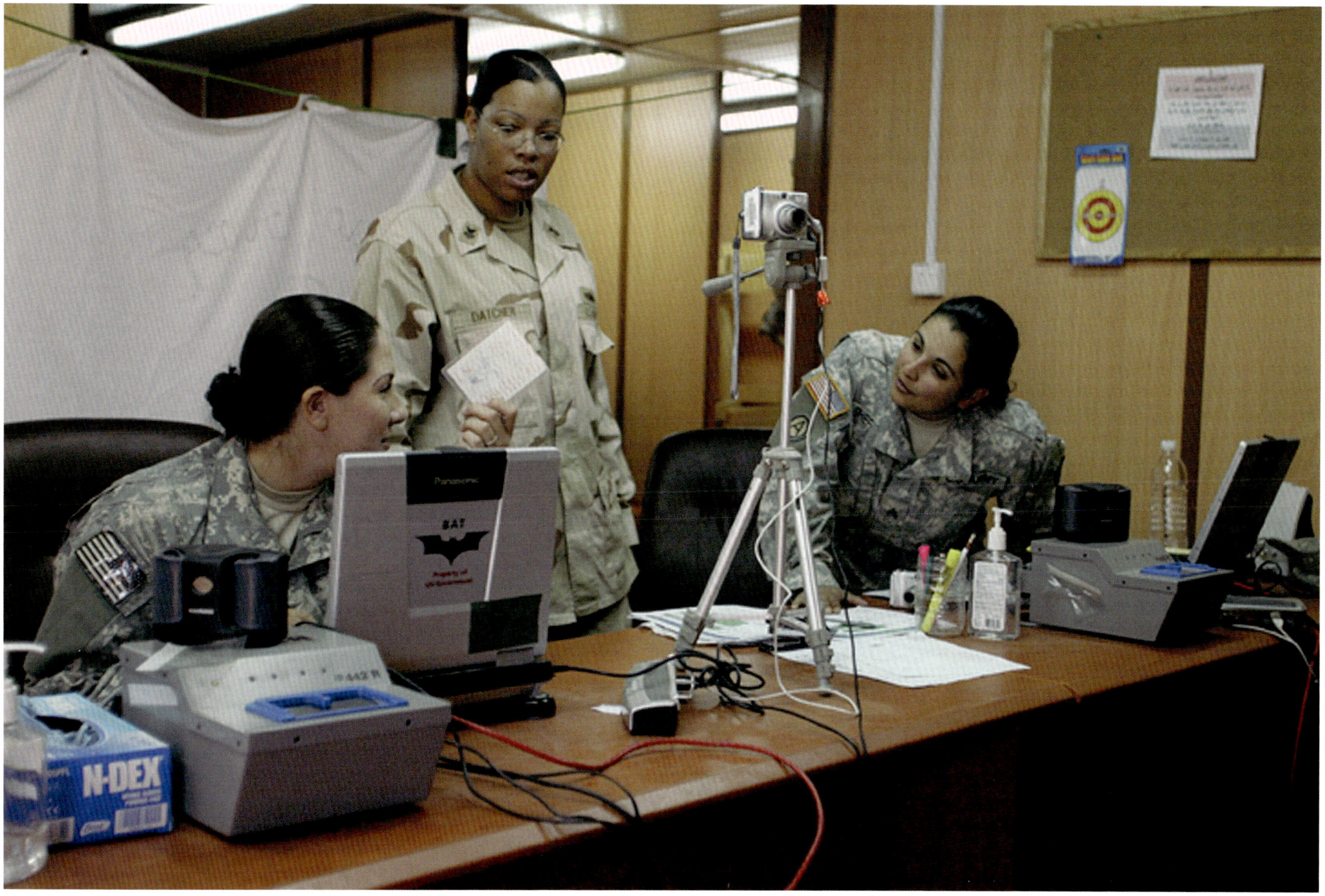

Female soldiers register Iraqi civilians visiting their relatives being detained at Camp Cropper, Iraq.
Visitors had to be photographed and screened before being allowed to visit with the detainees.

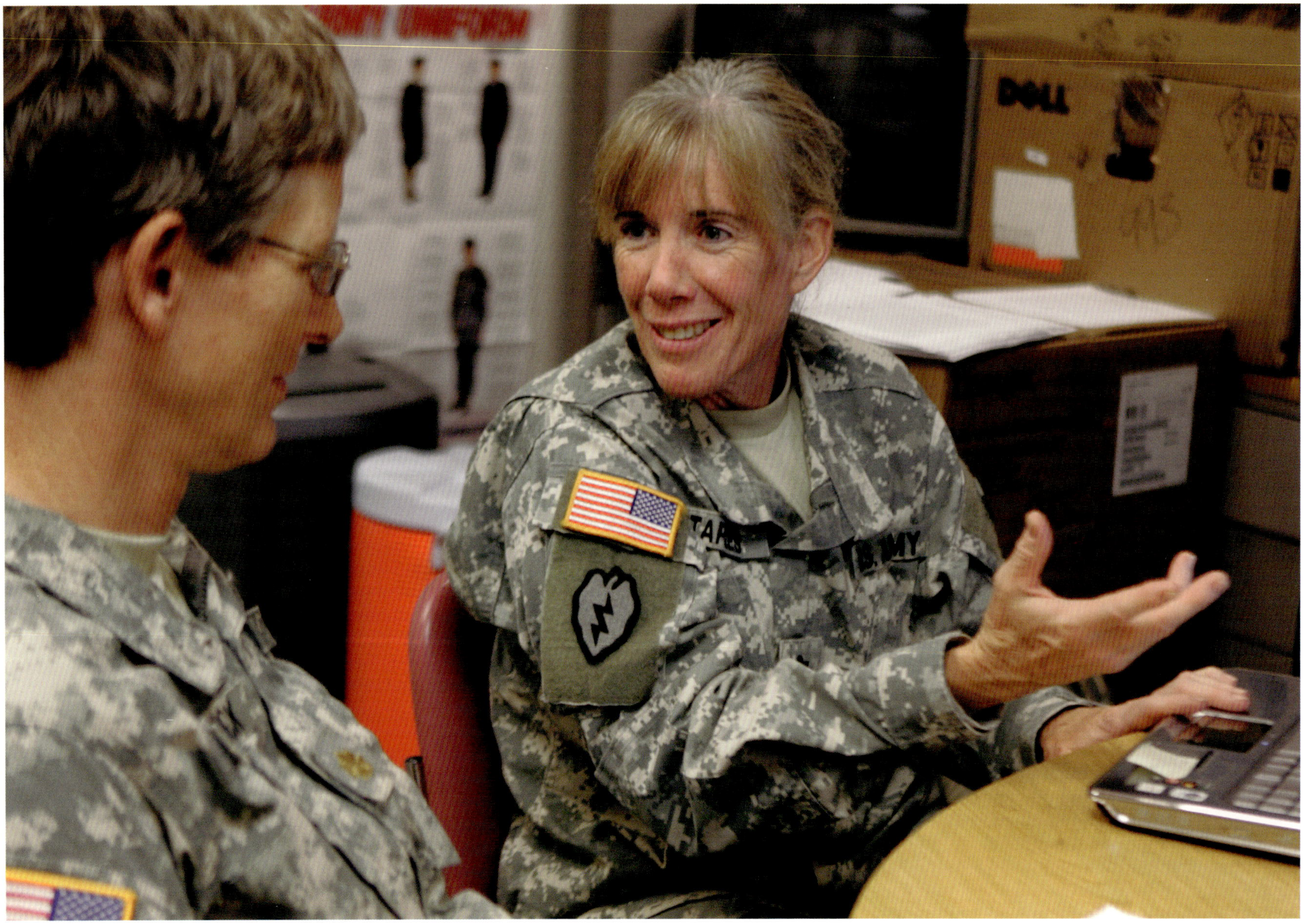

While planning an upcoming deployment to Alaska, COL Staples gestures while speaking with MAJ Westrick as they go over the inventory of veterinary supplies needed for the mission. The meeting took place at US Army Reserves Armory in Aurora, CO, on November 5, 2011.

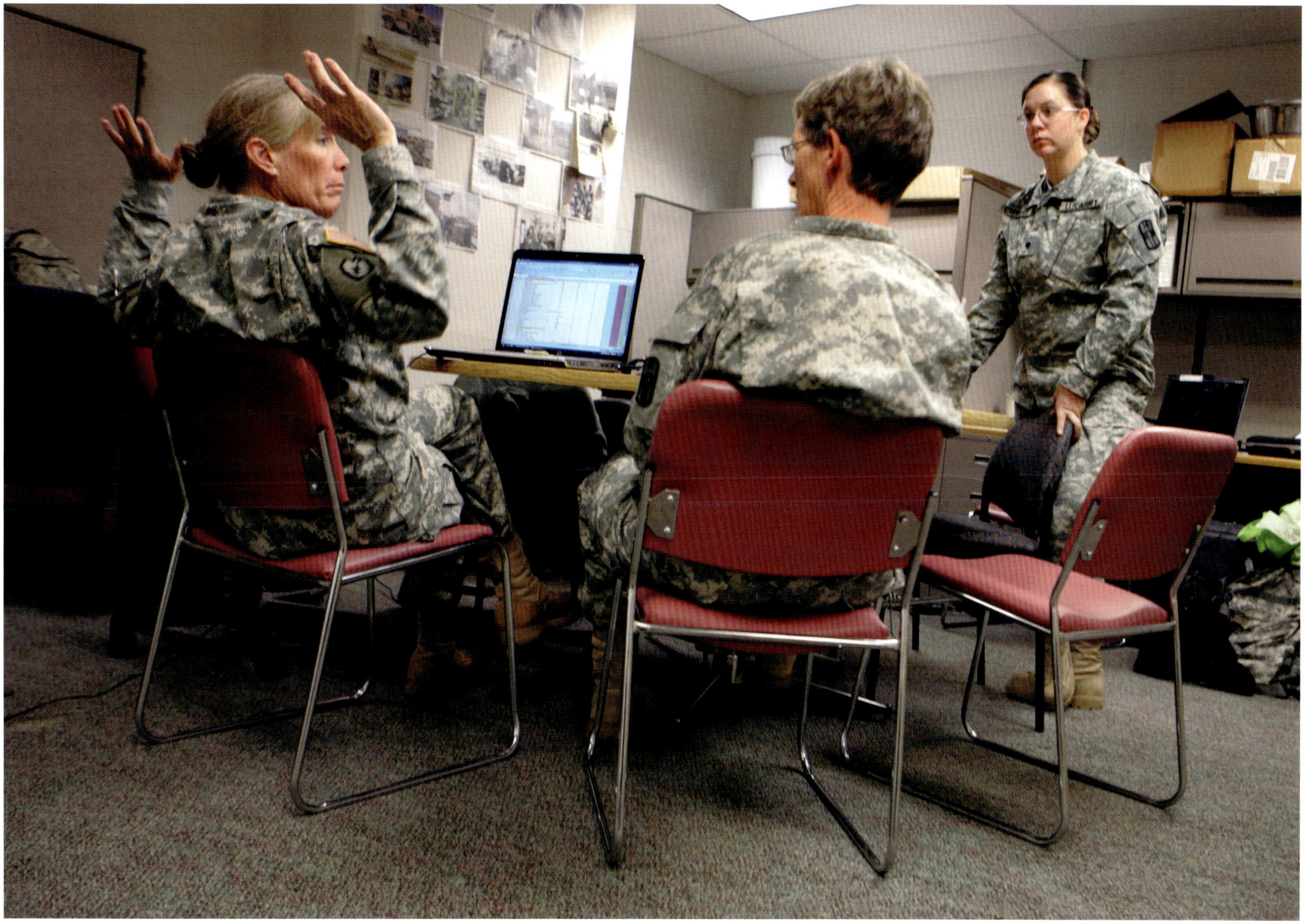

COL Staples and MAJ Westrick discuss inventory at the US Army Reserves Armory in Aurora, CO.

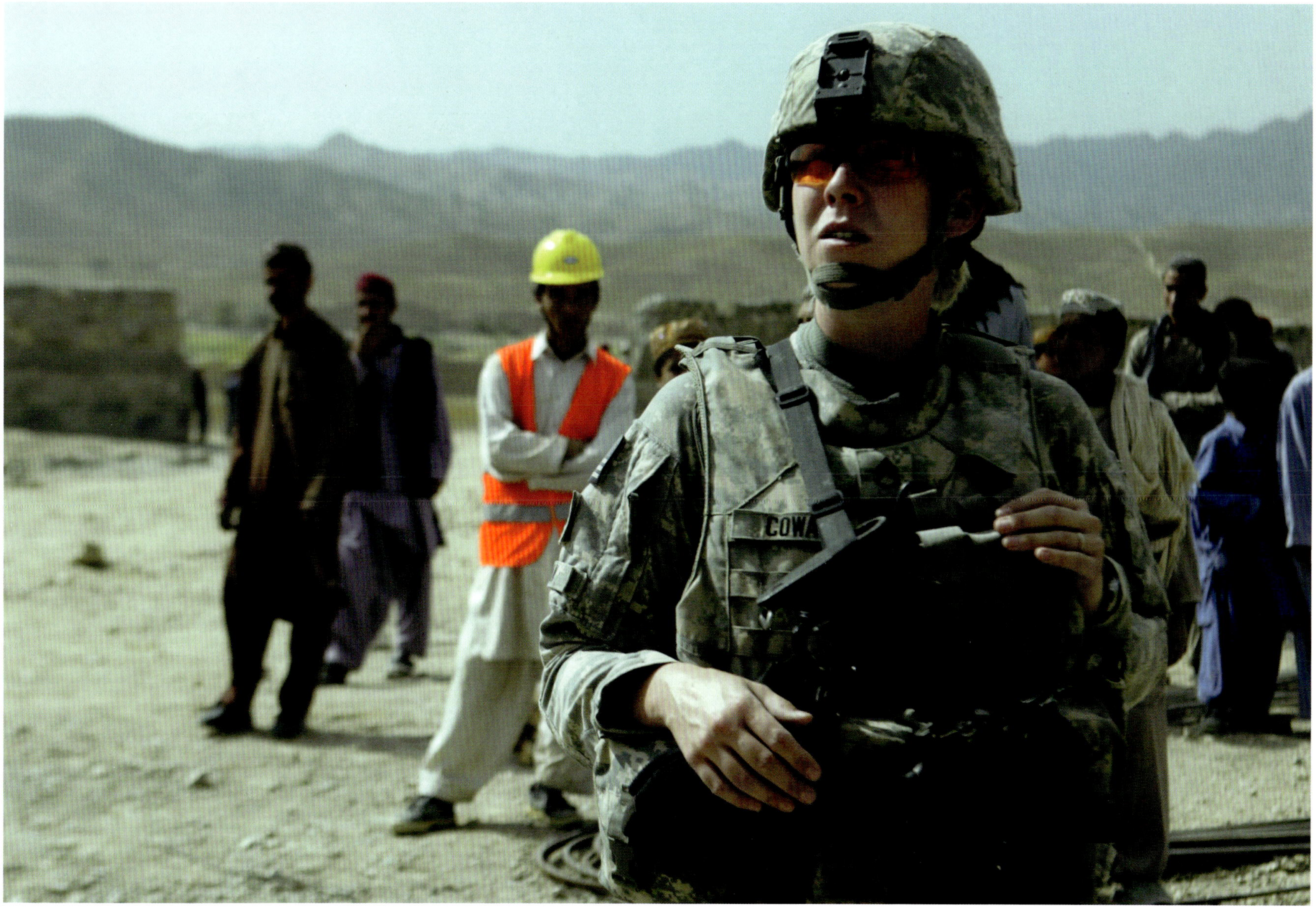

SSG Victoria Cowan counts broken windows in an Afghan school built by an NGO near the village of Margha. The Provincial Redevelopment Team [PRT] was at the site to inspect a wall being built by an Afghan contractor. The construction methods on the wall were found to be substandard. The PRT issued the contractor a warning to perform repairs or risk a fine.

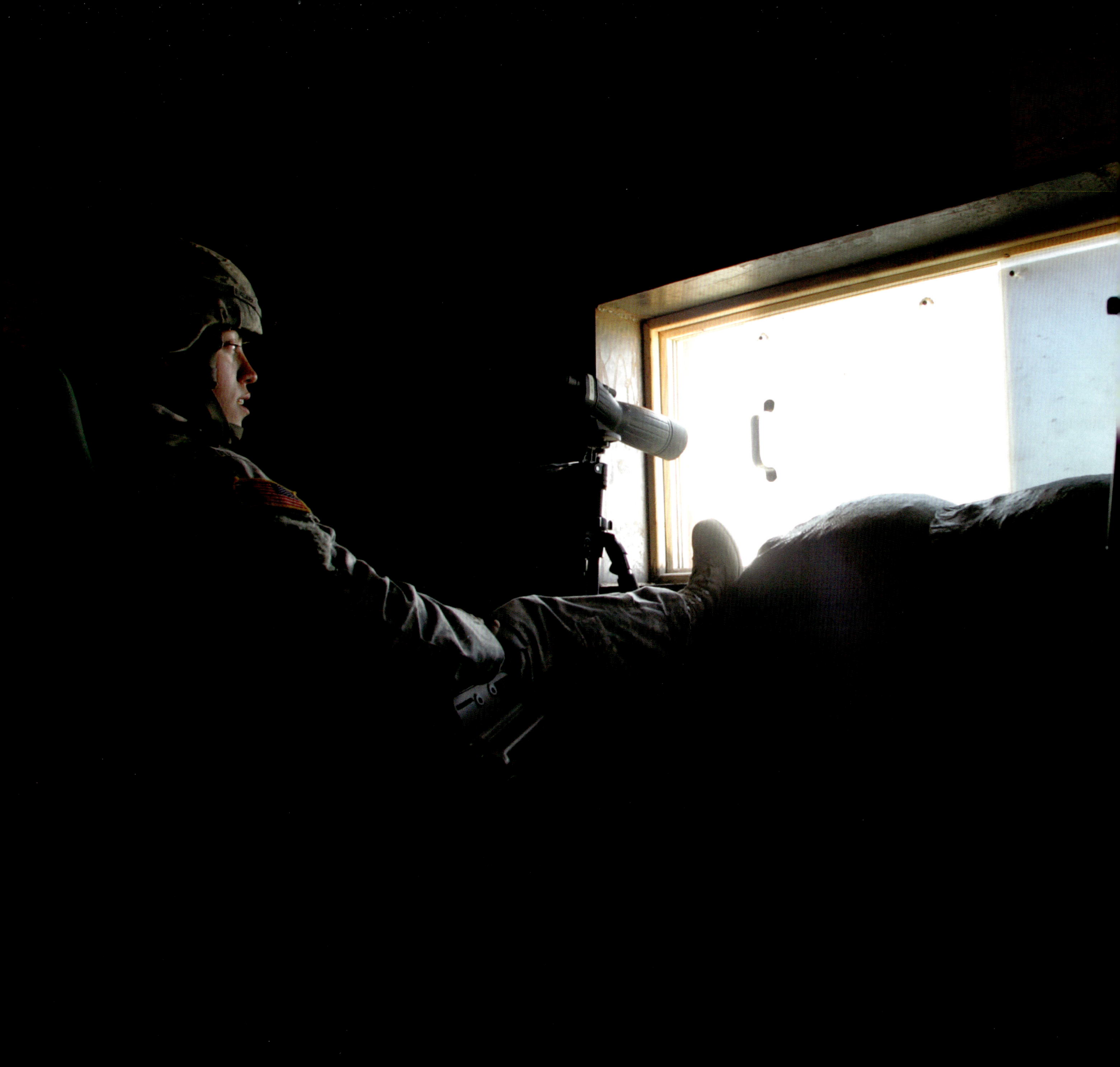

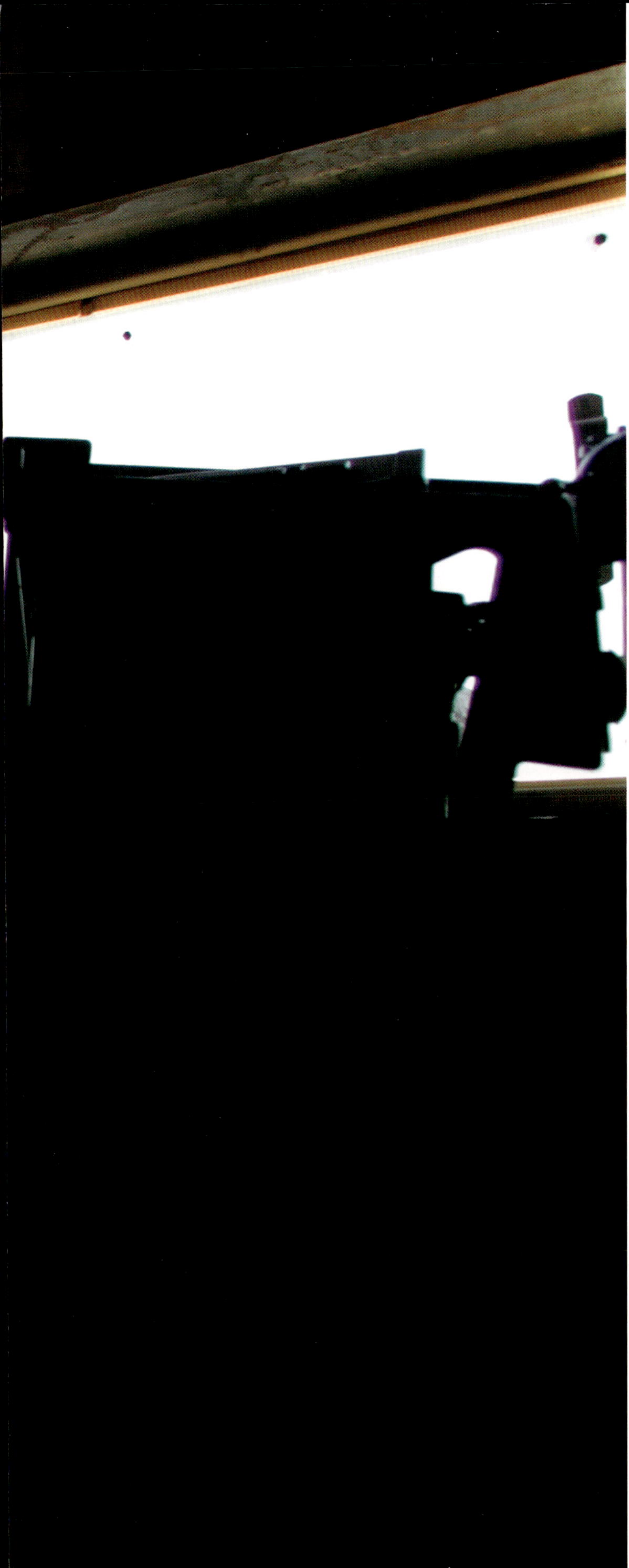

SG Clark uses a spotting scope to observe detainee visitors. She is watching for suspicious behavior among the visitors lined up for entrance to Camp Liberty, where they will visit relatives who have been detained.

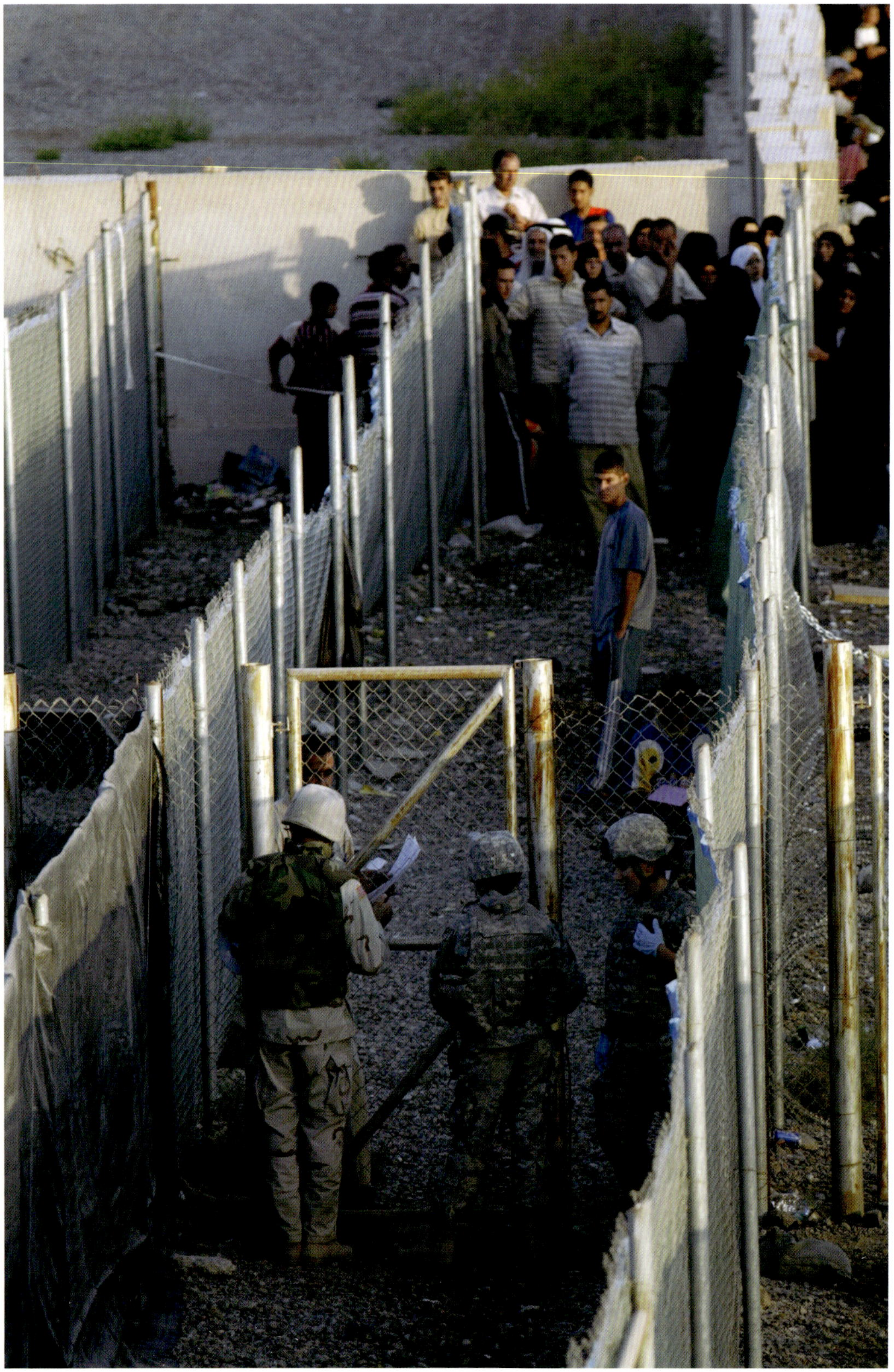

Female members of Company A, 2nd Battalion of the New Mexico National Guard, clear relatives of detainees for visits.

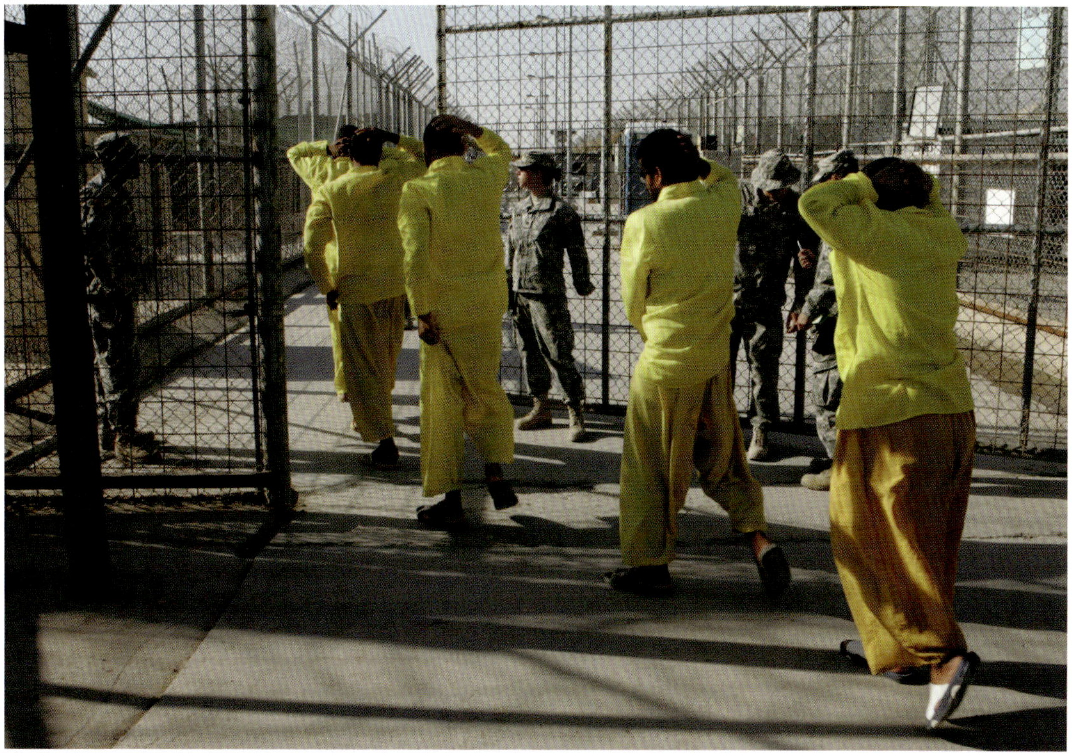

US guards, male and female, transfer detainees from one location to another.

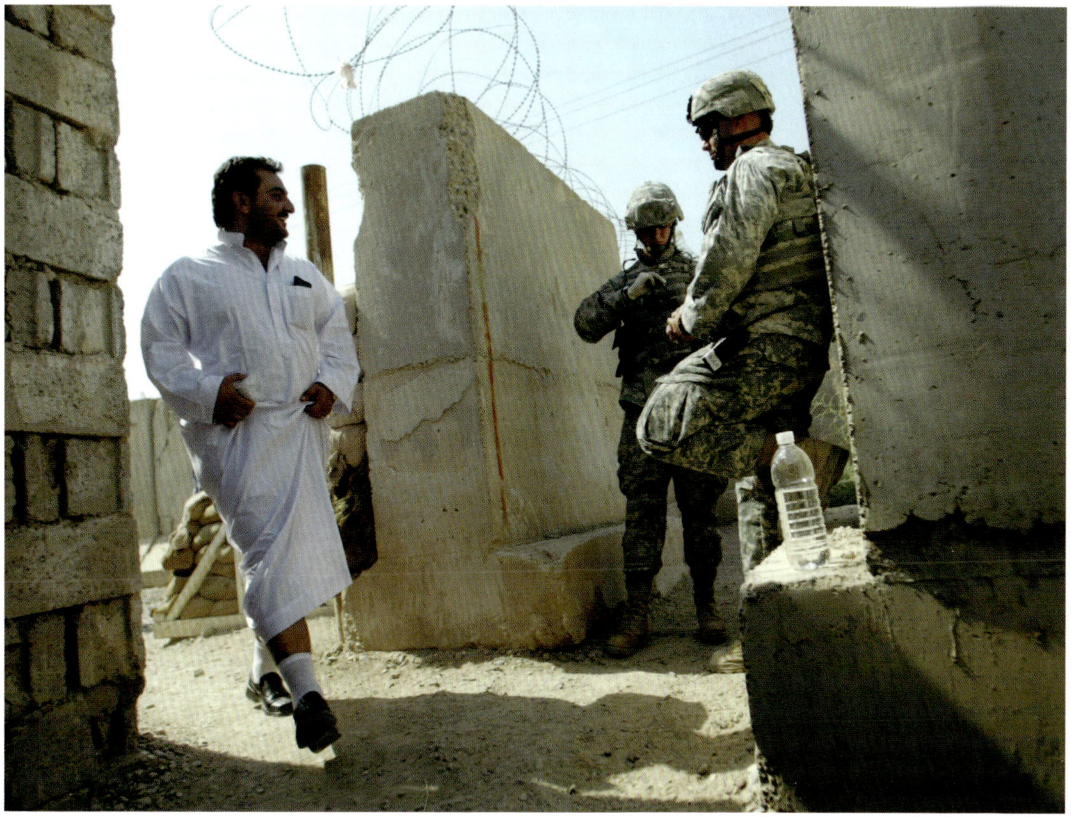

A released Iraqi detainee joyfully leaves custody. Earlier he had made a pledge not to participate in the insurgency and to obey laws. The release coincided with Ramadan.

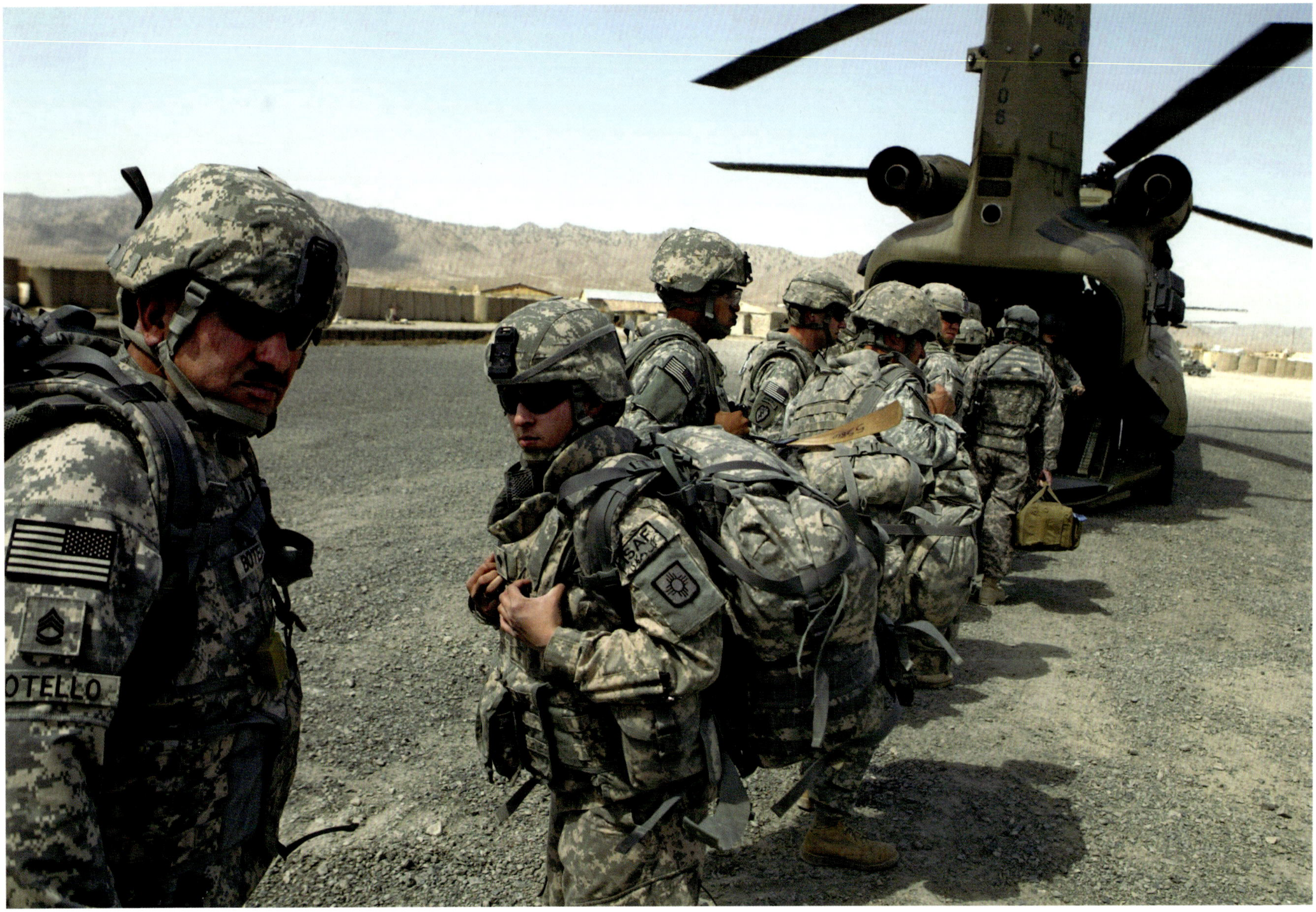

New Mexico National Guard members SG Andrew Botello and SPC Krystal Ramirez turn away from the prop blast given off by the helicopter they are about to board. The two are part of the 920th Engineers New Mexico National Guard based at FOB O-E in eastern Afghanistan.

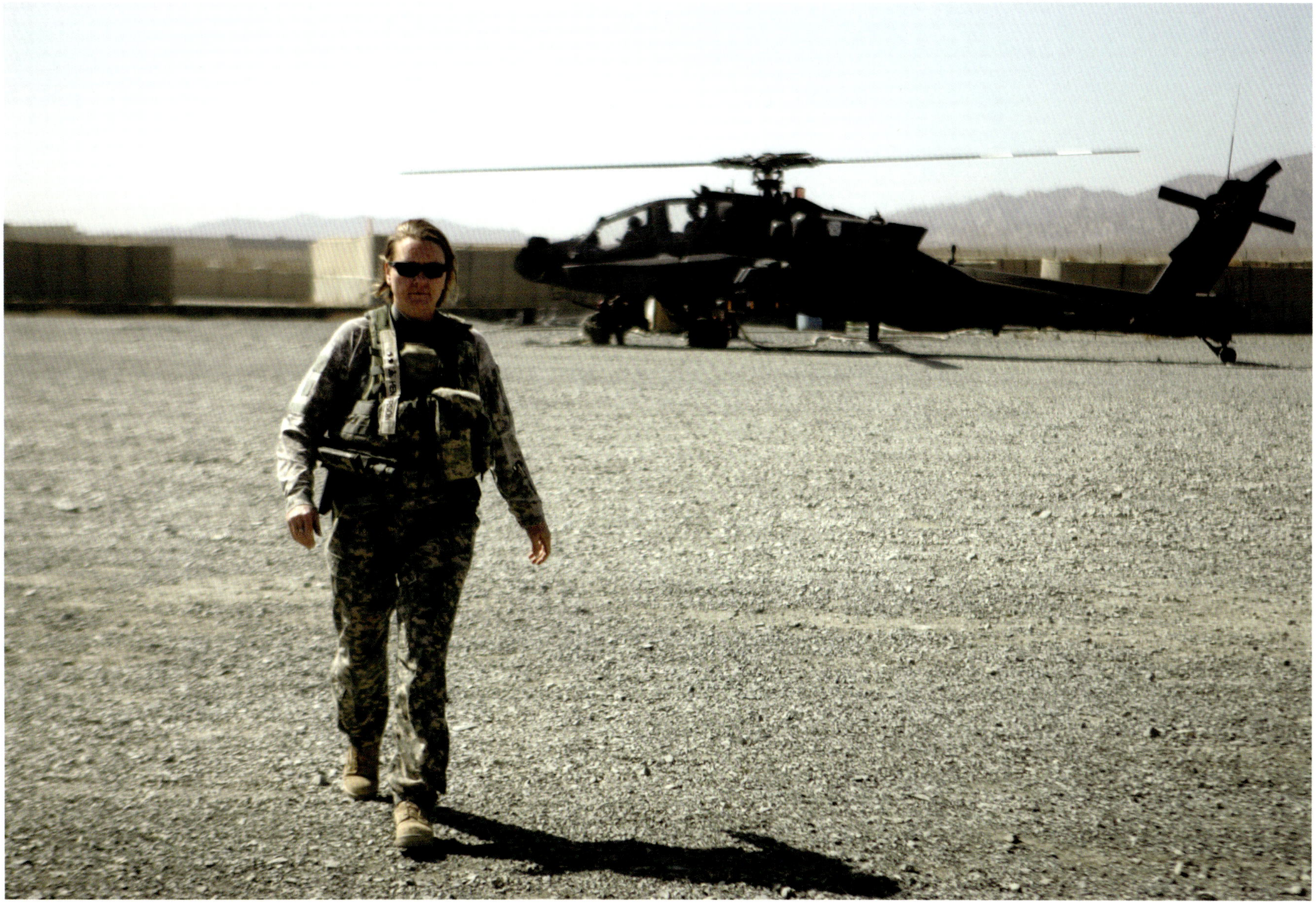

A female Apache helicopter pilot takes a break during a refueling and rearming stop at FOB O-E.

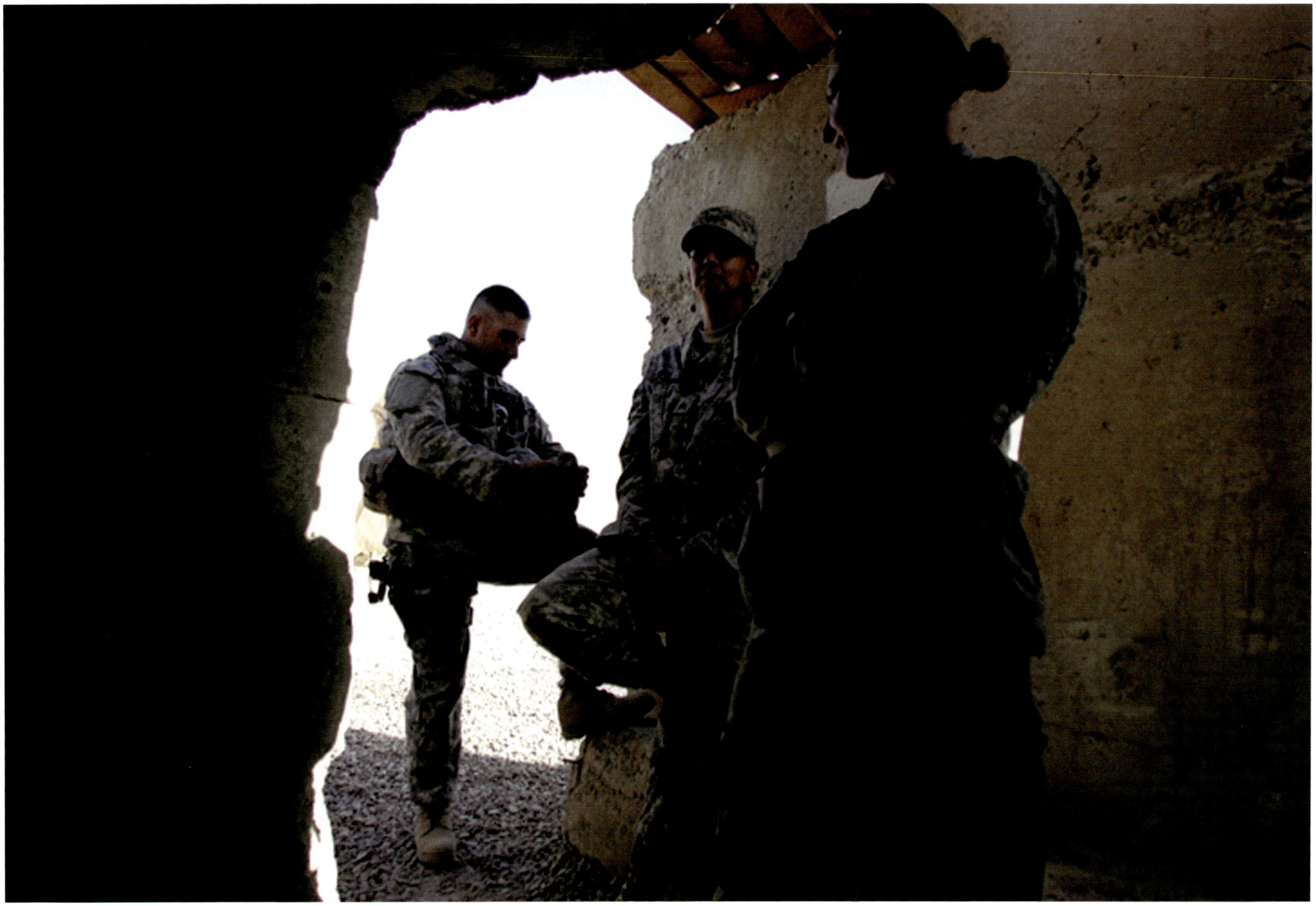

CPT Ali Dipor, left, takes a break with two of his female soldiers. The two women were part of a group of female soldiers charged with searching Iraqi women visiting their detained relatives.

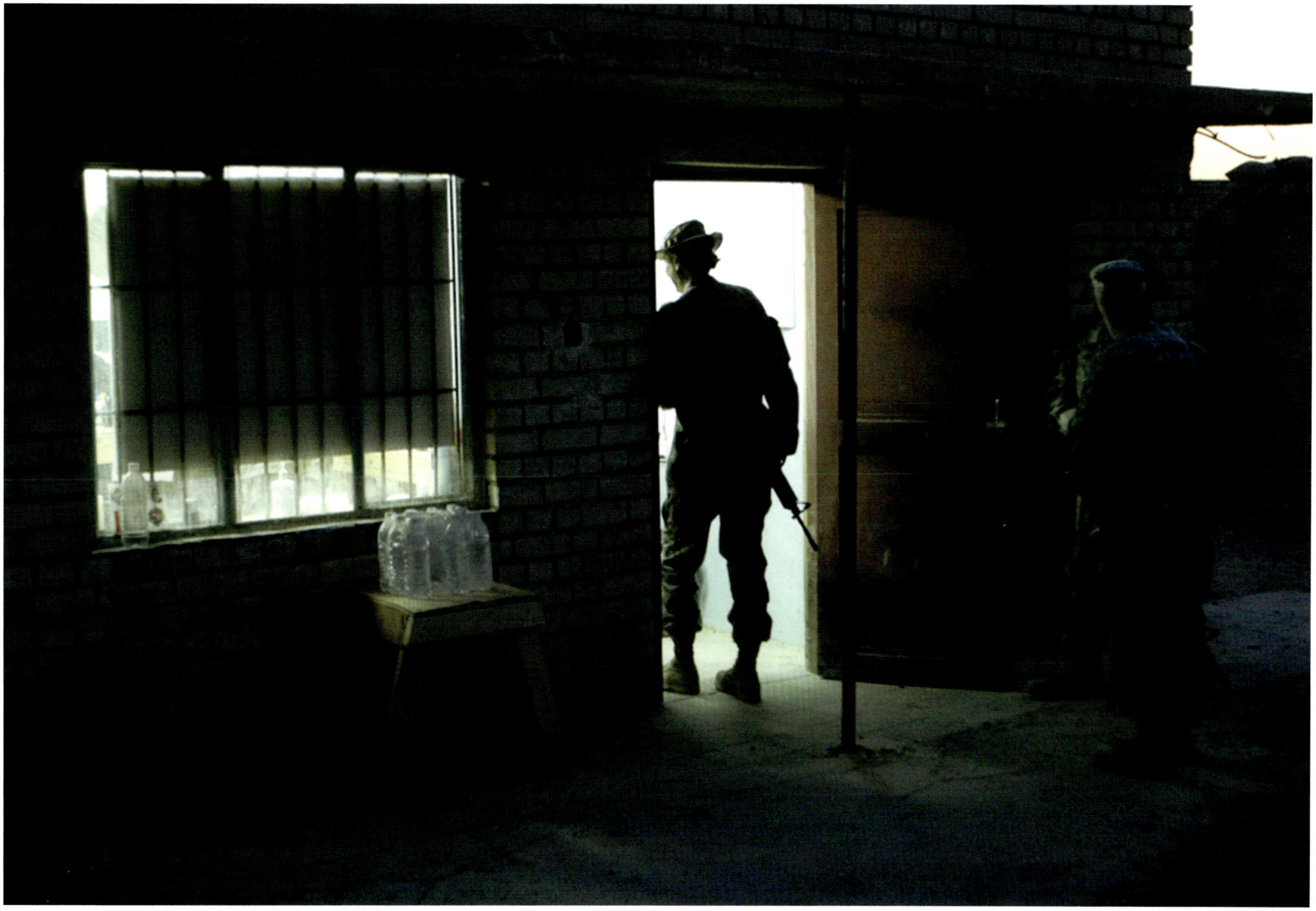

SPC Daylene Marsh checks in with the sergeant in charge of the morning shift at the detainee visitors gate servicing Camp Cropper, Iraq.

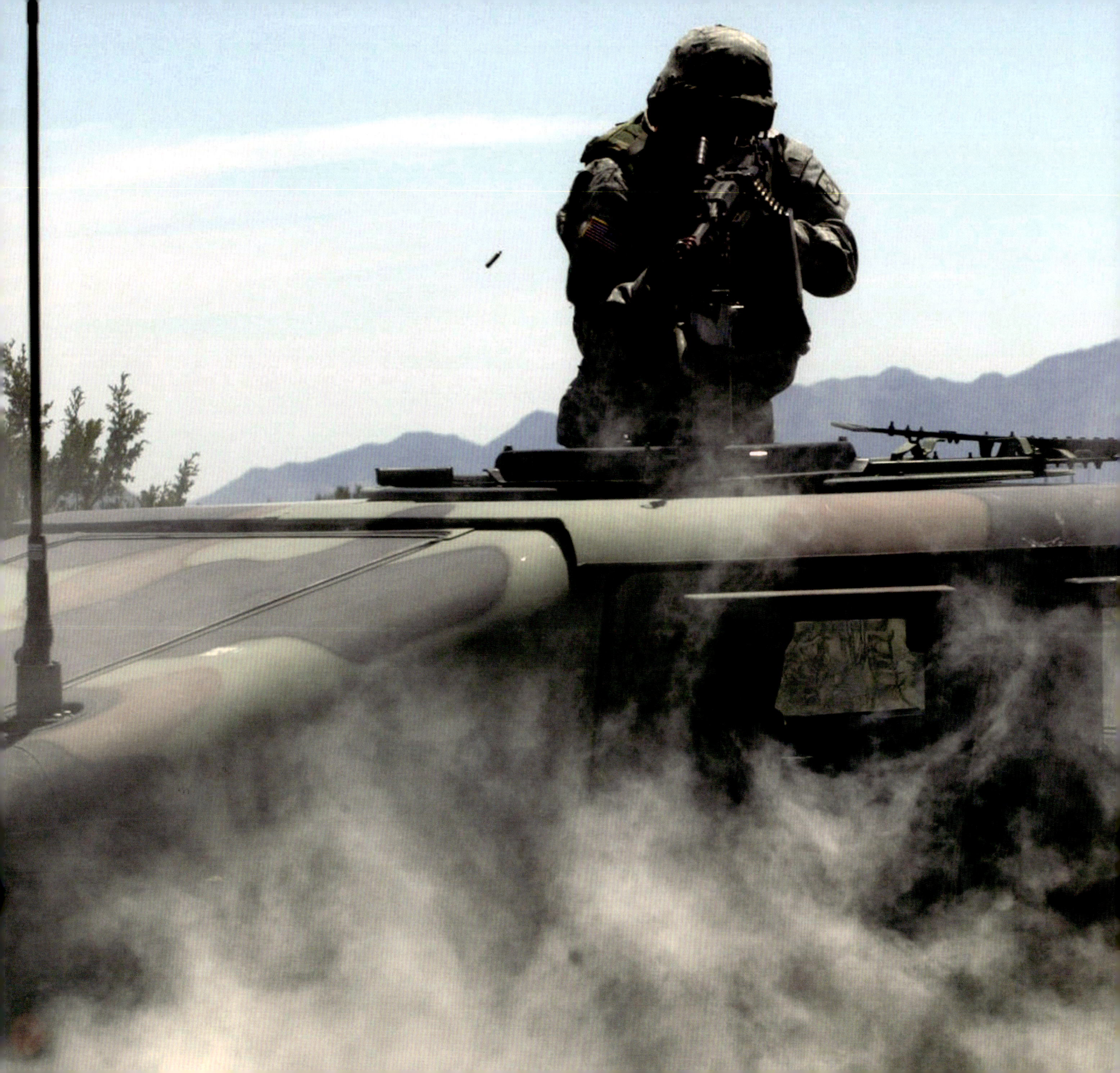

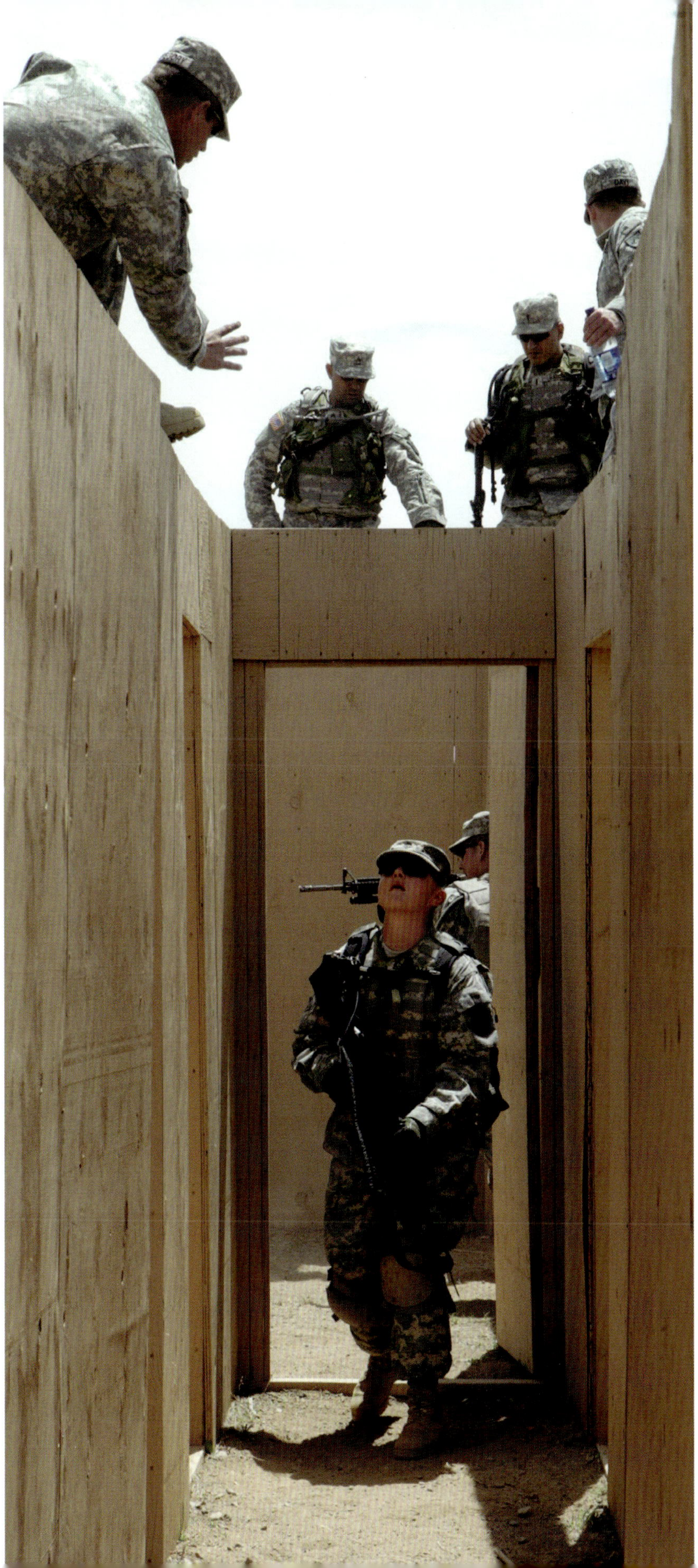

opposite: New Mexico National Guardsman SPC Angelina Maria Espinoza fires an M240 machine gun during a training exercise near Santa Fe, NM. The unit was training for deployment to Afghanistan.

left: SPC Angelina Maria Espinoza undergoes house clearing training during an exercise near Santa Fe, NM.

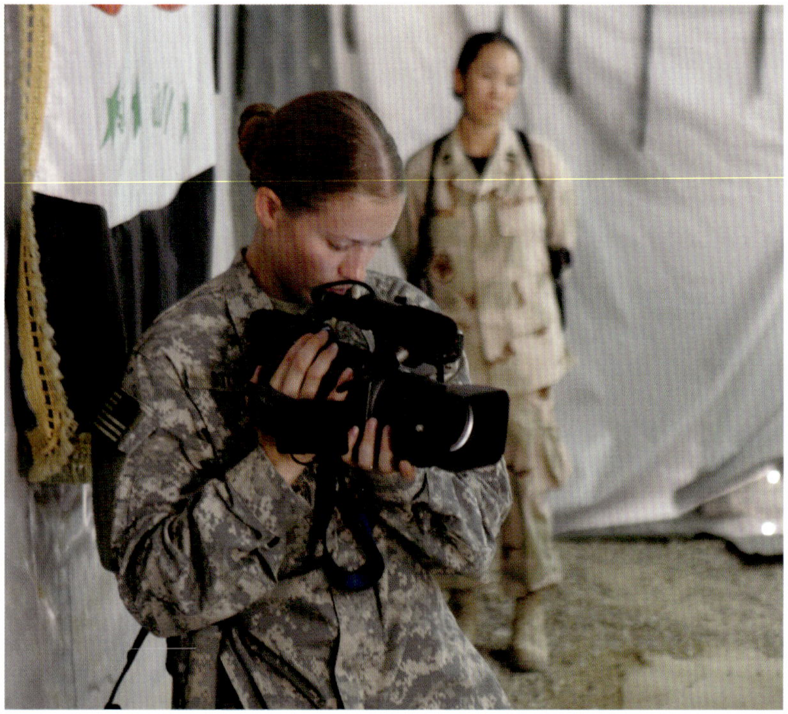

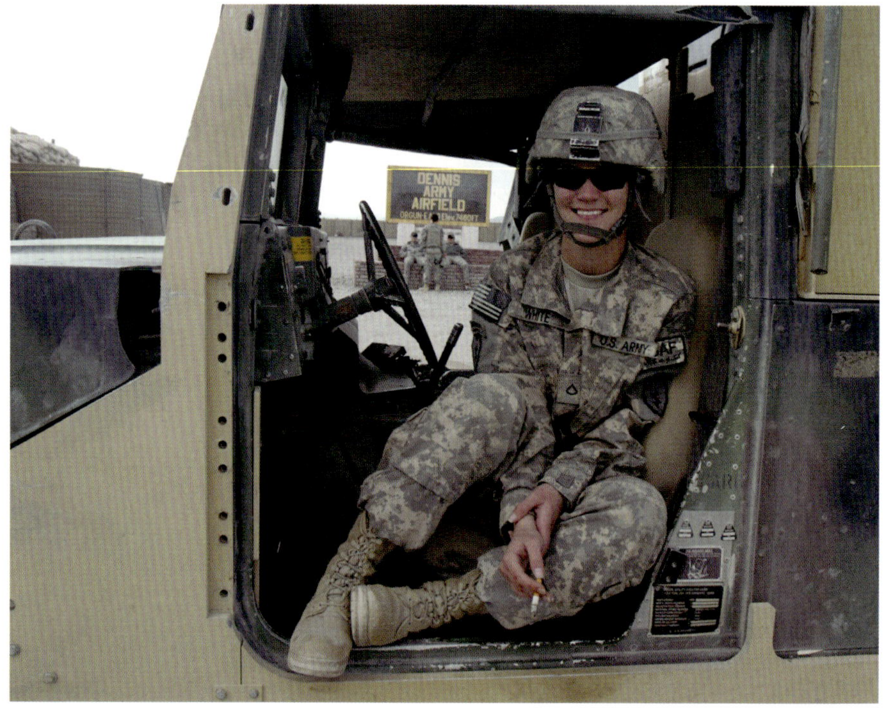

above, left: US Air Force videographer Stone documents a prisoner release at Camp Liberty, Iraq.

above, right: SPC White sits in a Humvee while finishing a cigarette. White is part of the flight line crew at the helicopter landing area on FOB O-E in eastern Afghanistan.

right: SPC Ramirez works on her nails while waiting near the helicopter pad at FOB O-E for a chopper ride to another FOB.

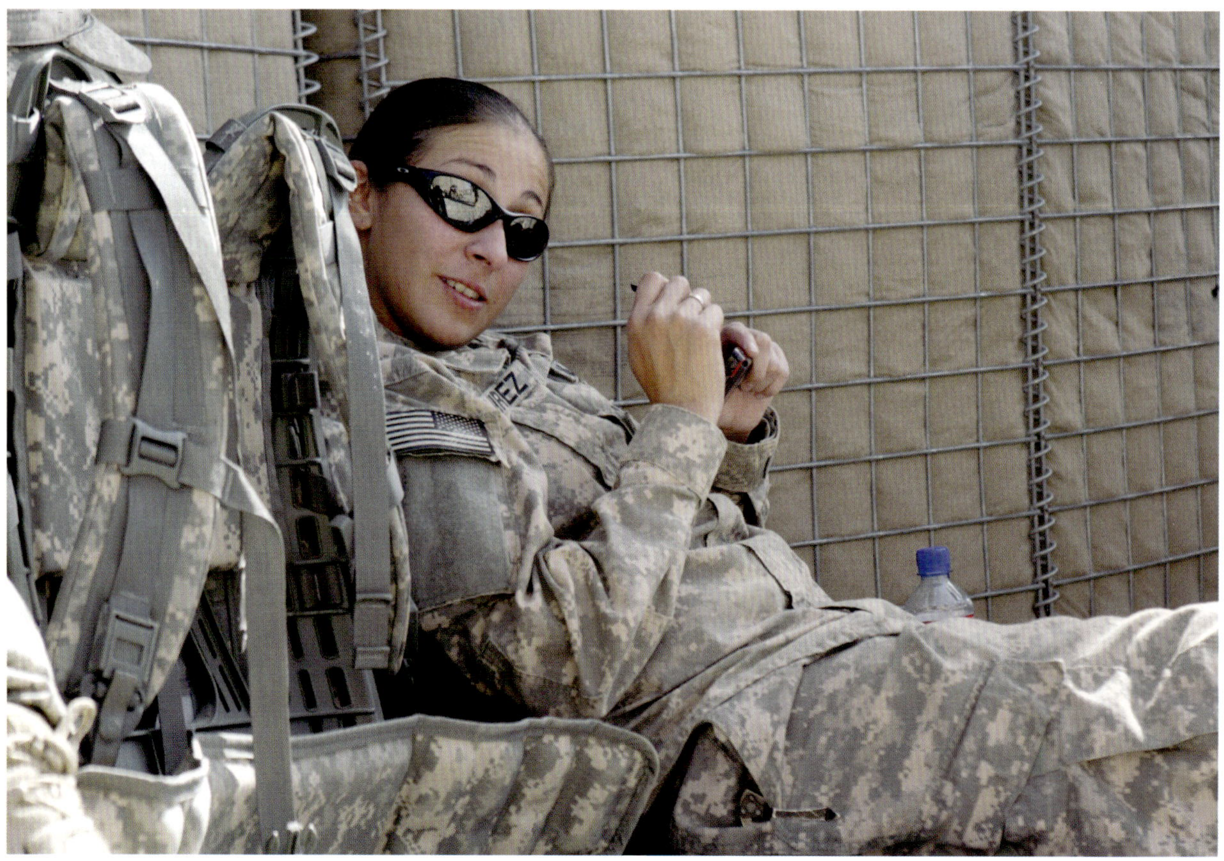

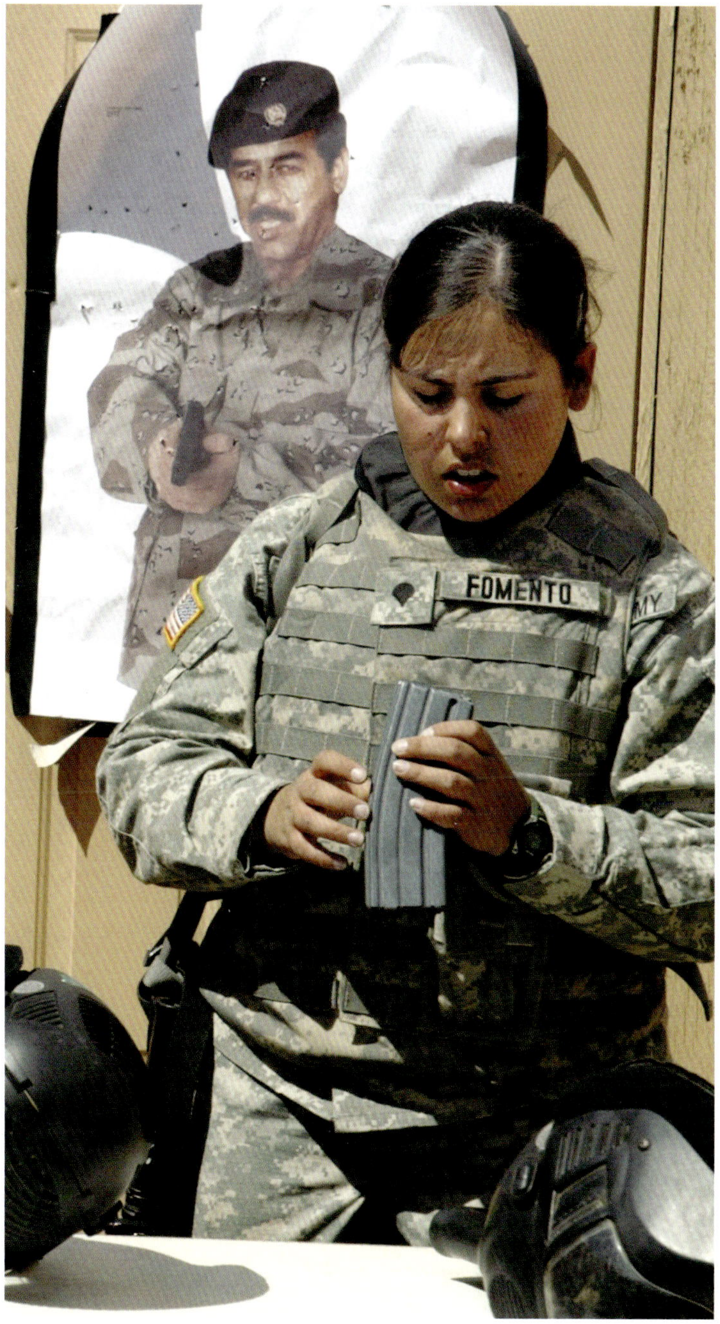

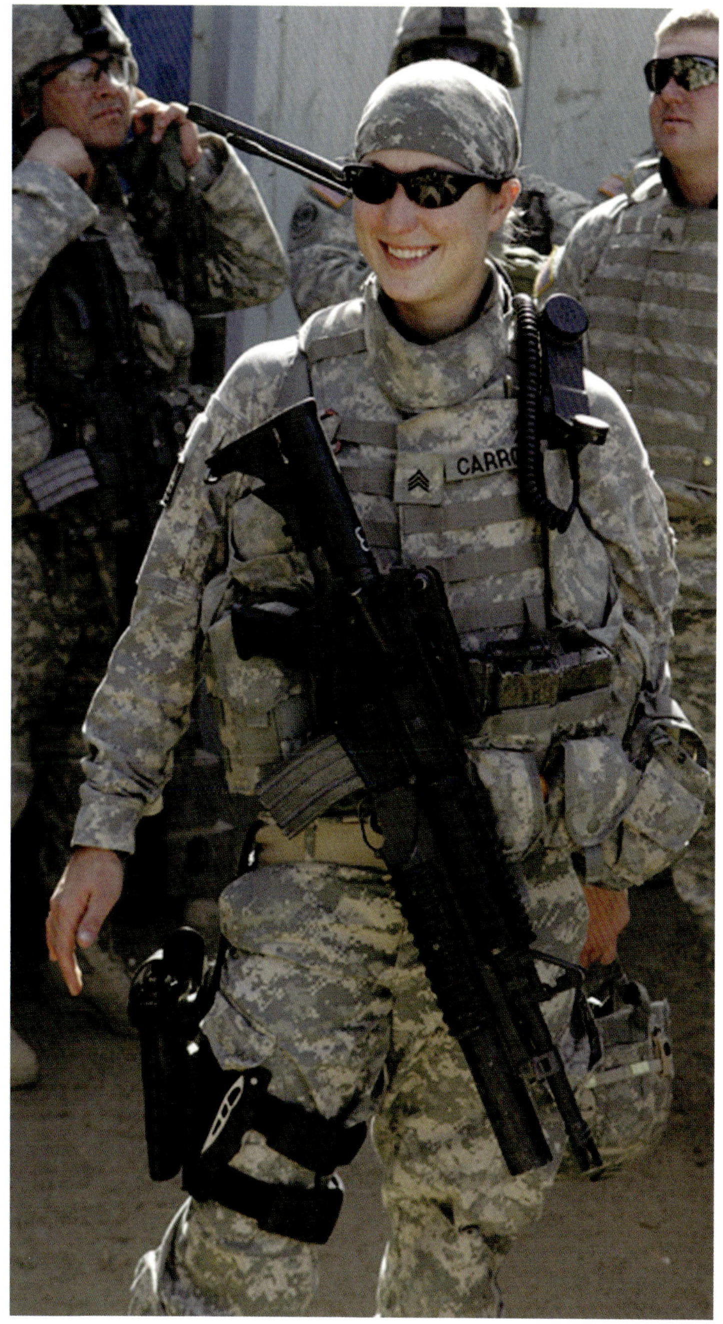

PFC Evonnie Fomento checks the number of rounds left in her magazine after undergoing room clearance training in preparation of deployment during the summer of 2009. New Mexico National Guard members underwent training on room clearance in a structure built for that purpose. Protective head gear and paint ball ammunition was used during the exercise.

Civil affairs SG Carro stands down during a patrol in Sauder City located in eastern Baghdad, Iraq. She accompanied the patrol to canvas Iraqi citizens for their opinions. The patrol unit was able to rest in a palace formerly occupied by members of Saddam Hussein's family.

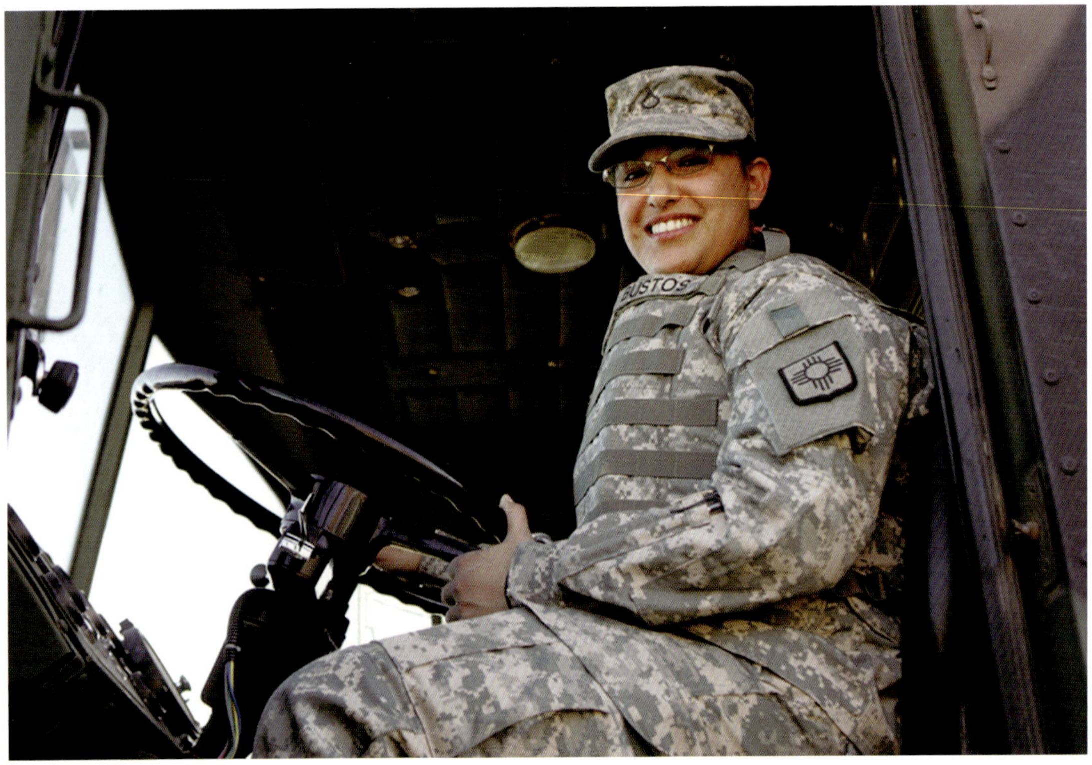

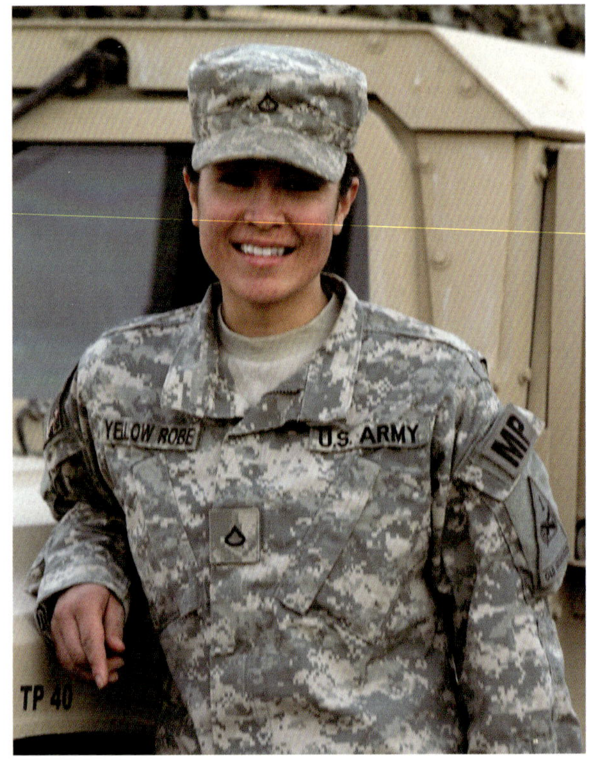

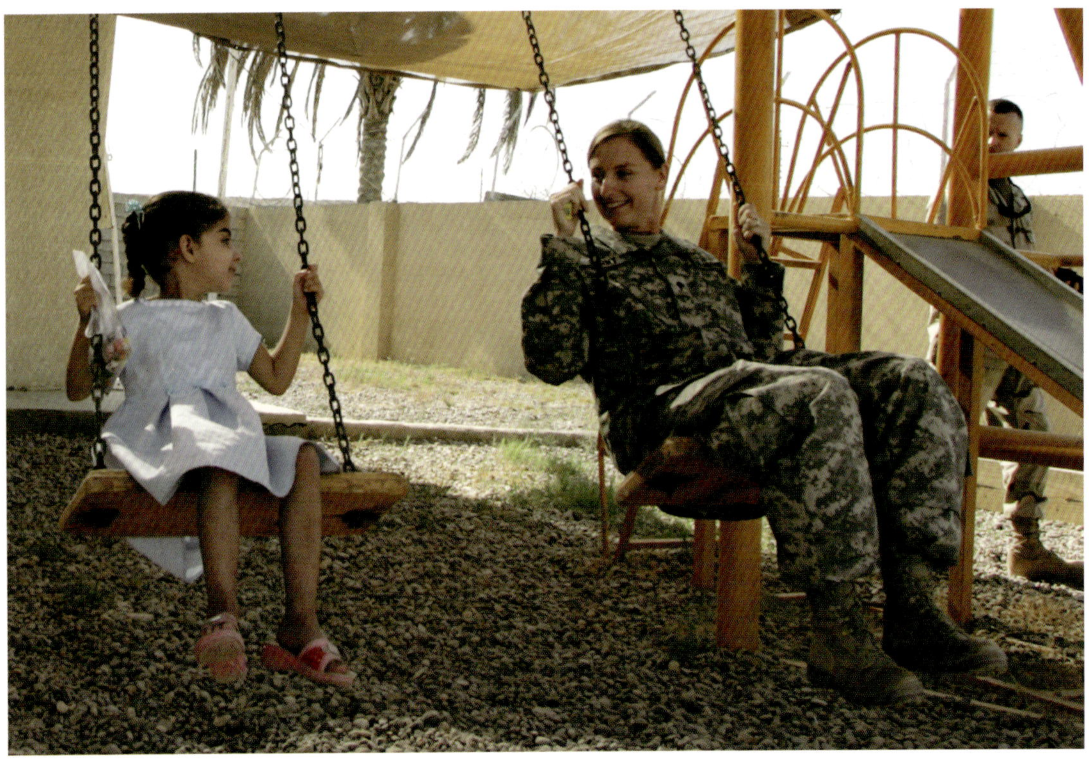

above, left: A New Mexico National Guard soldier practices operating a truck before her deployment to Afghanistan.

above, right: Sioux tribal member Amanda Yellow Robe stands beside an armored Humvee. Yellow Robe performed the job of turret gunner in a Humvee as part of a US Military Police company. The following day she participated in Operation Iron Harvest, an effort in 2008 to clear al-Qaeda from Diyala Province, Iraq.

left: A US soldier plays with an Iraqi child following the child's attendance at a US-sponsored health clinic. The weekly free clinic was open to local residents. Soldiers wishing to interact with civilians attended the clinic on a bi-monthly basis and presented toys to the children and hygiene products to the women.

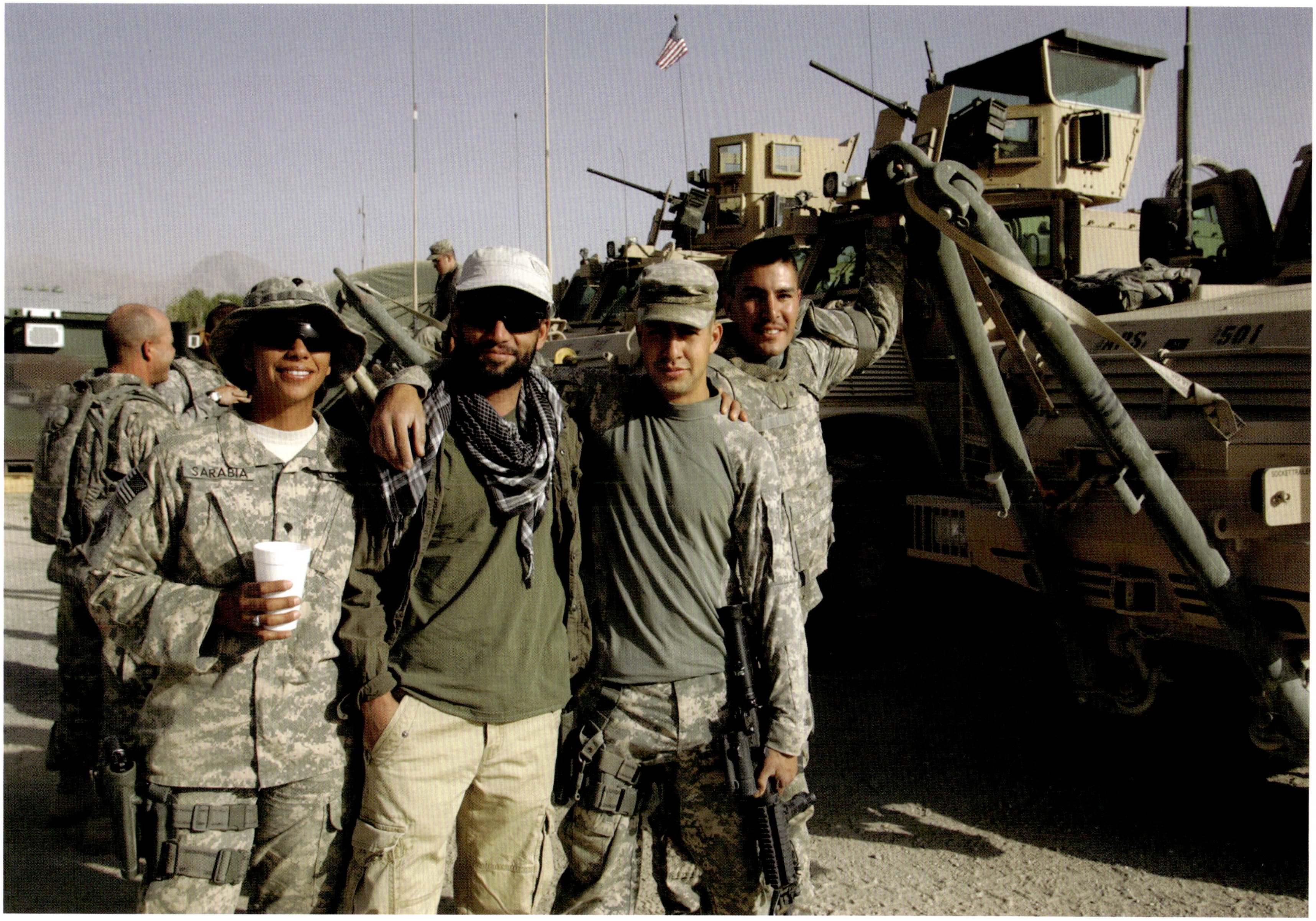

SPC Jazmine Sarabia of the New Mexico National Guard poses with fellow members of her guard unit at FOB Warrior in Ghazni Province in Afghanistan. The man standing next to Sarabia is an interpreter working with American forces. The Americans were there building guard towers and expanding the perimeter defenses. While FOB Warrior was an American base, it had been defended by Polish Armed Forces.

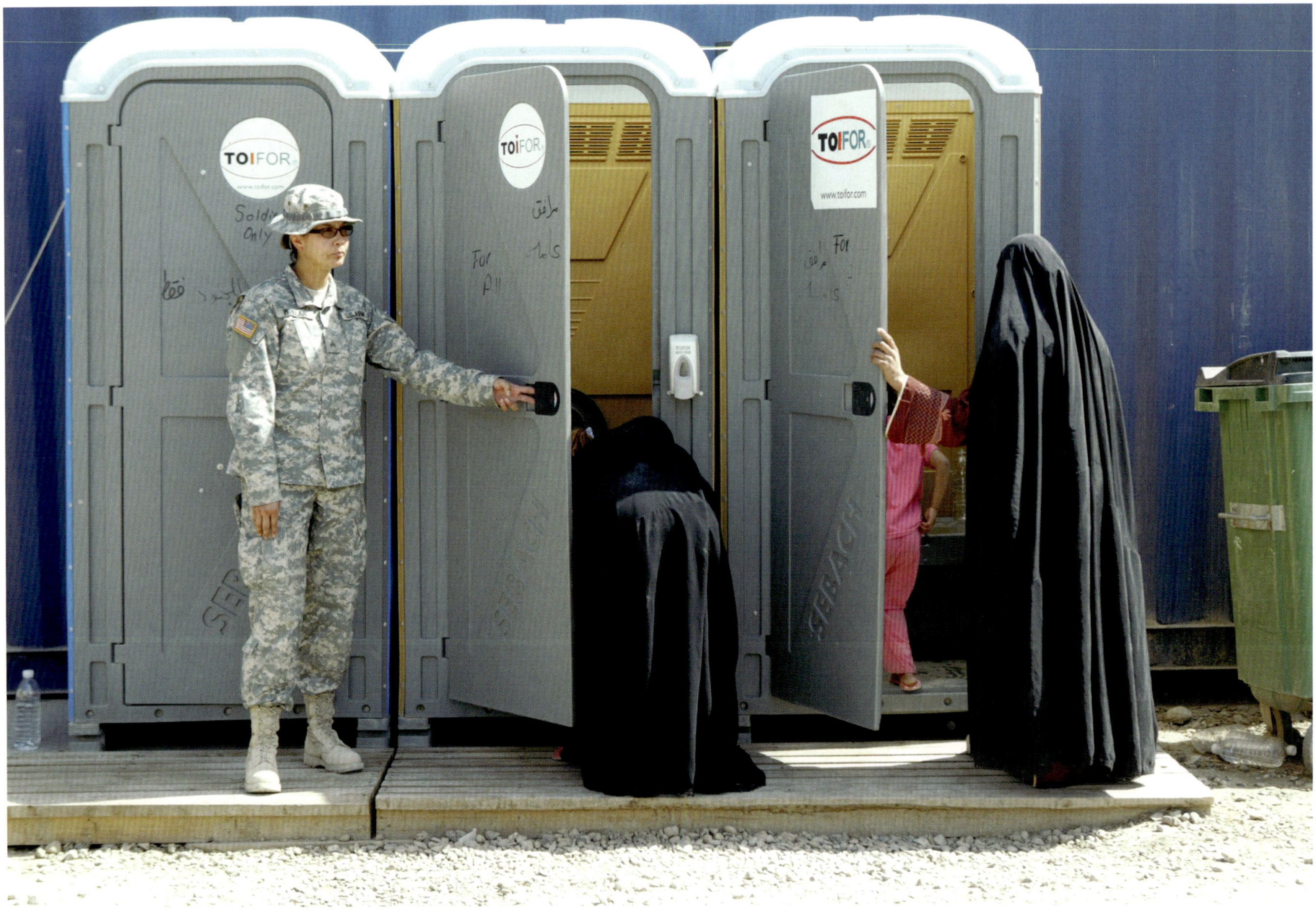

SG Whelan holds open the door of a portable toilet so an Iraqi woman is able to assist her child. The women and children in this photo are visiting detained male relatives at Camp Cropper at the Victory Base Complex in Baghdad.

Interviews

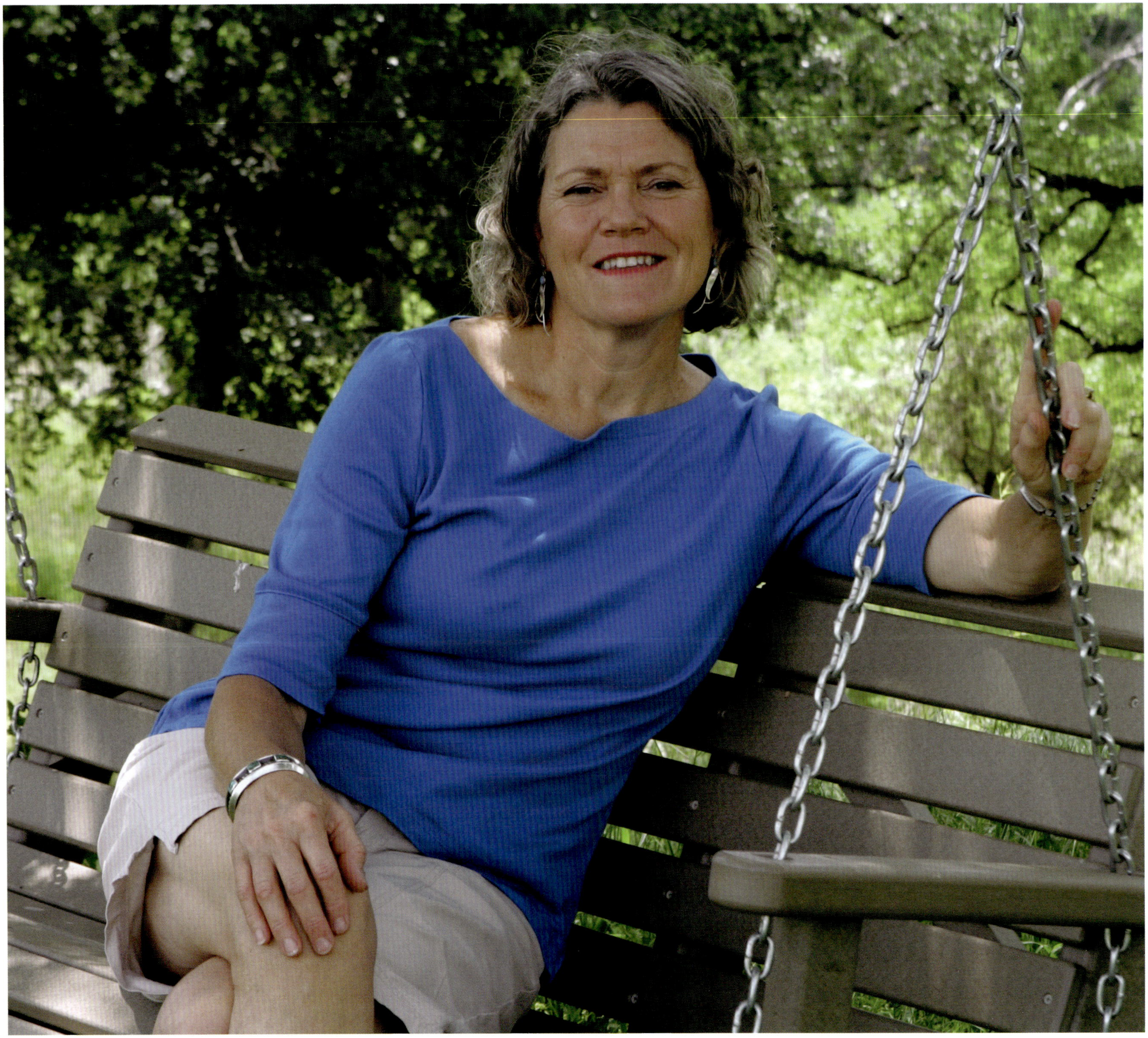

Retired US Air Force COL Kim Olsen sits on a swing at her Texas home.

Kim Olsen

Interviewed: April 22, 2013 in Fort Worth, Texas

Could you tell me a little bit about your career?

Well, I spent twenty-five years in the United States Air Force. Went in in 1979 and retired in 2005. My career consisted of mostly [being] in aviation. I was in the first generation of female pilots the air force had. I spent twenty years in the cockpit. And the last five at the Pentagon, which is very classic for an aviator in the air force. You fly for a number of years, command, and then you go do your staff job.

What did you do at the Pentagon?

I did a couple of things. I was in the Joint Staff. They call them J5, which is the Plans division. I had countries that I watched. I had Iraq and Afghanistan. It was an interesting time. Then I went over to the Office of the Secretary of Defense and worked on the Hill on budget issues. And then went over to the Inspector General's Office within the air force.

Were you there before 9/11?

Yes, and during.

You were there when the plane hit?

Yes.

So, you were aware of what was going on in Afghanistan before 9/11 happened?

We had run drills. We have these "comm lock" drills or desk drills. The one we'd run the summer before was around a nuclear device going off in New York. It was interesting because the death toll at that point was three thousand. That's what they simulated. So, they do a lot of those things just to watch your reaction, what you would do. And to kind of process through with all the agencies how you would handle catastrophes. Because they knew it was coming, but they didn't know how.

That's interesting.

They do them today, probably.

What inspired you to join the air force?

I have to blame this on my mother. When I graduated from college, I had a degree in teaching. At that point in '79, early 80s, a lot of career fields were opening for women, not just in the military but in all walks of life. And that was because of Title 9. We were sort of the generation that was benefiting from Title 9. We got into sports and we got to go to college, get leadership skills, and we then had career fields. So, I'm riding the wave of Title 9 women. And the air force had opened up a lot of its careers for women. And I had a choice:

I could join the air force, or I could teach in Homer, Michigan. Those were the two job offers at that moment [that I had] at the ripe age of twenty-one. I was walking down the beach with my mom. And I said, "You know"—because my mother was a teacher, my dad was a teacher; I come from a long line of educators—I said, "I think I'm going to follow your foot-steps and go into teaching." She kind of stopped and spins on me and kind of thumped me on the head. And she goes, "That was my only option when I got out of college. So, I want you to think again." [I replied,] "Well, I guess I'll go into the air force." She said, "Look, try it out for a while and if you don't like it, you can always go back to teaching." And I said, "OK." Twenty-five years later, I'm retired from the military. So, I guess I made the right choice. At the time.

How did you manage to become a pilot?

That's a whole long story. The gist of it was at that time in the military, I went to Officer Training School. I got my college degree and managed to get a commission somehow. There are only three ways you get a commission: the Academy, ROTC, or OTS. We call it Officer Training School. I was going to OTS. At the time, I was going to be a radar weapons controller. I went somewhere and watched what they did and I thought, "I don't want to do that. I think I want to be a pilot. I think I want to be a pilot [but] you're twenty-one. What do you know?" So, there was this whole process you have to go through to try to swap what you came in as to change your career field. To be a pilot, you have a physical test; you have to take a writing test; you have to have an aptitude test; you have to get letters of recommendation; blah, blah. So, I did all that. There were five slots. And I did this while I was in this Officer Training School. Of the five, all the guys got it, but I didn't. And I was the only female to apply. So, when I asked why because I knew I had a better record than some of the men, they said, "Well, we just don't let women do that." I said, "That's just not fair." "Well," [they said] "you need to go talk to Colonel Rush." I go down to his office and I say, "Sir, this isn't really fair. I'm just as good as the boys. And I think women should—" He kind of looks at me as if I'd lost my mind. And probably in his eyes, I had. Long story short, what I had inadvertently done was file an IG [Inspector General] complaint in the first three weeks of being in the air force. [He said,] "Yeah, you're right. We don't have a good reason to keep women from doing that." So, I was the first woman to be allowed to do that. I changed air force policy at that moment in time, unbeknownst to me. I just sort of stumbled into it. What was interesting about that is once you become the trailblazer, you are always at the tip of the spear. You are always going to be first to do X and then Y and then Z. It's not unusual that I became the first female to graduate from pilot training base. Then I became the first female to command this unit. I became the first female to do this. The first female to do that. Because, again, the military is a closed personnel system. Everybody enters at the bottom and works their way up. So, if you are the first at whatever career field, you are always going to be the first. That sort of defined me as an officer and an aviator. I became the first of many, because of the timing that I had. It's interesting because . . . we were all kind of running up at the same time. There weren't many of us and there certainly weren't many ahead of us—maybe twelve. But we all sort of rose at the same time. We kind of took those doors off the hinges for women in the military, such that a month ago, the secretary of defense said, "OK, women now could go into combat." I look back and it took them almost thirty years for that [to happen] from the first wave of women who entered combat-type aircraft. It took thirty years for them to do it. It's very interesting. It's interesting to watch. It's interesting to be in a position to watch history get made and know you contributed to that. For the ability [for women] to [go so far].

At what point did you realize that you were helping other women like that?

That's a good question. Number one: my epiphany to get through pilot training as the only female there, first and only—it was a struggle. Because men [kept saying,] "What? No." And that defines you too, because you are always proving yourself. You can't just be average. You'd better be better-than-good. Better never make a mistake. Just think about it: If you are one of two women flying a certain airplane, and one of you busts a check ride or does something [wrong], then 50 percent of the women [in your field have just] failed. Think about it. Your percentages are just so outnumbered. You just are always in the limelight. And so, you really had to watch what you did. It steels you. My husband used to say, "You're just like a turtle. All hard and then you have a soft, mushy side." I'm like, no. Because that's what protects you. It's your armor. Because it's tough—military service is tough anyway, but it's really a struggle for some of these firsts that we had. But that's OK. We made it. And thank goodness I had the personality so I could do it. A lot of women couldn't. [They'd say,] "I've had enough." And they left. That's OK too.

My two epiphany moments were [these]: The first one was when I took command, because I took command of a flying unit, an operational flying unit. I was one of the first to take an operations unit, KC 135. The first woman on the base, the first woman in that place. It was a big deal. What it told me at that moment was the military finally really validated you to begin commanding their airplanes and their men and women. You can always fly, but to give you aircraft and to give you America's sons and daughters, and to say, "They are yours now to command. And you take them to war and you take them and deploy them. You do what you need to do." [That's] a big deal. That was my first epiphany.

And the second was in 1994. They lifted some of the combat exclusion laws for women in the air force so that women could fly fighters. Before, we had not been allowed to do that. But in 1994, they changed that law and then women became fighter pilots. And I think those of us in the first cusp of women flyers proved that women could fly high-performance aircraft. I instructed in one for almost five years. And that work helped that.

Anyway, it's just interesting. And [actually another epiphany] was when the man who was picked by the president of the United States to go and rebuild Iraq—General Jay Garner, a great guy—they called him up: "Come help us to rebuild Iraq." He goes to the Pentagon and . . . he could have picked anybody in our three-million-person force we had at that time. I was just there, just to kind of help move the Pentagon thing because I was stationed at the Office of Secretary of Defense at the time, and we held the purse strings. He who owns the money wields the power. I was trying to help [General Garner] get his whole organization to deploy to rebuild Iraq. He could have picked anybody and he picked me. He was army and I was air force. He was a ground pounder; I was a pilot. None of it goes. He saw what he needed at that moment in time. And I hope I served him well. History will say whether we did [well] or not.

While you were in Iraq working with the general, what were your duties?

I was his executive officer. So, it was classic executive duties. I ran his schedule. I kept people at bay who wanted to waste his time. I kept him alive for all intents and purposes. I had seven other generals that were on his team. So, I helped orchestrate their days and their nights. Because we kind of worked around the clock. I went on all the night runs with him. He was kind of a man of the street. He drove around Baghdad; he drove around Iraq. He was all over the road. At that time, we didn't have a Green Zone. They weren't shooting at us yet; they weren't blowing us up. So, we had access to the country, and he understood the lay of the Iraqi land. We had to get to the different tribal leaders. We had to get to the different religious leaders. He knew he had to go see them, drink tea. Do what you do in that part of the world. And I was by his side for all of it.

How did the Iraqi men react to your being a woman?

I think it depended. The Sunnis were much more cosmopolitan, I think. Their daughters went to school. Their wives were allowed to have jobs. So, they had a different view. So that's the Sunnis. The Shiites are a lot more restrictive in their religious beliefs. So, dependent on where we went, if we were going to a Sunni place, I would sit next to him. No big deal. I would take notes. If we were in a Shiite, especially a very conservative Shiite area, I tended to stay outside because they always met in a parlor. The women disappeared. They segregate in that part of the world. It wasn't about me. It was about him and trying to keep peace inside this country. So, I watched and I asked; we had interpreters. I would ask, "Is this appropriate. Can I do it?" But I didn't cover [myself]. I wouldn't do it. Some guy challenged me one time—of course we had bodyguards on the street. I was being smart. He said, "You need to cover." I said, "Have you ever heard of an occupying power?" It was not very diplomatic, I can assure you, but I didn't care. When you have the weapons, you pretty much do what you want. It was an interesting time.

I can understand why you didn't always go inside for meetings. Why complicate things?

Yes, this was hard work. We were doing heavy lifting, as it was.

How long were you there?

One hundred days.

Did you have any idea of where it was going?

Yes. [General Garner] knew. He knew and could kind of see it. It was a lot like when Russia busted apart and all those small countries next to it—[Russia] was sort of the five-hundred-pound gorilla in the room that kept everything in check. Kept them from fighting each other. And if you are a student of history, you know Iraq was created after World War I by the Brits. They sort of drank too much one night and drew all these lines. How did [they] come up with that? Because it's not divided along ethnic lines. [They] did that on purpose so one place wouldn't rise against another. But the problem is, if you have a dictator, the dictator keeps the Kurds, the Sunnis, and Shiites all in check. You know how they do it. And you lift that off and they begin to find their equilibrium. So, if you look at the country in that it is three separate countries, they were pretty much on their own. And they were pretty much a democracy before we got there. Saddam left them alone. Nobody messed with them. They pretty much had things fine. They were poor, but they were fine. The Sunnis, of course, were created because again they were the middle class. They were the civil servants. They congregate around Baghdad. They got their power; they lost their power based on who was in power. They were the educated clan. The educated group. Then you have the Shiites, who were kind of in the south. It's interesting in that that's where the oil is. They had the wealth, but they didn't have the education. It was the Shiites who mostly died during the Iran-Iraq war. It was the Shiites that the Sunnis crushed after our failed Bush One attempt after Desert Storm. The uprising. They wiped out about a million of them. So, they were the poor. If you didn't fix that rub, that was going to re-erupt. And it did in 2006 and 2007 right before the big push. And again, if you were wise and a student of history, you would have seen that coming. And maybe played your hand differently. And it's easy to sit here and [be the] Monday morning quarterback. It is what it is.

How did your knowledge of politics develop? I'm sure as a twenty-one-year-old, you really didn't know much.

I didn't know anything at twenty-one. Let me tell you. As most twenty-one-year-olds don't. They think they do, but they don't. The military is set up such that you enter in at whatever career field you are going in. You get the best of that career field. So, for me it was flying. But within that, they send you to school and they promote you in rank. As you get promoted, you get more responsibility. And they widen your perspective of not just history of military and history [of] what the military was used for as an instrument of political power, but they widen it as to, "OK, where does the United States sit in this world?" And if you are going to exercise the military arm of it, what are the repercussions? And what does it take? And you get that as a young captain. You get that as a major, and you get it again as a colonel. These are different schools you go to. You go to squadron officer school. You go to intermediate service school. You go to senior service school. I was afforded all that opportunity. Right before I became a colonel, after I commanded, you go to senior service school and they make you a colonel. Because they now want you to be that adviser to politicians. Because politicians run the military. We work for civilians. As it should be. And being in the Pentagon, you learn a lot. I learned a lot in the first three years I was there. Pretty eye-opening.

Do you think the instructors were pretty objective? Or did they have their own slant?

I think where you sit is where you stand. And so, if you were in the National War College and you were taking a course from someone, say, from Israel, which we had, [that person] always slanted it towards their history and what worked for them. But your hope is, as you train up our officers today, that you get this broad perspective of all the different opinions and perspectives that people bring to the table. Because that's what you're going to deal with. If you and I are Shiites having a visit, you would have a whole different perspective of what Iraq is for you, [whereas] if I am a Sunni, I kind of want things to stay the same because I'm OK the way it is. You have to balance that in a country as you rebuild it, just as you have to [do so] across the world. Any political leader has to do that.

Did you at times find it all overwhelming? Getting those people to cooperate?

Well, I don't know if it was overwhelming. I think the task at hand, that was given to us, was a little unrealistic. When we went there, we had three charges. One was humanitarian assistance. Two was: lay foundations for democratic processes to take hold. And three was to kind of repair the country. The first one, there really [weren't] humanitarian issues. There wasn't widespread disease. The war didn't take a lot of casualties. There really wasn't a huge refugee movement. And people weren't starving to death. So that got taken off the table right away because there really wasn't any need for it. The laying down foundations for democratic process to take hold really isn't a military function. It's a state, it's an inter-agency, it's a non-governmental-organization kind of thing. [We] were like: *What do we know about writing a constitution?* That's not what we do as a military. So that was number two, that is long term. Look how long it took to get them to vote. To get the constitution, to get the parliament set up. And then the third thing was to repair what we had bombed. We just did things like, "Uh, really?" A good example would be [when] we knew we were going to take over a certain palace, have that as our headquarters. We knew that going in. So, you want to say, "Why did you bomb the air conditioning systems, you idiot? You are sending us into Iraq in May, June, and July. And we don't have any AC because you guys bombed it and took it out." You feel for the target here because you've got to make them miserable, but you've got to go in there now and live. Here we are ten years later—we had to rebuild [everything]. They had no sewage systems. They had crappy electric. Half the transformers didn't work. Any where he lived, Saddam Hussain and his cronies, yeah, it was great. But anywhere outside of that, forget it. You were on your own. That was a kind of lesson. [You] just kind of shake your head sometimes. But we were smart and didn't take out all the bridges, like we did in Europe. Remember, we took out all the bridges?

Let's talk about the role of women in the military. As you said, you went into the military during an interesting time. Things were just opening up for women. Did you ever communicate with the women who were already there and discuss how things were changing?

I don't remember making a conscious effort. I had another woman—there were only two of us who were pilots on the first base I was stationed at. And so they put us on alert together, which was good because I sat nuclear alert as a KC 135 copilot. You are just kind of surviving because you are there with all these guys and you're the first and you just kind of visit with one another and . . . bond. Holly and I are still friends today. I don't remember sitting with her at the age of twenty-two, twenty-three and saying, "Oh, we've got to change this." It was all you could do, was to do your job. I think the important thing was first to prove women could do [the work]. Because really all the military cares about is readiness.

What do you think women bring to the table?

I think women bring a collaborative leadership. Not all, but I think many do. I think women—just the way we process information, think differently—if you study the differences of genders, I think women bring [that difference in leadership]. The reason I was good for General Gardner is that I didn't think anything like General Gardner. I saw things he didn't. I could speak with women on the streets and he couldn't.

We'd go and sit in a man's living room and have a hot cup of tea, which is what you do. And at one point we go to this apartment complex and he goes in and he's talking to this guy. The guy was a retired Republican Guard colonel and he's yammering away at the fellow: "I don't want you guys shooting at us now. How can we reform you? Is there something you want to do?" In the meantime, I go into the back and was talking to the wife, who had disappeared to the back of the house, and I asked, "What do you need?" "You've got to get these kids back in school. You've got to get some normalcy back. These kids have been in our homes for almost three months now. Prep for the bombing, the bombing and the ending of the war." I said, "You are absolutely right." I went back out front and said, "Sir, we've got to get these kids back in school." "Oh my god, I didn't think of that," [he said.] And here's why [getting kids back to school was so important]: That means mom can leave the home, go to the market. [Consider] the economics of the market because [the women] do [the] shopping. That shows local normalcy, and men start to work. [The colonel] wouldn't have thought of that. I'm sure eventually he would have. That's a great example of what a female can bring to the table. I might have been the one to say, "OK targeters, if we are going to have to occupy this country, let's not bomb the hell out of their infrastructure because we've got to use it [later]. And if you bomb it, that means that I've got to send all the CE guys [combat engineers] in to repair the thing and that's going to jack the cost up about threefold," which is exactly what happened. I just think women help have the answers. I think the combination of the two is the best answer.

They complement each other.

Exactly.

At the moment, you are the CEO of Grace After Fire. Could you tell me what it is and what inspired you to take on that job?

I will go back to my opening doors for women. Those of us who took those doors off the hinges for women to open up all those career fields for my part of the world for the military and specifically the air force—I think the piece we missed when being trailblazers was, we didn't ensure that women who would do these high-end things like fly jets [would not] get in harm's way, make sure there was a safety net under them. Just like there had been for many years for the men. That safety net for a woman is probably going to look different from the safety net for a man. I'm not saying the bureaucracy isn't the same, because it is. But what women need to recover from war, because they process combat differently, is going to be different than what men need. And what happened was because of this perfect storm where we had a third of the entire force going to Iraq and Afghanistan for a decade-long conflict, you have a large number of women, almost 300,000, who've been to combat. And the system set up to take care of those vets who've been to combat had never really dealt with women who had been in combat. And so, what drives me every day is making sure they get cared for after they've been there. Women like me should do that. And we can't do it alone, and that's why I'm a huge advocate for just bringing forth [this idea]: "OK, look. Women vets are different." They just have different needs. Not [necessarily] biologically. But they've got different things going on in their lives [than men do] at the age of thirty. That's what drives me. I'd like to say I created Grace After Fire, but I didn't. The founder was a woman who was working with [recovering] alcoholics. She had been an alcoholic and recovered. And in her work, she had found that 50 percent of her clients had been veterans. She said, "Hmmm, something's going on here." So, when Texas had the big shooting down in Killeen, and all the issues and the huge suicide rate—bless the governor's heart; he dumped a bunch of money into helping vets and us. She kind of happened to be in the right place at the right time and said, "I can help you with that." She put this organization here in Texas. Since 2008, it's been here. I joined in 2010. . . . She wasn't a vet, but she was smart to know she needed a vet if she was going to run [an organization focused on the needs of] female vets.

What kind of services do you provide for the female veterans?

I have outreach coordinators in places like Houston, San Antonio, Austin, Dallas, Fort Worth, Richland Hills, and then West, where I'm from. We've trained people in El Paso. And what we do is have a warm body out there. If a female vet needs a referral, we have a large network out there to help her so she doesn't have to navigate that by herself. [We've] had [vets struggling with all sorts of issues] from suicide to homelessness, to domestic abuse, to financial—it runs the gamut. That's one thing we do, referrals.

The second thing that we do is we have a website and [a] blog, and once [vets] get in, they can talk to each other and find [other female vets for support and community]. We have an 800 number [too]. [We've also] created a peer-to-peer model in which women sit around a table and they go through a structured program about how to reintegrate back into the civilian world after being deployed or in the military for a length of time. It's called Color Me Camo. Table talk. We're pretty proud of it. What's cool about it is a lay person can get trained up as a facilitator, and then they start their own small groups in their hometowns in Texas. So, it's not that we are counselors or shrinks or anything; we are just regular female vets who have gone through their own transformation and aren't in the middle of dealing with whatever. And we can help you if you are struggling at all with your transition or help you with wherever you are in your life. [Our] focus tends to be the under-thirty crowd, and it's the Iraq and Afghanistan group.

At the meeting where I met you, the main topic was about sexual harassment and sexual assault.

I think it's disappointing that this is what our young women are dealing with. And men. It's 2013, and I remember getting sexual awareness training when I was young in the early '80s. But I think what it takes is a fundamental change in the leadership and what is tolerated within units. And I really believe that sexual assault, harassment, racism, prejudice—any of those things—impacts readiness. Sexual assault impacts readiness. It does. I mean, we no longer tolerate racism within the military today. So, my guess is that we have to treat sexual assault with the same sense of urgency that we treated racism back in the day. I think leaders have to be held accountable for assaults within their units. I think young women who are sixteen, seventeen, eighteen years old who enter the service where there are predominately men, men [who] are trained to dehumanize an enemy—think how we train them up. How we teach an eighteen-year-old to kill another human being. Well, we do a little bit of psychology on them. We have to prepare her and make her smart about what to watch for. I think females have to be trained to protect themselves. And the [other] thing is—and this is critical—you have to have men hold other men accountable. You're not going to solve this [problem of sexual harassment and assault] if it's [only] the women trying to hold the men accountable. You have to have other men hold men accountable. And the good news, I think, is that this next generation of men and women are so used to men and women together as they grow up, they aren't going to have the issues that, say, my generation has had. I really hope so, because men today are being raised by strong women. They've got sisters who whip up on them on the soccer field. They sit in their engineering class next to other women. And now with combat exclusion coming down, they will have women with them in combat and it won't be this unique unit of all guys. [Men] will be used to women as an integral part of the team because [a woman] brings a talent that makes you better as a whole. I think that is one of the—I hope—good consequences of getting rid of the combat exclusion for women.

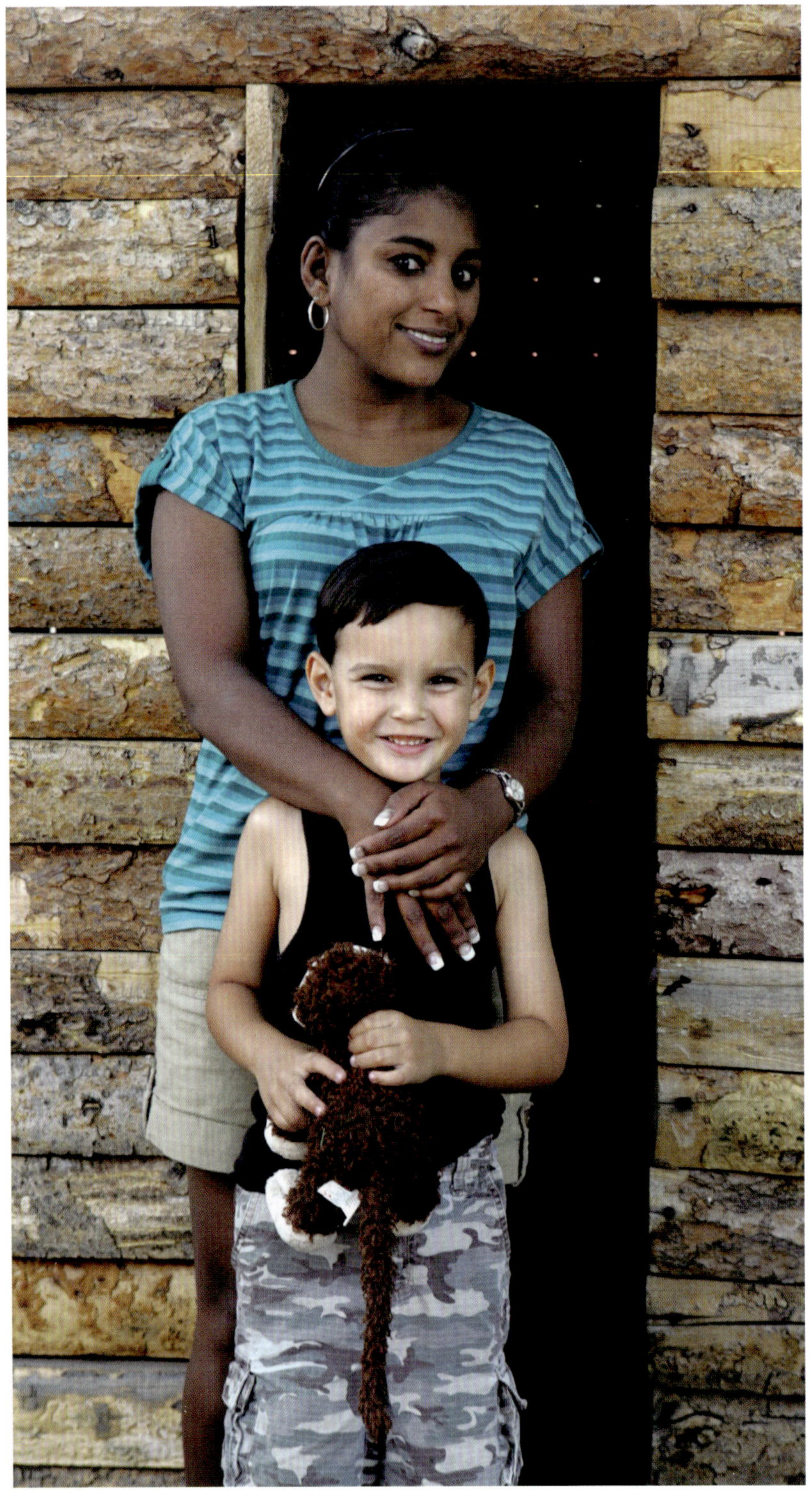

Miriam Beg stands with her son Michel at the door of a playhouse located at a shelter for women in Denver, CO.

Miriam Beg

Interviewed: August 17, 2012 in Denver, Colorado
at the Volunteers of America Homeless Shelter for Women, Brandon Center

Author's note: Ms. Beg is a twenty-seven-year-old foreign-born female veteran living in Brandon Center, a women's homeless shelter, with her five-year-old son Michel. While in the army, she met and married Michel's father. They later divorced, with the husband staying in the army, stationed at Fort Riley in Kansas and Miriam moving to Denver for schooling opportunities. She enrolled in college, majoring in history with the intention of becoming a history teacher. Her government checks for school weren't being delivered on time. Her landlord became impatient with the late rent payments and told her she was going to be evicted. Not having enough money to move to another apartment, she began to search for a shelter to take her and Michel in. None of the area shelters offered more than single-night housing, which wasn't suitable for Miriam and Michel. She learned about the Volunteer of America's women's shelter and was offered a room for the two of them. Under a government program, she is able to live at the shelter for a maximum of two years. At the end of that time, she should be finished with her course work and able to find employment. She currently has finished two years of college.

You are from India originally?

My family is, but I was born in the Fiji Islands. Most people hadn't heard of the Fiji Islands, so they would say, "Indian, like from India?" or "Indian, like Native Americans?" And I would say, "Indian like India." Because it was easier for them.

When did you come to the United States?

2005.

Where did you learn your English?

I learned it in kindergarten.

When did you join the military?

The same, July 2005.

What motivated you to do that?

When I was back home and I was in the last year of high school, I saw on the news about the Twin Towers and other stuff, and people were horrified and everything. And at the time when we talk about coming to the US, we think, "Oh, the US, we'll never go there." It's hard for people to apply to go to the United States. It's like a lottery to apply. Only a few certain people get chosen. I said OK. After high school, I applied to come here and I forgot all about it. I applied and forgot. And the US Embassy back home contacted me a year later and said, "We have your paperwork and you have been set up for a[n] interview." After three interviews, I came to the United States. I came here to make a new life for myself. Make a better life for myself.

Where did you land in the US?

Los Angeles.

And that is where you were living when you joined the military?

Yes, for a month and a half. About two months. I was also looking for a job. And they would tell me my English is not good enough or I didn't have a diploma or degree. My uncle and a friend of my family, they said, "You know the military will take anybody if they have a high school diploma. Go and talk to them." So, I went to talk to them on the same day and signed up.

Did you find a lot of other immigrants in the military?

Quite a few when I first went in. Quite a few.

Where did you do your training?

Fort Jackson, South Carolina and Fort Lee, Virginia.

What was your military occupational specialty [MOS]?

92 Alpha. Supply. Automated logistics specialist.

You deployed to Afghanistan?

Yes. 2007 to 2008.

Where were you based?

Bagram [Air Base].

Did you ever suffer rocket attacks?

I . . . the base . . . we had mortar rounds coming onto the base and stuff. Because the enemy will attack the three things that you depend upon: your food (the chow hall), your medical, and then your supplies. If they can eliminate the things you rely on, then you have no weapons to fall back on. So that is why always mortar rounds were coming to us.

How did you find your military service?

I liked it. Considering I was scared of heights. Scared of weapons. And all the violence stuff of growing up. I'm used to it. It becomes part of you after doing it for so long. For quite a while, I mean, you become used to it. It becomes like second nature to you.

Did you make lots of friends?

Yes. Buddies. Battle buddies.

How were you treated in the military being a non-American?

It was OK. I was new to a lot of things because I didn't have a chance to be a civilian that long. And then I joined so soon after I came here. It [was] a culture shock for me, being in the States itself and then the military. And then it was straight off to basic training, shipped off. It was totally new. They were yelling in your face. Oh, my mother yelled at us all the time. My mother always [yelled], "Come here right now." But it was different here. They said stuff meant to toughen you up. But most of us [started] crying. I said, "These people sound just like my mother." In the early hours, we grew up, you know, waking up early, walking to school all the time. The marching wasn't all that bad because I was walking to and from school all the time. All the way to school and back. The marching was OK. The early mornings were a piece of cake, waking up early in the morning to help Mama in the kitchen. So, the early mornings were a piece of cake. Instead of four o'clock they said three o'clock. I say, one hour earlier—what could be wrong? Just one hour earlier than I woke up as a kid. The marches were OK. The push-ups and sit-ups—I had to work on that, but it was OK. The running. Oh my gosh. I cannot run because my legs are short. I was always, like, falling out. And somebody would grab my hand. The people I went to basic with were really good. They knew I was new to the States. My African American friends, they would use these African American colloquialisms. What does it mean? Like somebody said to me one time: "How are you hanging?" And I said, "I'm not hanging. My feet are firmly on the ground. I'm not hanging." "That means 'How are you doing?'" "Oh, that means 'how am I doing.' I'm good." Or they [would] say, "You're fine." And I would say, "Yes, I'm fine," and they would say, "That means you look pretty." "Oh, thank you. OK, I'm fine, thank you."

But now I speak a lot [of] slang. The language, yeah. They helped me out. They said, "Oh, we have a mall." They took me to a mall off the base one time. "This is a mall?" They said, "Yes." They would get a kick out of watching me oohing and aahing over everything. Yes, I went to a mall for the first time. But it was good. They were supportive and helpful. The drill sergeant said, "You are going to pass basic training. I'm going to make sure of it. You got the early hours down pat. You got the walking and marching down pat. I just have to get you on the running, running, running." So, on the weekends he would run with me. The sergeant would help me. He was supposed to be off, but he would come. That was really big-hearted of him because he had a family, I found out. But he would come and run with me. He would run with me to make sure I could run within the time. Within an hour, two miles.

This was one of the trainers?

Yes, he was one of the platoon sergeants. He was really good. Sergeant Valentine, I believe. He was really a good guy. A drill sergeant and everything. Caucasian guy. "OK," he would say, "we are going to run with you." Everybody was supportive. They were nice. It wasn't easy, though. I wouldn't say it was easy, but the people were willing to help you to get you to where you had to be. They didn't want anybody repeating basic training. They want you to succeed. Do what you need to do. It's harder for them to do the whole basic training again. You want to help to get through it. You can do it. They want to help you get through this. They say, "You are going to do this. You can't fail." One time, he said to me, "If you fall out of a run, you are lagging behind. If you are in a combat zone and if you are not on it, you will let down your battle buddies." That was in my mind, so I always pushed myself.

Did you become a good shot with the M4?

Yeah. M16 at my time. Later I got the M4. It is good. The first time I fired the weapon I flew backward, OK. I was holding it right. You have to nestle it really tight in here. I'm thinking, "They said it's going to give a kick, a big kick." "What kind of kick?" I said. You have to sight it [so you] won't jerk it. It will not go places, the round. I said, "OK." The next thing you know, it jerked the weapon out of my hand. Everyone got a laugh out of it. But I improved on it.

Did you find that same attitude during the rest of your military career?

Everything they said, don't take it personally. It isn't criticism. It's meant to build you up. It's not meant to hurt your feelings. If you get your feelings in the way, it interferes with your doing your job. Especially when you get deployed. Male or female, it doesn't matter. Whether you are on the front line or you are on the FOB [Forward Operating Base], it doesn't matter—the enemy will attack. The man on the front line, he is relying on the things to get him through. He can't go on patrol if I don't supply him with [what he needs]. If I don't supply him [with] the parts for his .50 cal. Right? Even a small thing like a firing pin. Come on, you need that. He relies on me, and if I can't supply him with the things he needs, how is he going to function out there? And fight the enemy with his weapon empty with no magazine rounds? Back here on the supply team, if I can't do my job, he can't do his job. We rely on each other. We support each other.

Oh yes, it's a critical job.

They say the job is not critical, but I think differently. I think it means just as much. I would not say this, but I think we get attacked way more because every day we have a hole in the roof or stuff like that. Or the wall has been breached. They say we have mortar rounds coming in. We have to go hit the bunkers and account for everybody. Hit the bunkers to see if no one is missing or is stuck in the Port-a-John at the wrong time or the wrong place.

Did you ever suffer casualties?

Yeah, we did. We had to help. Not going into much detail [because] I don't wish to go back to remember it. We did help. I went to help the medics, help them to transport the people on the stretchers. I forgot the military term for it. They said, "We need available personnel to help us pick up casualties and the person who has a missing limb from the assault." Some of us had to stop on the way out of the warehouse and grab our weapons and our flak vest and Kevlars (helmets) and take off and help them and do that. And you don't want to give into it, you want to throw up, [but] after a while it becomes normal. It's like, you've seen it, OK. You know what to do. Help them breathing. The first step is to see if we can still help him out. I can just talk about it and not altogether can talk about it. If you dwell too much about it, then you break down. You just have to talk about it in a neutral tone of voice. Otherwise, if it affected you, then you can't function in life. And then I have to take care of him. And I can't let it affect me. And that's the way I think of it. Does it make sense to you? Am I going off on a tangent? I hope not. I am saying a little too much. I'm sorry.

When you returned to the States, how much time did you have on your contract?

They extended me again when I came back. They were talking about extending me to deploy again for a second tour. They moved me from my unit to—I was in 4th Brigade; they moved me to the 1st Brigade, to a different unit. They said something about we couldn't be in the same unit [because] it [would] interfere with our work. Our schedule and everything. Who is going to pick up the child from day care after work? It's going to affect my concentration to do my work. And his concentration to do his MOS. Move us to different units to get us prepared to deploy again. We had only one year in between. They didn't give me much heads-up. And 1st Brigade hasn't deployed since 2003. And they are talking about deploying me in 2009 with them. This unit hasn't deployed since 2003. They are only going to deploy for the clean-up mission, so we all can get out of Iraq. They said, "You won't be using your MOS out there, but you will help round up the stuff, leftover stuff, and bring it back to the States." Pretty much the situation is security, women going out on patrol standing guard and all that stuff. I said OK. And then I started thinking when I moved to the unit and they delayed the deployment again and everything. And you know what, [my husband] was in my family still, back home. I never had a chance to go to college full-time and get an actual degree. Back home after [I finished] high school, my dad couldn't afford for me to go to college. So, I got a job during the day. I got a job during the day and I went to night classes. But it was sporadic. It was not an everyday thing. It was like a part-time college class. Here a college class, a college class there. How could I afford to pay? But now I want [to] go to college full-time to get something. Not something saying high school and some college. It doesn't sound so good. I talked to my commanders . . . [and] I said, "I want to get out. I want to go to school. And I want to be able to spend time with my child because when I deployed, it was four months after he was born. The first time I deployed, he was a baby. Give birth to William and take him down south to my in-laws. They were going to be his guardians when I deployed. They wanted my family care plan when I deployed. My husband and I both deployed. He was down south with my in-laws and they [experienced] the firsts, the teething, the walking, the first everything. I told them, "Don't extend my contract." They were going to extend my four-year [contract]; it was going onto five years. I said, "You know let me get out. I want to go to school full-time. I might come back. I will come back when I have my college [degree]." That was my dream though, to go back in as an officer, so all these tall people can look down on this little, small officer. I'm just kidding.

You want to return to the military?

Yes, I want to, if I could. Before, when this situation came up, I did call the military and said, "Can I come back in?" I called the army recruiter. They said, "The only people we are taking back in right now are air force, Air Assault, Special Forces, and the guy I talked to on the phone said [the positions are all for] males, so you can't come back in right now." I said, "Oh, OK, well then, I guess I'll keep calling them. I'll keep trying." They won't let me come back in. I can use [a] steady job, steady pay [and] secure a future for [Michel]. That would be good.

He was born while you were in the military? You met your partner while in the military?

Yes. At Fort Riley, Kansas. When I got out of the army, I stayed in Kansas for a couple of months. And I then moved to Colorado. Also, with the child custody thing, they said I didn't want to be too far away, but I didn't want to stay in Kansas because Kansas [was home to] all the memories. The negative memories from the marriage. At Fort Riley, Kansas. I wanted a new start, but not too far away that he couldn't come see the child. So, I said, "Colorado is right next door." And Colorado gets good education reviews for college. Education they said in Colorado is one of the best. So, I said OK.

When did you come to Colorado?

Late 2010. I went to [the] community college of Aurora for a while. And then I did one semester at Red Rocks Community College. I moved from Aurora to Wheatridge [and] back to Aurora. I went back to community college [in] Aurora and I've been there since.

What are you studying?

Bachelor of history. I love history.

You didn't have enough money from the military to live on your own?

They usually pay you a housing stipend to go to school for full time. They pay you during the break. But they passed this new law. They stop paying you during the summer semester break. That kind of put a dent in my finances. And when they pay you the housing stipend, usually when you get paid is [the same time as when] the rent is due, between the 1st and the 5th [of the month]. They deposit every month, but it's not like on the 1st of every month or the 2nd of every month. It would be nice. It's every month. Sometimes it's on the 2nd, which is good because I can pay my rent. Sometimes it hits your account on the 12th. So now you are behind on the rent and [incur] late fees. They start mounting up. So, long story short, I am here.

You were in an apartment?

I was in an apartment.

And they said you have to move.

You don't pay, you move. Late charges and everything. I didn't have the money to pay [my landlord].

Were you able to come here straight away?

No, I had to call a lot of places. I called the Delores Project. I called the Salvation Army. I called all these places and they said, "You know what? Some of them you go there, you spend the night, and in the morning, you've got to leave." And you keep calling throughout the day to see if they will let you come back at night. I said, "I can't be doing that. I've got a child. I got a storage [unit]. I put all my stuff in storage. The landlord, the leasing manager, was giving me a lot of hard time about pay. I said, "You will get your money. I told you. I will put you on the phone with the VA people; they are responsible for putting money in my account. And I will let you talk to them. And they will explain to you that yes, the money is coming. You will get your rent. It might not be between the 1st and the 5th, but you will get your rent for the month." But [he] was very unreasonable. He was very, very unreasonable. He wouldn't listen. He [threatened to evict me]. I said, "I can't have my son go through the humiliation and the embarrassment. Or myself—I've never been evicted." I said, "There will never be a first time for that." [He] drew up a notice . . . [that said] on the morning of the 20th of March, the sheriff will come, so you be gone before then or the sheriff will put you and your stuff outside. I don't need that, so I got a storage [unit]. I had friends [at] the college I went to. This lady I had become friends with at the college, her and her husband had a truck and they helped me put my stuff in a storage unit. I started calling the shelters. That's all I did.

Stayed in an empty apartment. I still had the internet service on. I looked online. Got all these numbers. Called them. Some of them said, "You can stay the night, but then in the morning you have to be gone." You call all day to see if you can get your spot again. Some said, "We only do lunches. We only serve lunches; we don't give places to spend the night." Some said, "Three nights." I called them. I had to go to the VA all the way down in Denver. My friends took me down there and I talked to them. [They said,] "She is homeless. Can you help us? She is about to become a homeless vet." They said, "Has she been homeless for a year?" [My friends explained,] "No, but she is about to be on the street. As of really soon she is going to be on the street." This a week before the 20th. So, I talked to them and they referred me to the homeless vets on the third floor of the VA. I talked to Miss Colleen Kollen. As Ms. Ashley knows, she is my case manager. And she helped me out. She said, "You have to call the Brandon Center." At that point it slipped my mind I had a child. They called me on the 18th and they said . . . "We have a bed for you." I said, "I have a son. I said I have a son with me too." They said, "OK, then we don't have any rooms available. But if you are by yourself, we have a bed available. I said OK. Oh my god, I've got to be out by the 20th. What am I going to do? I prayed so hard. I looked online. On the afternoon of the 19th, I got a call from these people and they said, "We have a room for you and your son." I said, "Thank god." So, I came. My friends dropped me off in the vicinity and I walked here. I have a place now.

And you are able to continue going to school?

I had to leave in the middle of the semester because my grades went a little—my A went down to a B. It was really hard for me to concentrate in school with all this other stuff on my plate. And my son, I had to think about my son. I didn't want him to think, "My mother can't take care of me." And my family. I talked to my family and I said that everything is fine. I didn't want to worry my parents. My parents are getting old. I didn't want to worry my father and mother; they have made enough sacrifices for me growing up for me to go to school. They went without so my brother and I could have. For that I am eternally grateful. I said right now I am going through some hard times, but God's will be done. I will be good to go in a while. I have a conditional stable home or a shelter—I didn't [tell them] it was a shelter. I said, "A home that lets vets stay there." Which is as close to the truth as possible. Because I don't like to lie to them. I said it is a place where a veteran can stay; veterans with children also can stay here. My mother said, "OK, this is for helping a veteran out?" I said, "Yes." She didn't fully get the whole idea. She said, "OK." I said, "I'm OK." I don't want to worry them too much because they have enough on their plate. So yes, I'm here. I tell them I am OK. They have been really good to me here. Ms. Ashley has been very good to me. [Giving me] good advice, taking care of me. Helping me to be self-sufficient. I thought nobody was going to help me. I thought nobody is out there to help a veteran. I said, "No, they will help you, in the homeless vets program." They are helping out too with other resources. What you need, transportation and food. And it's good; we don't lack for most things and we have a roof over our head. We have a lot to be grateful for, right? Roof over our head and food on the table. Clothes on our back, shoes on our feet, and a way to get around. That is more than most other people out there can say. So, I count my blessings every day. Every day.

Are you going to move to Claremont Home? [The Claremont Home is a stand-alone residence for female vets who are being prepared for leaving the care of VOA and living on their own.]

Yes, I am thinking about it. It is a thinking process right now. I'm thinking. I haven't thought one way or the other, to be honest with you. But I'm thinking about it. I'm thinking it would be a good stepping stone from here to there and then my own place finally. They help you with your money. They help you with financial management, helping you with how to save money so you have pocket money when you leave. And a conditional home. You can get your own place not going broke after the first month's rent and deposit. So, you will still have money in your pocket for a rainy day. It's a good stepping stone. I'm thinking about it. I haven't made a decision one way or the other. But I'm thinking about it.

Have you gone to look at the house?

Yes, I have. They had an open day. I went to look at it. It's really good. I'm thinking about it. That's what I'm doing. Thinking.

Rhiannon Leigh Carnahan

Interviewed: October 23, 2011 in Woodland Park, Colorado

When did you join the military and what age were you?

I joined the military in 2004 right after I graduated out of high school. I was eighteen years old.

What motivated you to join?

My middle brother, Zack. He was my hero growing up and he had already joined the military and I was following in his footsteps.

You say your family has a history of military service?

Yes. My grandpa was in the army, air force. My stepdad was in the marines, my uncle was in the marines, my brother was in the army, and my other uncle was in the navy, retired.

The Vietnam era?

One of my uncles who was a marine and my dad, yes. And my other uncle who was in the navy retired not too long ago, a few years back.

As a child, did your family members share stories with you about their experiences, and were you told it was a good thing to be in the military?

For the most part, yes. I never really heard any bad stories from anybody. But the military was always a good thing.

Was it about serving the country or making yourself a better person?

It was a little bit of both. Most of the time everybody else [in my family] served [because of timing] and the draft and everything. But as I got older, it was about making yourself better. And also serving our country.

Your stepfather was a marine. What kind of influence did he have on you?

He had a lot of influence. He was the one who raised me. Him and my mother got married when I was five years old. So, he was basically my dad. I grew up with him. He helped make me who I am today.

Did he talk about his experiences in the military?

Not to me. Not much.

I have been told that as a child, you were taught about weapons.

Oh yes. Very much. Both my parents were NRA instructors. There were always guns in the house. We learned how to shoot them, to take care of them, to clean them—all that fun stuff.

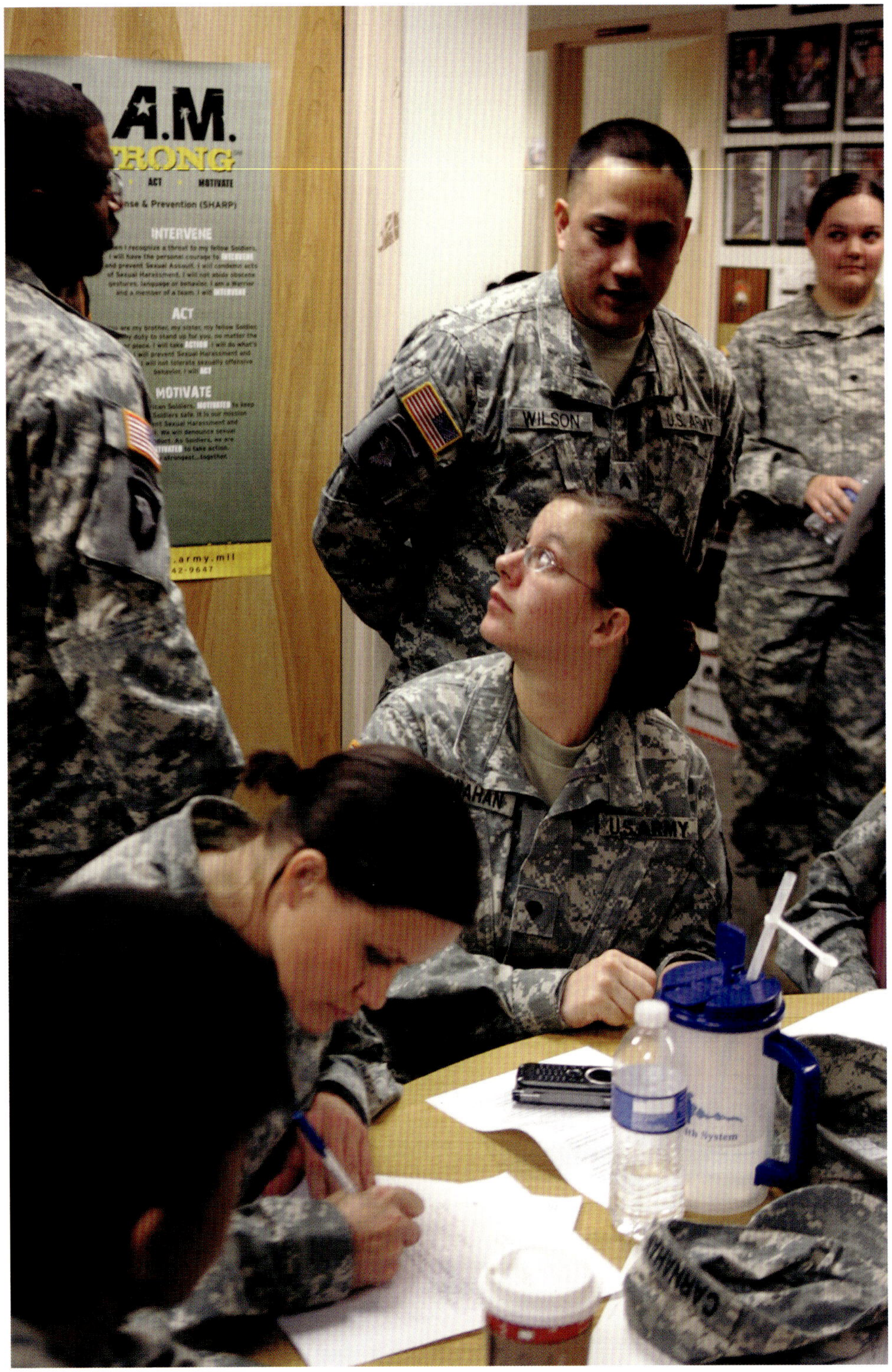

Rhiannon Leigh Carnahan looks up at a fellow member of the National Guard during a meeting at the National Guard Armory.

Did you think a lot about joining the military?

No. In my senior year, I decided it would be the best thing for college, school. Get out of where I was. I didn't want to live like a lot of the other kids living in Cripple Creek who haven't really done a lot with their lives.

Are they still there?

Some of them are. Yes.

Living disappointing lives?

I was proud because I got to Germany and see many things at eighteen years old that I know half of my friends will never see in their lifetimes.

What was it like in basic training and the first few months in the military?

Basic training, I thought, was a lot of fun. I had fun with it. Kept my head up as my brother told me it—it's a mental game they play with you. [If you] let them break you down, they will. We both had fun in basic training and really enjoyed ourselves. AIT [Advanced Individual Training], the schooling, it was fun. From AIT, I moved straight to Germany and that's really were I started my career. It was fun and scary at the same time. I was eighteen, nineteen years old moving across the ocean away from my mom. I didn't want to leave. It got better as time went on.

So basic was an extension of your life in Cripple Creek, Colorado in some ways?

Other than the yelling from the drill sergeants. But yeah. Going out into the woods, not necessarily hunting. Doing our soldier skills. Learning how to be a soldier, what needs to be done. Everything else. I thought it was a lot of fun.

Did you feel that the skills you learned growing up helped you in basic?

A little bit, yes. Talking to some of [the other soldiers] who never went out into the backwoods and played, never saw a wild animal before in their life—I thought I had a little bit of an advantage over that, knowing how to take care of myself out there. And knowing what to deal with and how to deal with it.

Did your instructors notice that and give you additional responsibilities?

Not really with being out in the woods. But they did notice with my shooting. Growing up always shooting. [Among] a lot of the females in my platoon, I shot better. But at the same time the recruiters and drill sergeants looked at it as, "She already thinks she knows." And they would get on me to make sure I wouldn't go back to my old ways, but my old ways were taught military style.

What was your MOS?

My MOS is a 92 Alpha, which is an automated supply specialist. I worked in the warehouses and in the motor pools, putting vehicles into service or issuing out parts and stuff like that.

How long were you in Germany before you deployed to Iraq?

I was in Germany for about three and a half, four years before I deployed. I had gone through two different duty stations. I was in Hammel, Germany to start. That was from 2005 to 2006 and then from 2006 to 2007, I was in Bamberg. Then I deployed to [Balad Air Base in Iraq] and came back in 2008.

You were doing the warehouse job in Iraq?

My company ran the forward redistribution point, which is [for] any other companies leaving Iraq and the stuff they left [behind]. We would go through it and put it back into the military system, so it could be issued out again. We had a few of the warehouses on Balad, and that is where I mainly worked.

What kind of equipment would they turn in?

It was mostly miscellaneous stuff. Expendable parts. But they were still in the [original] packaging, so we could re-use them.

Were you at all apprehensive before you deployed?

I was slightly nervous, but I ended up deploying three months after my full company did. There were three of us who ended up leaving three months afterward. The guys that I was with, because I was the only female—there were two other gentlemen with me—they really kept my head up and we had a lot of fun going through the training in Kuwait, which you have to do before you got deployed. We just stuck together, and [when] we got down there, I was with my battle buddy that I had been with for four years. We got stationed at the same place every time. I was nervous at first, but it got better.

What was life like for you there? Were you in hardened housing units?

We had hardened housing. We had our hooches or pods or whatever you want to call them. There was two of us to a room. We were surrounded by concrete barriers and everything. Living there was fairly easy. I mean, Balad's nickname was "Mortaritaville." We were mortared at least once a day. [Our warehouse] was on the fence line, so we were one of the main targets.

Any close calls?

Before I got there, there was one mortar that hit in our yard and ended up sending [home] one of our TWN [Third World National]. He got hurt pretty bad. None of the [other] soldiers got hurt—he was the only one. We ended [up] moving facilities about halfway through the year, to a brand-new facility. We ended up getting a mortar through that one. We were lucky because it never went off.

So, you did have reason to be fearful?

At times, yes.

Most of the time it was routine?

That was one of the biggest things they warned us [about], not to get into a routine, become lackadaisical—because we were in a war zone.

You had to wear your Kevlar and IBA [individual body armor]?

No, not all the time, no. There were times we were still in a war zone, but most of the time you could walk around in your uniform with your weapon at your side.

So, you did have to carry your weapon at all times?

Yes. The only time we didn't carry our weapons was when we were going to the gym. They weren't allowed in the gym.

What were the relations between the female soldiers and males?

In our company, we were all very close, so we kept a good, tight bond. Most of the people, there was never any fighting, I guess I could say. Especially between the male-female [relationships], more male-male or female-female. But [in this] combination, everybody got along. [Everybody] had everybody's back.

There wasn't any sexual harassment or sexual assaults?

Not in our company. None at all. There [were incidents] around the base. Females weren't allowed to go anywhere by themselves, especially at night. I know my battle buddy and I in our little hooch had a scary moment one morning [when] someone had tried to break in. There were hand prints pushing up on our window and there was a knife laying outside our hooch.

Why do you think your company got along so well?

I would guess [because] everybody knew better. I mean, most of the men were married. And then there were a few females [who] were married. Nobody tried to cross that line with each other.

Was your CO very much aware of policies?

Our CO was female, so it helped keep everything down.

Sounds like you were in a good company.

For the most part, yes.

Were there threats from outside your company?

Yes.

Did you hear any horror stories from other females?

No, we really didn't talk to a lot of other companies. We were the only company in our pod. We really didn't have to converse with other people. We all stayed close. They would have announcements out and stuff [about] things that happened. Our first sergeant would let us know what was going on.

How do you feel about your service looking back?

I'm glad I've done it. It has helped polish me as the person I am now. Especially going to Iraq. I have grown up a lot. I have learned a lot from my experiences. It is very eye-opening.

Do you think differently about America now?

Parts of it, yes. I still think there is some reason for us being there, but not as much as people think there is. This is the deadliest war we've had, and it's almost for no reason in a lot of people's opinion. So, it's hard to say if my look at America has changed because I'm on both sides of the fence.

Have you become more politically aware?

No. I don't do politics. My mom tried to get me to do politics growing up, but I just never got into it.

You don't pay attention to the news?

I pay attention to the news, but I don't necessarily care. I care more about the little things going on, not necessarily the big war things. I don't like listening to what [politicians] say after being [in a war zone] because what they say is not necessarily true.

You have a different opinion than the politicians?

Yes.

What about the high command?

I would prefer if we actually had in our higher command more on the civilian side a person who [has] been in the military—[sound of baby crying interrupts the interview]—and has seen because the difference between those who have and have not has been drastic.

Maybe we should mention that we are not alone.

I've got Skylar Ann. She is almost five months old now and fussy.

Is there anything else you would like to say about your experiences?

I think it's good for younger people to go through at least the minimum requirement, which is three years in the military, because it does help you grow up. You learn a lot and the benefits you get from the military are worth it—college and everything like that is worth it. They will pay you to go to college, no questions asked.

Have you taken advantage of any of the programs?

I started to when I was on active duty, but then I got deployed and the classes were all in [session] so I could no longer continue. Now that I'm out of the active-duty side, I have my—I'm 30 percent disabled from active duty, and they have their vocational rehab [program] through the VA that will send me to college. I have my Montgomery GI bill that will pay for my college.

Were you injured?

Before I deployed from my first duty station, I had torn my ACL completely in half.

About your reserve duties, did you separate from the military or just transition into—

I just transitioned straight from active duty into the reserve. Once I got out of it, I came home. It was December and I had three months before I had to report to my duty station. But I reported in 2010 in January to my reserve duty station in Denver.

You're in Denver and not in Colorado Springs?

I was trying to get into a medical unit because I want to become a nurse eventually. It was the closest medical unit they had, but I'm actually in a veterinary unit. So apparently vets fall into the medical system.

Have you considered becoming a vet?

No, I still want to work with humans.

How do you think you'll be able to do it?

I can do it because while I'm still in the reserves, they have a joint assistance program that also helps you pay for your college. But I've got to find time between Skylar and work and everything else to be able to go to school. I probably will wait for a bit before I go back to school. I'm going to get my CNA, hopefully working with Memorial Hospital in getting a contract with them and have them send me to school instead of using my money now.

What is CNA?

The first level of nursing. Then you pick up your RN and everything else.

Was this desire something you picked up in the military?

No. I was fifteen years old and my mother and I had gone up to see my brother up in Fort Irwin. We were driving back and we were talking about what I wanted to do, and this big nursing billboard came up and we started talking about it. My uncle, who retired from the navy, is a pediatric nurse. He has really been my influence to go into nursing.

When you and your brother get together, do you talk much about Iraq?

In the beginning, we did. Especially right before I deployed and a little bit after. We don't talk about it anymore because it confuses everyone around us. Nobody knows the military lingo like we do.

Do you feel as if you relate to each other now that you've both been to Iraq?

Very much so, yes. My brother and myself and my uncle—that part of the family, we are very, very close. I think it has to do with the military and that we've all served.

Do you feel that you have a disconnect from civilians?

Not necessarily. Some of them yes, because they will just sit there and go on and on about the war and how horrible it is and everything. But, I mean, this goes back to the Constitution. Because if it [hadn't been] for the soldiers, we wouldn't have what we have today.

Do you find you're often defending the war?

In some aspects, yes. Bush had done a good thing by fighting back, but I don't think he did it in the right way.

Do you have anything else you would like to say?

Not really.

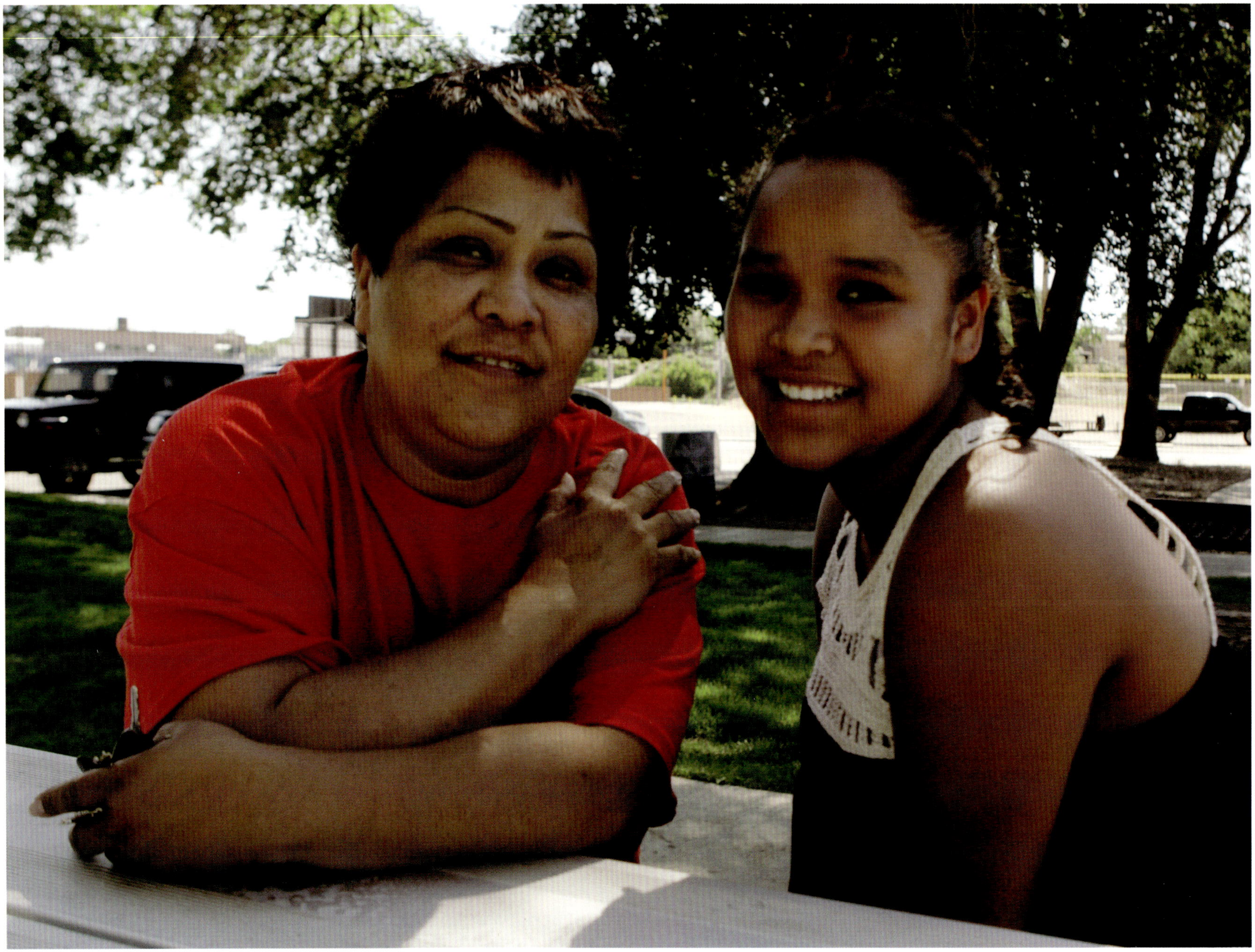

Beverly Charlie and daughter Kiara relax in a public park near their home in Farmington, NM.

Beverly Charlie

Interviewed: January 29, 2009 in Farmington, New Mexico at the local New Mexico Workforce Connection Center office

My name is Beverly Charlie and I am Navajo. I'm [from] a family of eight. Four brothers, four sisters. My mom raised us, not necessarily [with] the old traditions, but we still abide by and know of some of the traditions. I'm the first out of my family [who] joined the military. When I first thought of joining the military, a lot of [my family members] were really surprised. ...But they knew I was independent anyway, so they kind of supported it to see where it [would] go. I think my brothers kind of thought, "We'll see how far she lasts."

I think the most surprising part of the military was living with a bunch of women from different backgrounds because here in Farmington you've got Caucasian and the Navajo and the Spanish people. When I got to Fort Jackson, I was still a minority, but [there were] a whole bunch of different races as well. It was a culture shock. I started to learn a lot of the different ways of how everybody carried themselves and [how] everybody talked. I called home quite a bit and let my mom know I felt pretty lost. My mom taught us that we don't look at different colors; we don't call people "white people," "black people." We never talked like that. I was brought up to never say things like that, because my mom grew up back in the day when there was a bathroom to walk into and she [had to say] she was a Native American [and ask] which bathroom [she could] walk into. She didn't want my family to be like that and to talk like that because she's been through it. My mom told me to pray and believe in God; [my problem] would eventually work itself out. I found my way through it. One of my first duty stations was overseas, which kind of surprised my family because they didn't think I would go too far. But I went to Germany. I think my brothers were surprised I was still hanging in there.

Of course, I still got myself in quite a bit of trouble, but at the same time I think I was learning. I always called home. I kept in touch with everything. When I first joined [the military], I got an eagle feather [from my family]. They blessed me, saying I was on my way. On my journey. They had some kind of little ceremony. My grandfather was a shaman. He would go through the whole thing too. If my mom knew things weren't going too well [for me], she would have him do a little prayer, ceremony prayer. He would tell her, "Everything will be fine. She just needs to keep her feather, take care of her feather. She'll be OK." From Germany I deployed to Somalia, Africa. I think that blew my family away again because it would not be close to home.

Was there fighting?

No. We were on the outside of it. We were in Mogadishu. We would come into town in Somalia and you could see gunshots all over the place. Even at night you could see the flares and stuff, but I think we were well protected. They wouldn't let us go too far. The military police came in and took over that part. If they knew that something was going on this side, they would have us go on this side. It was really surprising. I think that was my first duty station. My first deployment. And I think just seeing it as a soldier who had first joined—you don't know which way to run. Even to take a shower. They told us we couldn't take a shower because of all the rounds going off. And they literally told us to get under our cots. It to me, it wasn't scary because I had just joined. When you are young and just joined, you want to see something. It was kind of interesting. When I wrote home, I scared the heck out of my mom. We were an aircraft unit, so we were out at a good distance from everything. I did tell her about the good things too. I got to see that. I got to ride in a helicopter. The good things—giraffe, zebras running wild, the R&R [rest and recuperation] part. Eventually we came home. I wrote a lot. My next duty station was Fort Drum, New York. After New York I deployed to Hawaii for about three years. My mom got to visit me there. And when I got to Texas, Fort Bliss, I got into an accident.

You narrowly escaped serious injury in a five-ton truck accident. Doctors felt you might have long-term memory loss. Your family traveled to Fort Bliss to pick you up from the military hospital and took you home to recover. Can you tell me more about that?

When my mom came in, they told her not to freak out because they had shaved part of my head and I still had road rash all over the place. My eyes, I could barely open. My brother stayed outside, he looked and he didn't want to come in because he didn't know how to handle it. The company said, "Let her go home. Somebody has to take her to the bathroom. Somebody has to take her pants down." I think I was back for three weeks. My sister drove me back down to the post. When I came home, I think my whole family freaked out. My family was very supportive. My brother would sleep on the floor by my bed. [My grandfather] was telling my mother again, "All she has to do is heal. She'll go back [to the military] again. All she has to do is heal." It was like a regular prayer, but he had the fire and everything [in] the traditional way.

He had the eagle feather and blew smoke over you?

Yes. When I went back to Fort Drum, that's when I was told that me and the driver were going to be charged with the accident. Me *and* the driver. And we went on a year-long investigation with that. It kind of made me mad. I told my grandpa about it, and he said, "That's the military. Let them do this. Everything is going to be fine."

Did you find that reassuring?

Yes, I think so. We all felt reassured.

Later, you were stationed in Haiti. What was the mission over there?

To uphold democracy. You would see kids running all over the place. Blood was a big issue [because of AIDS]. If one of the kids was bleeding, we couldn't touch him. We were actually in town when we were there. We had warehouses that we were living out of at that time. That was kind of interesting. Once again [I] wrote home and told [my family] what happened. When I got home, we did a light ceremony. I got more of the blessings, more people praying just to make sure I'm in good health and I'm safe when I'm overseas or I'm doing fine. Even today I could not be feeling good and I [contact my family for ceremonial help]. [My brother] was learning how to become a shaman. Normally I would go to him and have him do a prayer and talk about why I want the prayer done and how I feel today. I'm glad I got to see my family. On my deployments I would bring my medicine bag and my eagle feather. I wouldn't normally take it out because I didn't want it to get damaged, but my medicine bag would stay on me wherever I go. My mom would always ask me, "Do you have your medicine bag? Just keep it on you. You'll be OK. Everything will be fine."

Do you think that over the years you've come closer and more connected to your traditional ways?

I think so, yeah. I've grown up a whole lot more into it to where my daughter knows how to do it. She knows how to pray, she knows how to bless herself, she knows what it's for. She's seven. I know it's become a big part of [life for] me and my daughter.

She knows the morning prayers?

I won't say she's well-trained, but she knows how to go through it. I left Fort Bliss and went to Germany, and that is where I had my daughter. I had my daughter six months, and then I redeployed. That's when Iraq happened. I was still pregnant when I went to Germany so I think my family was pretty scared. I had my daughter all by myself. I had nobody holding my hand. I could do this by myself if I had another child; I wouldn't need nobody. I was told by a [German] doctor that you shouldn't have to scream: "That doesn't do nothing." Now I took all that I learned and I am more mean and to the point. "Why are you screaming?" No one held my hand. I had my daughter. My mom and my uncle and aunt came up to see the baby. They left a week before the towers fell. That was really weird, how everything came into place because of what happened with the flights. I think it scared everybody. I was really amazed— "Wow, I was just on those planes." Everybody was calling left and right, asking what are we going to do with the baby, what's going on. Then they told us we were going to deploy from Germany.

To Iraq?

We were one of the first units. We were an ammo unit, . . . so we were one of the first ones to go to Iraq. The main function of our company went up in October of 2001. We were up there just after the Twin Towers fell. I went up in December because I had to figure out what to do with my daughter. And my company there was one of the best companies I was a part of because they allowed me to come all the way back here. I flew my daughter home and we stayed in Albuquerque. My next flight was in two days, so I got to spend two days with her here. I think she was six months old. And I had to leave her. I left her here with my mom for a year. My mom made sure that I had my medicine bag and that I was good. I took all that with me. Of course, it was on me every day. So, we deployed to Iraq and stayed up there for the whole year.

We were out in the middle of nowhere. It was interesting the way different cultures were a shock to everybody. Sometimes when I watch TV or I see something even on Kuwait or any other of the places I've been to, I think, "Wow, I've been there." Or something in a movie that reminds me of something, which some would call PTSD.

Did you talk to your grandfather about that?

My grandfather passed away, I think after the truck accident. So, he didn't get to know what happened when I went back to Germany.

Anyone else in the tribe to talk with?

My brother does more of the praying now, but we went up to my sister-in-law's [house] on my dad's side because her dad is a roadman. My brother said it was too strong for him. He wanted someone that knew a little bit more than him.

Your problems were too strong for your brother? You called this man a "roadman"?

Yes, I guess like a shaman. We went to him. That was in Arizona. We drove out there and talked to him about what was going on. He said he would pray about it. He brought out the fire, brought out all kinds of stuff. He told us a little bit of what he saw, which was good. Everything was pretty good. I think anything that goes on in our lives is just like sitting down and praying with the Lord. My opinion is when the Lord made all the different people, He made different ways of praying. Different ways of us believing who He is. And with traditions or culture, everybody has their way of having their own church. To me it's the same God. We just have a different way of doing it. The Lord didn't make just one person or one tribe. . . .

Going back to the military, I got back from Iraq and got back with my daughter again. She remembered me but not remembered me. She wouldn't go near me. She was hiding behind my mom. We had everybody at the airport, which was kind of cool. After that, I took her back to Germany. I went back to Germany and finished my tour there. After that, I ended up going to Kansas. When I got there, I had to go to school for another month and a half. So, I had to bring my daughter back here [to my mom]. I was constantly driving back and forth. That's when one of my brothers passed away. I have four brothers. My company was getting ready to deploy and my mom was getting ready to go into surgery, so our family doctor asked if I could push off my deployment. At her age, I wasn't sure she would make it. [The doctor] said, "I'll write the letter, I'll do something." If I could [have gotten] just three months to six months to push back my deployment, I [would have stayed in the military]. I told myself after fourteen years [in the service], I wasn't going anywhere. I fought with [my commanding officers]. I think what made me mad was that they said they could find a family here in Kansas to take care of my daughter. I've never been treated like this since I've been in the military. If I had been treated like this a long time ago, I would have [gotten] out a long time ago. And I said, "I'm getting out now." I wish I could have stayed if things could have been different. I only had six more years to go. I think I was very fortunate. I got home with my family. I got my job here and I still help veterans. I'm not in the military, but I still help veterans when they come out of the service now. I've gotten involved with the veteran community, which I never thought existed, the VFW, the DAVs, AMVETS. I'm in the second year with the AMVETS as commander. We've got thirteen ladies in our organization, which is awesome, being a voice for women. Everyone knows that women have PTSD as well. There are things that happen to our women out there too. It's not even the enemy; it's the friendlies that are hurting our women. Within the home.

I know that a lot of our women have a lot to say. A lot of them have gotten the courage to actually say something to the VA and bring it to their attention. But the only thing I see as a problem there is that they want proof. I don't understand that part. What if something happened to me out in Iraq? Do you think I would tell anybody about it? I wanted to hurry and leave that place. Once I got out, I wanted to leave well enough behind me. But how do you show proof when you are trying to walk away from it? I think that a lot of the ladies I've talked to are in the same situation too. I've had one lady—she's trying to figure out how to get counseling statements or any kind of information on stuff like that. I don't know where to guide her. Unless she kept something.

Was this a rape?

Maybe something to that effect. It could be anything. I don't know.

Another thing I do see with a lot of our veterans, like with me, is that it's hard to get your own home. The military provided me quite a bit when I was in the military. Which was great. But now that I'm home living here [with my mom], [I'm] looking at the pay and not making enough to earn for the economy. The cost of living is expensive. I could say I'm somewhat homeless. A lot of [vets] I know are living with their families until their families get tired of them or [the vets] get tired of them, and they move out. Where do they go now? Because they obviously can't afford it. It seems like you have to have the income of two coming into the household. I've stayed with a couple of people in my family, me and my daughter. My storage is full of stuff from my own home. For the price of an apartment, you could pay for a house. I'm hoping to see an end to that soon. Every time I go somewhere, [I get asked], "Do you have a husband?" Why do I need a husband to get me a home? So they are looking for another source of income. And I think it is really expensive. I think [high living expenses] are hitting a lot of the new soldiers that are coming out. A lot of them are turning around and saying, "I'm not used to this," and they go right back into the military.

What inspired you to go into the military?

A long time ago I used to see on TV that the men were the warriors. That kind of irritated me, and I think since I was young until today, I've always [had] more of a boyish side. I wanted to do sports. I wanted to do the boy's role more. I didn't want to sit and do dishes and cook. That wasn't my thing. And then when I joined the military, I looked at it and I thought, "I want to be one of those warriors that gets up and fights instead of staying and keeping the house warm."

Was there any tribal influence?

I don't know. Maybe because I'm Native American, I would see warriors and [it would be] a bunch of guys. Our Native warriors. Where are the women at? I think girls are as good as guys. And I think I'm growing up with a newer generation too. I thought, "I want to be one of those people. I want to be able to hold the flag." I'm hearing in some powwows the women cannot hold the staff when they bring the flag in. Why not? She was in the same war he was in. I went to Iraq just like the next person went to Iraq. How come I can't hold the staff? I have interest there too. I think I would like to be that person too. Especially if I can deploy just as much as him. I've seen people who have probably been in the military the same amount of time I have and have never been deployed. I see some males come in this [Work Force Solutions] office and they look at me as if I've never been in the military. And I tell them I was [here and here]—where have you been? They kind of back off and they talk to me differently after that.

In your tribe, what were the women like?

I think that Navajo women are very quiet, even some of the ones who have gotten out in the past are still quiet today. I know I tend to take the quiet role too sometimes. But I know I've got a voice. I've seen what the world has to offer and I want to be a part of that. And I think even our Navajo people, we could move forward and we could do something. I think that our women should get more involved and go forward too and use their voices. But I think we've always been quiet. Even in my family, my brothers and the men in my family always say, "Just because you've been in the military doesn't mean. . . . " And I say, "You've done nothing for your country." It kind of makes me mad because, yeah, I'm a Navajo but yet I think I'm part of the veteran community now. I stood up for my country. One of my sisters was married to a guy from the air force, and when I came back from the military, I had something in common with him. But I never thought about it at that point because it was just my sister's husband. And he'd sit there and he'd go, "You guys did this and did this. You were in the army and you got deployed. What did you see?" They would have friends over and my sister [would say], "Why do we have to talk about this?" So now I hardly get invited to her house because she knows if I come over, that's all that they are going to talk about.

You find it hard to relate to people who haven't shared your experiences or at least show you the respect you deserve?

Yes. I'm still the younger person or they look at my age and they are like, "You don't know."

When the Native females come back, are they treated with respect?

No, I don't think so.

It's still the man's world?

Yeah, I think it is still. I just went over to a [veterans] chapter house and told them I wanted to be part of [it]. I talked about changes. I talked about what the world has come to today, as well as what I do for my job and that I'm willing to help move forward. But I don't think they want to move forward, at least a couple of the people in charge, and these [people] were men. [They said,] "Well, this is the way we've been doing it, and this is the way we will continue."

Were they veterans?

Yes. They are veterans. My grandfather, he's a veteran and I didn't even know. But I hardly know him anyway. And he stood up and he talked on my behalf and he introduced me to them. And he talked to them in Navajo. He talked about all the places I'd went. Some of it I understood; some of it I didn't. I had another guy telling me what was going on—"He's talking about you and he's telling them who you are and what you did, and you would be good for this community." I'd brought newer veterans [with me that day to join]. I said, "You're holding us back. We are the next generation." It got to the point where [the chapter leader] said, "You want my spot? Here." I said, "Don't tempt me. I will take it. You are in that spot for two years. And you see me in two years. I'll be right where you are at." And he says, "You're very confident," and I said, "Where would I be if I wasn't?" At the end, my grandfather, he hits me on my back and says, "Way to go. Good job. Good job."

Do you think things will change?

I don't know. You know, the last couple of meetings I haven't gone to because I've been busy with my job and then my mom went to the hospital, so I kind of back off from a lot of stuff even with the current organization I'm in now.

But they won't change unless you push it.

Yes, you've got to keep pushing the same way I kept doing it [when] I got shot down like that. But if it was another guy saying something, they listened to him. They did whatever. I even brought that up. I said, "You're going to get more female veterans. They are coming out of the service. They are going to say something." I said, "We're not shy no more. We're not quiet like we used to be. And the guys go, "We don't want a class on that." "I wasn't giving you a class," I said, "I'm telling you this is what is going on. This is who I am. This is how old I am. And I will be right where you are sitting. That's my goal." He just looked at me and didn't say nothing. There was another chapter house [I visited after being invited] to speak. I told them who I was, what I did, just let them know that there are other veteran communities out there that are looking for people to be a part of their group. I went out there and I talked to them. It seemed I was getting quieted. "Shhh, we'll take it from here." I said, "I'm not done talking." The guy made a joke to everybody and said, "She still wants to talk."

Are other female Native veterans going through the same things?

I think females over all are still fighting to get to where they need to be. I have a bigger mouth. That's kind of like my joke. We have one guy over in Shiprock and he is very, very supportive of our organization and invites us. But when we do stuff with him and his organization, I tend to—I say, "Why are you doing it like this?" And I just start doing it. And he just looks at me. One day I said, "I know I'm overbearing, but can you listen to my reason first and why I go this route? I'm willing to listen to you too. We both want the same thing but just in a different way." I'm trying to kill two birds with one stone. Now it's OK [and he says], "I know Beverly's got it."

I have veterans come [to the chapter] and start crying and talk about what's going on in their life: "I just need to talk to another veteran today. You know what I'm talking about. If I talk to my wife—what is that, what is this? I don't have room to cry. I'm still trying to answer, 'Why am I crying? Why do I want to cry?'" Sometimes I do see a big difference being a female. I've had guys come out and say, "I've killed twenty people." No dude, there has to be more to the story. And they're like, "Oh, you were in the military?" Their whole demeanor changes. I say I was in for fourteen years, and I think they don't know where to go with that.

Do you want to see you daughter in the military?

You know, I want to leave it open to her, but I told her I want her to be better than me. I think any parent I guess [feels that way] too. She was like, "When I join the army—" and I said, "How about you join the army after you go to college." And she goes, "Well, you didn't. I [told her], "Your rank will be higher than my rank in the long run." And she said "Oh, I didn't know that." I said that you get more rank, you get more money. And she goes, "I didn't think of it like that."

I've had a lot of the veterans speak of esteem, esteem of the tribe. Do you feel that as a female veteran? Or is the amount of sexism still too high?

I think the sexism is still a little bit too high. Like I said, I think the majority of women are quiet. But that is my personal opinion. Father-wise, I'll tell you right off I have no respect for mine. I don't really care for him. I know he is still here, alive. But the tribe, the Navajo tribe is the largest tribe, so if we were a smaller tribe, I think we would have a tighter community. Tighter to where we would help each other. But I think it's so large that we are kind of scattered. We don't know each other well enough to help each other. Because we've got part of the Navajo tribe going into Arizona, up to Colorado. It's so big, they don't even know of each other's chapter houses. I know they used to have a medallion that they would give to the veterans to recognize them. I've never seen that happen again. You know the majority of our code talkers came from the marines. And the majority were

Navajo. When I first got out of the service, I had a Navajo friend. He was a veteran. I was working at the Motor Vehicle office at that time. I didn't even call myself a veteran [then] because when I looked at veterans, I always [thought] of World War II, Vietnam, the Korea era. I never thought that I could take that place—just step in and stand side by side with one of those guys. I said, "Wow, you're a veteran!" He said, "You're a veteran." So, we started talking while I was doing his driver's license. And he goes, "Did you know you could get this; did you know that—" No, I didn't know. He was actually the first person who ever taught me what I needed with my benefits. Told me about the VSO here. And when I went to the VSO, that's when I started going into the community and that's how I became the founding commander for AMVETS. And thinking we should get one for all females. There are female organizations throughout the Navajo reservation, [but they're] scattered. Not loud enough to get help or be recognized. I've had Navajo women come up to me and say, "We've already tried that, that doesn't work."

They were veterans?

They were veterans. But I think they were kind of mad because [our group was] being heard and we are loud.

Do you have a War Mothers society over here?

As far as that goes, I think it's just Gold Star. I haven't seen anything else. I've seen Daughters of the American Revolution. I am kind of learning about them. In Farmington, it's like everybody is involved in that, which is kind of cool. But on the East Coast, the Daughters of the American Revolution is the majority of one [skin] color and they won't let any other colors get in. I've brought this up to these [people] because, I said, our veteran women organizations are of all different ethnic groups. If you don't accept one, then we will not be there. And the lady goes, "I am a veteran. I know that veterans are of all different ethnicities. So please come and be part of our flag day." I was interested. I'm still learning. Even with the chapter houses. Each chapter house has its own veteran organization, [funded by] their own money that was allotted by the federal [government], I guess money that is given by the Navajo presidents or whatever they do over there. And how much is allocated to each chapter house.

What is the Lady Warriors?

A subchapter of the AMVETS. Our post is the 1912 Lady Warriors AMVETS. Right now, we've got thirteen [members]. We've got ten lifetime [members] and three [members who] are coming from Albuquerque.

Are these women all Navajo?

No. Of all different ethnic [backgrounds]. We have Zuni women, a couple of Navajo girls, one from Oklahoma. She's Cherokee. She's [fair-skinned]. She says, "I might look white, but I'm not. I'm Cherokee." She's very proud. We've got an African American woman. A few Caucasian ladies, two or three.

You don't have to be Native American?

No. We are an all-female veteran organization and whoever wants to join, we want to get them involved. I always think that at the front line, you don't have a bunch of Navajos standing in one corner and then a bunch of white people in one corner and a bunch of blacks. It's not like that. So why would we do it for the organization? The ladies, they are just as happy and content with everybody joining because the more the merrier. We are all women veterans, and we all have something in common. We visit with each other. Now we can say we have friends. I know before [getting involved in veteran organizations], I never went outside my family. A lot of my old friends, I don't know what they do. If they have kids or are drinking or whatever.

Do you feel that you've changed so much, it would be hard to relate to them anymore?

I saw one friend and I said, "How many kids you've got?" Probably the wrong question to ask. I saw about ten running around. She said, "Let's go to the club, let's go do this." And I was like, "I don't even want to go, I don't do that." I want something different. You're right, what would I have to talk about?

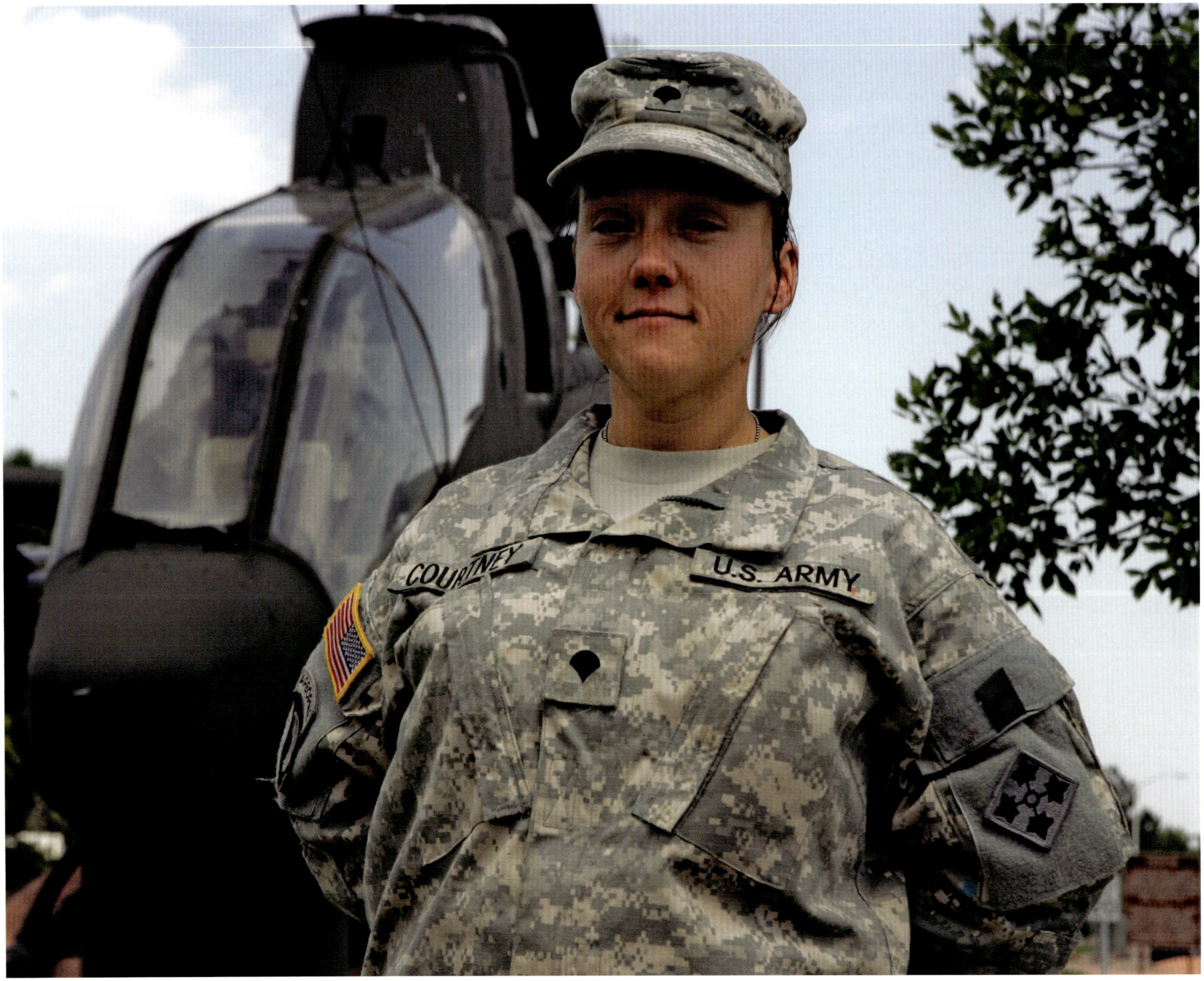

Sarah Courtney stands at the front gate of Fort Carson in Colorado Springs, CO.

Sarah Courtney

Interviewed: August 9, 2012 in Colorado Springs, Colorado
Based at Fort Carson, Colorado

When did you join the military?

January of 2007.

And you are still active?

Yes, I am.

What motivated you to join the army?

Initially it was an escape from the life I was living. Halfway through basic [training], it became more than that. It became patriotic. More or less. In basic training, they show you videos of the stuff that's happening overseas and what [happens] to our soldiers. It has the potential to change you. It made me more patriotic. It made me definitely appreciate what we have in America.

What do you think motivated your fellow soldiers?

Everyone has their own stories. Some people were just like me, escaping the life that they lived. Some people were army brats for their whole life. I have friends of different calibers. Everyone joins for their own reasons, I guess. Like I said: different people, different reasons.

You've stayed in, what, five years now? What is the average contract?

The average contract is three years. Actually, it's eight years, but they want you to do three active and then five in the inactive reserves [where] basically you are on call. You are out of the army [after three years], but if they decide they want you back, you have no option. They call you whenever, for five years. So, I joined for three years with the five-year hold period. I reenlisted after my first deployment, went for six more years.

What was basic training for you?

It was not as bad as I thought it was going to be. TV definitely overplays it. Or maybe it used to be that way. When I went, it was kind of hard. I'd say mentally harder than anything, being away from home and friends. Physically you do things you never thought you could do. Basically, great for me. It was something that opened me up to know I could do things on my own. And I didn't have to be afraid to try everything. I was very timid when I joined.

Were you treated well by your instructors?

I was treated well by most of my instructors, but you know, everywhere you go, there is going to be that person who just doesn't like you. And they are not really sure why they don't like you. They just don't. I had a drill sergeant [who] was like that; she just didn't like me. I had problems with her, but then they moved me. After that, basic went real smooth. I liked all my instructors, for the most part.

What was your first duty station?

Fort Campbell, Kentucky. First time being away from home. I was there for two months, and then they deployed me to Iraq.

What is your MOS?

I am a Chemical Biological Nuclear Radiological Operations Specialist. It sounds fantastic, doesn't it? Basically, I maintain and issue out equipment for chemical, biological warfare. In the event we got attacked, I teach everybody how to protect against it. And I maintain the equipment that protects them against it. That's about the short of my job. The long and short. There's not a whole lot to it. Radiological hazards, detection, decontamination. Stuff like that.

There wasn't much demand for that skill in Iraq?

There was at one point—when we first invaded over there, from what I'm told by other seniors, because I wasn't there. They did need it; they did have to wear it all the time. But the reason it's not such a threat [is that] chemical warfare kills thousands of people. The collateral damage for civilians and surrounding area is too great for them to want to use it. And that is in any country. And that is why we are on a kind of a Geneva-Convention-kind-of-a-truce with chemical warfare. Because the civilian casualties [would be] just awful. Not a big demand. Not right now.

But Saddam Hussein did gas his own people.

There is a bit of a call for it. But like I said, the fact the threat is small doesn't mean it's not there. [Learning how] to shoot my gun doesn't mean I'm going to go shoot it. I'd rather know how to do it and protect against it than not know anything at all.

You were telling me earlier that you were the only female in your unit. How did that go?

When I got to Iraq, most of my platoon, the other NBC [nuclear, biological, and chemical] people, you never are supposed to have that many in one company. There are extras of everybody sometimes. They put me over there, and being the only female was really, really hard. It's hard enough in the army. You have to earn the respect of your male counterparts as it is because you are a woman, you are weaker and supposed to be more emotional and all of those things. The males tend to not want you around. They don't want someone watching their back who is potentially weaker than they are. So, it was pretty bad for me when I first got there. It took me eight months for me to earn their respect as a soldier. I never earned it as a person. But I definitely earned it as a soldier. I just fought through it. It was bad. I've been through worse, I guess. Worse things in life.

What was your platoon doing?

My platoon was a security element for EOD [Explosive Ordnance Disposal]. Basically, EOD is the guys who go out and blow things up when they find bombs and stuff like that. When they get out, they obviously can't carry their weapons [while] they set a charge on something to blow it up [and even] working the robot takes two hands. So, they need a security element. I was a gunner in the second truck for EOD security. I was working the turret behind the 240 machine gun.

Were you ever called upon to use your weapon?

I never had to use it. I never regretted it for a second. I never regretted not having to use it. I don't want to hurt anyone. If I had to, I would. I never regretted it.

Showing up at the explosion sites, you must have been exposed to some pretty awful things.

Yes, I have. Everyone handles war in their own way. And everyone gets whatever they want from it. It never really bothered me to see people killed or stuff like that. I know that I'm going to die one day regardless, so it really wasn't that bad for me. But on the same token considering everyone handles it different, I know people who have had mental breakdowns from the same things I have seen. It's not that bad for me. I grew up in a hard neighborhood. I wasn't really sheltered as a child. I've seen worse things than someone blown up from a bomb. If that's how they went, it's probably better they went that way than some of the things I've seen.

You came from a rough neighborhood?

Yes. I did.

Where were you in Iraq?

I was between FOB Liberty and FOB Prosperity. Most of my time was on Liberty. I was on the FOB because we were always on missions.

When you were on base, did you have other females to buddy up with?

No, because I pretty much went on mission and slept. That's about it. If I wasn't doing that, I was with my platoon. One of the dudes was something. I was the biggest screw-up because I was a female and a private. My friend was the biggest screw-up just because he was. He was my best friend. That pretty much kept me grounded, having a battle buddy that I had to take care of. He was just so awful. He was a good guy, though. My best friend. No other females though.

How did the rest of the platoon treat you?

Most of them were indifferent. And the ones who weren't, tortured me by making me do physical things like push-ups, sit-ups. They call it "smoking" or "hazing" or whatever you want to call it. I did that for four hours straight one time, in this thing called The Sandbox. It was a sand pit in Iraq, ironically. Wow, sand in Iraq, but in the sand pit. That's what they called it. It was like a sandbox. And [one of the guys in my platoon] smoked me for four hours. He kept throwing water bottles at me every half hour and making me drink so he could continue. In an Iraq summer. It was awful. It was not the first time.

This guy just didn't like females in the military?

He was my squad leader and they just wouldn't listen to me. Every time I turned around, one would tell me something and I would try to do what that one told me to do, and the other would get mad at me for doing what the other one told me to do. It was, like, never-ending. It wasn't so bad because I've worked with females since then. I came here and now I'm with a lot of females, and I can say, personally for me, I'd rather work with males any day. I'd rather work around all males, I guess for the same reasons males don't want us in the army. Because some females are so preppy and prissy and shouldn't be in the military.

Was there much sexism?

Well, yes. There's sexism always, though. That's apparent everywhere. Not that I'm some female activist or anything. It's obvious in a lot of things. I mean everyday life. But in my platoon, yes, I was the only female. That's one of the reasons I got tortured. They thought I was there to bust up their little ball party. I wasn't—I got assigned there. It wasn't a choice. When after they realized I wasn't there to cry about everything, they kind of left me alone. They mostly left me alone. They were mostly indifferent.

It took them eight months to figure that out?

Yeah. It took them eight months to figure that out. I could have gotten them in trouble way before that. That's another thing men are afraid of [with] women in the military. We tend to possess the power that unfortunately they don't. It's segregated because we are the weaker species. According to everybody. [But] I've seen women who can out-PT [physically train] men. Mostly we are the weaker species. They tend to not want us around as much.

Power—what do you mean by that? Power to complain and get them in trouble?

Because rape and stuff like that, because we are the weaker ones. If you got a guy and a girl standing next to each other and the girl says he raped her, mostly society is always going to go straight for the guy. They're going to believe what she said. He raped her, he's bigger than her. They are going to take that at face value, before the facts. And that's unfortunate. Mostly, but not always, sometimes people are innocent. Men are afraid of us because all I have to do is run and say, "Oh, he touched me in an inappropriate place," and his whole career is ruined. That's all it takes, for one woman to say, "He did this to me" or "He said an inappropriate word around me." And now you have a complaint against you. That's why they are afraid of us.

Have you heard of that happening?

I have a friend who got put out of the army not too long ago because there was a young female soldier who was drinking underage, something she always does, drinking underage at the barracks. And she said this private raped her. This dude just got into the army. Twenty years old. And his whole life is ruined. He got kicked out for it.

Did he have sex with her?

No, he didn't, because they were all drunk. He was nineteen years old [at the time]. She was twenty. Because they were all drunk and they did actually do it. Well, he didn't. Because their friends saw the pretense. It was going to happen. Yes, he's out. I let him live with me for about three months after he got out and I went ahead and paid for him to go home. I tried to help him as much as I could. I know the girl. The girl is my friend. I don't hate her, but I think if you are the kind of girl who does this kind of stuff all the time, don't ruin a man's life just because you got touched. Don't put yourself in that position. It's all about what position you put yourself in. I mean, if you see a whole group of people with guns on one side and people over here with Bibles on the other, are you going to run to the people with guns? I mean, *What*? You are putting yourself in a position where you could get shot. So why not run to the people who've got books? So, she put herself in that position. And she got my buddy kicked out. It happens a lot, quite a bit in the army. A woman holds the power that a man can't touch in the military. That kind of thing happens quite a bit in the army. But at the same token men physically hold more power than we do. And they get to do a lot more stuff. I wanted to be a combat engineer, but because they stuck the word "combat" in front of it, I couldn't do it because I don't have the lower extremities.

Yet you can handle a machine gun in a turret?

That is another thing I don't get about guys. That's what I told them: "Why do I have to be strong to pull a trigger?" My son can pull a trigger, and he's seven. He doesn't need to train hard at all. But even then, there are tools. Like I told you all the time, I'd rather be smarter that stronger. On my first deployment, I was cussing. One of the NCOs [noncommissioned officers] in my platoon, he told me to get down. And I'm like, "Permission to know why I'm dropped." He said, "I told you about all that cussing." I jumped up so quick, and I said, "I'll quit cussing when you go in there and tell every man in that room he has to stop cussing." That NCO, he said, "What makes you think you're equal?" I said, "You put a tractor tire out in the middle of a field and put a chain on it and put a guy on it and he may be able to drag that. You put me on it, I'm not going to be able to move it an inch. What makes me equal is that I'm going to keep trying till you tell me to stop." I don't need to be strong. I'd rather be smart. You don't have to be strong to be in the military. I would prefer that people who join have some semblance of intelligence. That would be preferable. Because me and that 250-pound guy [in that hypothetical situation] dehydrate at the same rate. The difference is he's going to carry all that heavy shit while I'm going to build something to carry all that heavy shit. I have no problem with women in the military. I think men don't give us enough credit. I don't need to be strong. And they say the other reason is a man is quicker to save a woman than he will his male counterpart. That's bullshit. I promise you, if a woman and a man are dying, I'm going to save whoever I can get to first. I'm a soldier first. Gender means nothing to me. I like these soldiers. That's how I look at my male counterparts. We can all be naked in a room together and I don't care because we're all soldiers. That's really how I see them.

Since you were a gunner and keeping everyone safe, did that change their attitude about you? During the patrols, at least?

During the patrols they never talked to me. I just kind of did my thing and they left me alone. I did what they said. They said, "Turn it here," [and] I did that. If they said, "Turn it there," I did that. Even if they were wrong. It took me a long time as a private to figure that one out. Just: "Roger, check." Move on. Even if your idea is stupid. They didn't change their attitude towards me at all. I just did my job. They were just leaving me alone because I was doing my job.

Tell me the story about throwing out the bottle of water.

Everyone joins for their own reasons. And everyone stays for their own reasons. On my very first deployment, we were out on patrol. Soldiers like to throw candy and stuff to the kids in Iraq and Afghanistan because they don't have nothing over there. We were rolling through this neighborhood that looked like one of those neighborhoods on TV, like [something you would see featured on] Feed the Children. Stagnant water. There was a dead horse half a block away, just decaying in the middle of the street. There was a four-year-old and a three-year-old, brother and sister. I threw them a cold bottle of water. When they picked it up, they looked at it as if they had never seen cold, clean water in their entire lives. And the look in their eyes when they looked at me—that made everything I've done prior to that and everything since that in the military worth it. Every bit of it. It's not just about going over there to kill the enemy. You have people gung-ho to do that. I'm over there to help other people. In this deployment I just had, there was a five-year-old on our FOB. His brother worked in one of the shops on our FOB. He didn't have anyone to play with. So, I got some bubbles in the mail. And I took them over to the shop. And I played with this kid for an hour and a half with bubbles. He'd never seen bubbles in his whole life. He was in shock. I couldn't help thinking, "If you've probably never seen bubbles, then you've probably never bathed. You've probably never seen a sink full of dish water. You've probably never seen a bathtub full of bath water. All the things we take for granted. Even the smallest things down to a bubble. Brightened that kid's entire day. Probably his entire week. People who don't have stuff, they appreciate it so much more when they get it. So that makes it worth it for me. Hell, that kid is probably going to grow up. That's another thing about people in general—one act of kindness can change a nation. Maybe that kid was going to be the next Taliban leader, and maybe he's always going to remember that one female soldier who wasn't mean to [him] and who sat there and played bubbles with [him]. Maybe one act of kindness can save the entire world. People have got their heads up their ass too much these days to understand that. I don't. I understand I could have changed that kid's whole life by one act.

Both these stories came out of Afghanistan?

The first one was Iraq, the cold bottle of water. The second one, with the bubbles, was Afghanistan. When I was just there.

When did you return from Afghanistan?

I've been back for one year now. We got back in 2011.

Do you anticipate going back?

Yes, we are deploying again soon. Not there. I can't say where and when [but likely] in the next couple of months.

Can we talk a little more about sexual harassment in the military?

Sexual harassment in the military is a big thing. Something a lot of people don't know is that actually a lot of it is male-on-male. A lot of it is same-sex sexual harassment. That's probably because there are more males than females out in the middle of nowhere. It happens more like that. Everyone has a different take on it. And everyone perceives how they were assaulted differently. I really don't see it too much. But I'm a very lenient person. I'm in the military. I'm not exactly Susie Homemaker, Betty Crocker. Whatever you want to call it. I take it a little bit differently. I've never been assaulted. I have a few friends that have. I don't really know anyone who is a perpetrator. There's a zero-tolerance policy in the military, and that's everywhere in life. Don't touch anyone inappropriately without their permission. Don't cuss at people. And stuff like that. It causes issues. So, like, it's not really the biggest problem in the army. I would say more bullying would be the biggest problem in the military, to me. The fact that you have seniors that get to say whatever they want. Or because they have more credibility. That's another thing—just because someone has been in the army for twenty years doesn't mean he's not going to lie. Doesn't mean he has more credibility than I do. That's ridiculous. Sexual assault is so touchy, literally, it's a touchy subject because you don't know who is right. Anybody can say someone touched them. Now you've got to prove it. You don't know who's right. The zero-tolerance policy automatically makes you guilty, whether you did it or not. If someone says you did it, then you did it. It doesn't matter if you are innocent. It's a zero-tolerance policy. If they do find you innocent or something like that, they'll move somebody. They'll generally move the perpetrator before they'll move the victim. Sometimes it goes the other way—the victim is the one who gets moved. But yes, I think the policy on that is a little harsh, but it's necessary because there are too many loopholes if you're any kind of lenient on that. Too many loopholes: "Well, I touched him, but I didn't touch him there;" "I said this, but I didn't say that." I've never seen it go on. Maybe I'm lucky.

What would you tell a woman about joining the military?

I would tell her that joining the military is no different than working anywhere else. When I first joined, people were like, "Oh, you joined the army, you could get killed." I could get hit by a drunk driver as soon as I walk out of this restaurant. I could get hit by a drunk driver as soon as I walk out the door of my house. Life is a gamble. Any job you do is a gamble. You could be working at McDonald's [and] you could potentially burn your face off on one of the ovens. Every job has its hazards. As far as me joining, it was the best thing that ever happened to me. It changed me, for the better. Especially considering the life that I was in. But then it changed my personality. I was very timid. I was a book reader, a bookworm. Don't talk to nobody. Don't meet their eyes. I joined and I changed. I changed very much. I did things I never thought I could do. I definitely recommend it to anyone. Would I recommend you stay until you retire in twenty years? I don't know if I'm going to do that myself. So, I'm not going to recommend that to anyone else. That doesn't make any sense because I don't know if I want to do that. I don't want to wish bad things on people. Your experience is going to be whatever you make it. Your experience could be awful, or you could be one of those laid-back people who really [don't] care what anyone says. OK, you said something stupid to me—I'm going to keep on walking. Other than that, think of it as middle school. And there it is. And now you're in the army. Middle school with PT all day long. With Phys. Ed. class all day. That's what the army is. That's true.

Is there anything else you want to say?

I would like to say this to anyone who reads this: Just try to be happy. Enjoy the little things. Because there are people who don't have anything. . . . Enjoy grass, trees, flowers. The cool breeze on your face. Butterflies. All these things you don't get to see for years at a time when you are deployed. "Oh my god, there is grass!" So yeah, try to live and be happy even with the smallest things. The breeze in your hair. The sun on your face. Anything. Try to do that.

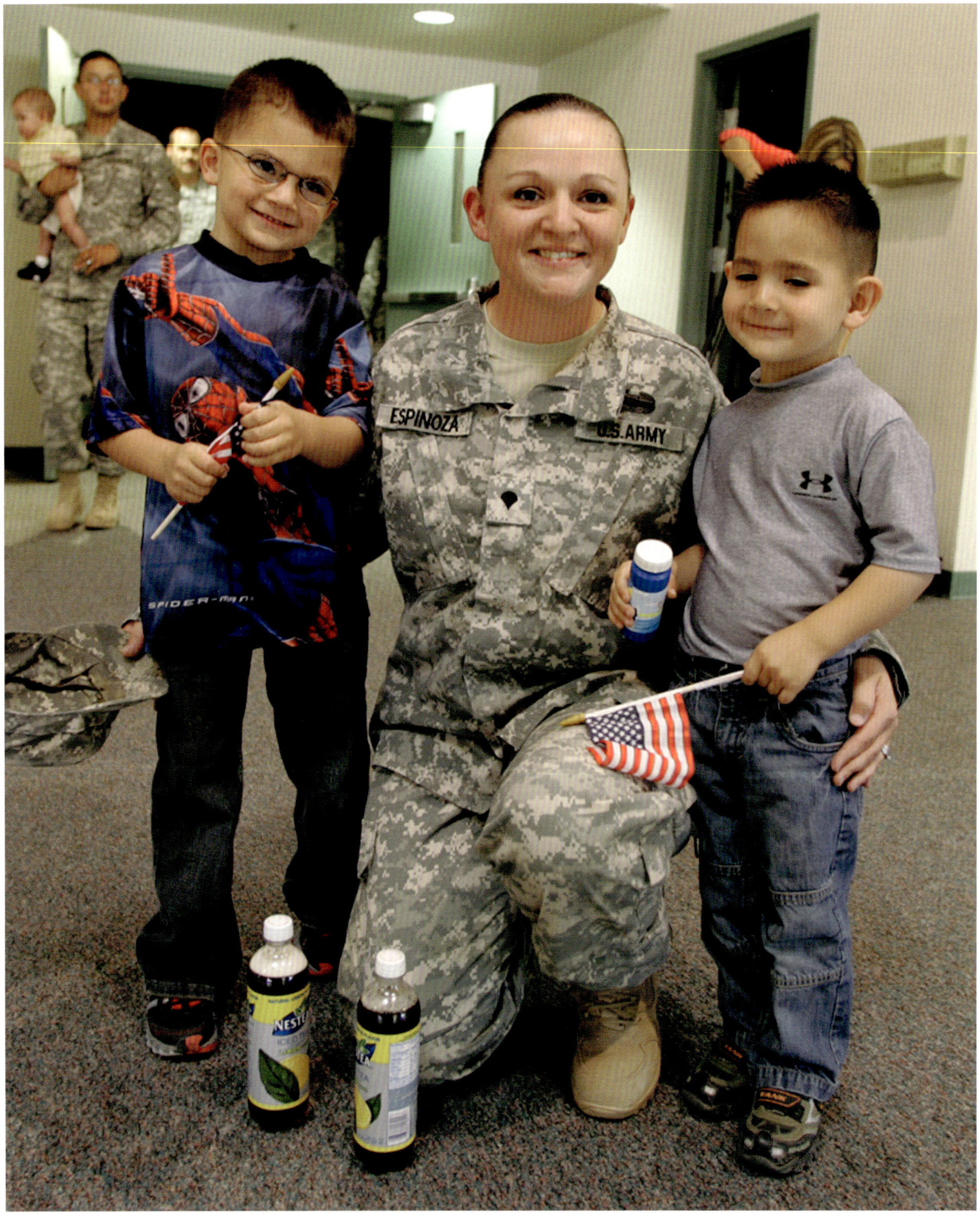

SPC Angelina Espinoza with children Justis, left, and Mickey, right, at the Yellow Ribbon ceremony in Roswell, NM.

Angelina Maria Espinoza

Interviewed: September 23, 2009
Stationed in Combat Operations Base Morales-Frazier, Kapisa Province, Afghanistan

Would you please give me your name, military affiliation, and age?

Angelina Maria Espinoza. I was born in Crow, Texas [in 1982]. I'm in the Roswell, New Mexico National Guard, 920th Horizontal Engineers.

You were in the active military before?

Division 3rd Brigade.

You did five years with them? What was your MOS?

Before that, I wasn't an engineer. I was a cook with the combat engineers out of Force ID.

What inspired you to join the military in the first place?

My life was going down a bad, bad road. And I needed to do something to change [it]. I changed over to the military.

You felt you needed a little discipline in your life?

Yes. I needed it.

Were you at all apprehensive about joining the military?

Oh, no. I had no money. I had no place to go. I was down to my last student loan. I had a drug problem.

Where were you going to college?

I was majoring in nursing. I was going to [school in] Brenham, Texas.

Were you at all concerned about the possibility of being in combat?

It didn't even cross my mind.

Were you ever deployed while you were in the active military?

Yes, I went to Iraq. We went in 2003. We were part of the first wave. We were part of the combat engineers. We went with them. There was a very small handful of females who went. It was a true experience. It was awesome.

You said you were deployed in 2003?

Yes, we deployed in 2003. Being a female in that situation, it was new. Especially for me—I was six months out of basic training. I had just barely gotten to the unit. I didn't know anybody. The few friends you did know, you barely knew. You barely got to see them. I was scared. I was twenty years old. I didn't know anything. I didn't know much about the military, my job, or anything. I was a fresh person. That's all I was.

Where did you go in Iraq? How close to the front lines were you?

We went everywhere. Tikrit, Fallujah, Kirkuk, down the Tigris River, all the way to Baghdad. We were in a lot, a lot of places. We went everywhere, it seems. But the main ones that stick out in my mind are the ones I just named.

Did you ever feel you were in danger in any of these places?

It's weird to say, [but] it was the unknown that kept you on your toes. You didn't know what was going to happen or anything like that. The unknown was what kept you aware of the situations. You didn't know what to expect till you expected it. I don't know if I'm explaining it right. Being out on guard duty and stuff like that, you don't know if that donkey is strapped down with bombs or anything like that. You are watching the donkey. You are watching kids. You are watching everything. Because you'd heard all the stories about, "This happened, that happened," and everything else. You are watching everybody. You were watching everything, so it kept you on your toes. It kept you more alert. It kept you alive.

This is an emotion that you think everybody felt?

I don't know if everybody felt it, but whenever I sat down and I talked with people we deployed with [or] with my husband's friends, [that seemed to be an emotion everyone felt]. I was closer to my husband's friends than the people in my own squad because I don't get along with many females. I don't like cattiness. I don't like the drama that some females bring. I get along better with males. But they felt all the same things, even though they acted all macho. They said the same things: stay alert, stay alive.

You mentioned your husband's friends—you were married at the time?

No, I wasn't married. I barely just got married this March.

Was you husband part of your unit?

Yes, he was. I was in headquarters; he was in Alpha Company. He was a combat engineer.

Was he out there at the tip of the spear?

Yes, he was always running missions and everything like that, clearing buildings. He was doing the stuff, good stuff. When they came off roadside bombs, he would be out there. He was doing things I'd be too petrified to do. I was scared for him.

Where did you meet your husband?

We met in the motor pool in Fort Carson, [by] Colorado Springs. It was snowing that day. It was cold. We were doing inventory, laying out all of our equipment. I kept running in and out of the building, trying to stay warm. I was blonde at that time. I had dyed my hair blonde, blonde, blonde. He spoke Spanish to me because at that time my name was Sanchez. I spoke it back to him. "A blonde girl. A little white thing like you. Why are you speaking Spanish?" And I told him my last name. That's where we met. [W]e've been together since then, January 2002.

Is he still in the active military?

No, he wants to come back in. I guess people get used to people telling you what you are going to do, what is going to happen. Tomorrow we are running that mission. This is the time we are going to leave. I think he wants to come back in because he misses that structure.

The military to both you and your husband feels like home?

Yes, it does. We both come from rough backgrounds and everything like that. Your background is what you stand on. That is your foundation of who you are today. That is where you come from today. I think that is where both of us come from.

You got out after five years and then you joined the National Guard?

Yes, I joined for a year for the Texas National Guard. Then I moved up to New Mexico. [This coming January], I [will] have been in the New Mexico National Guard two years. I have seven years in the service right now. I tried to do an interstate transfer, but it didn't go through. I had to wait my time out and then come into the New Mexico National Guard.

Have you bonded with these people?

I should say that the National Guard is not the place for me. Active duty would be a better place for me. The mentality of [each] of them [is] different. They have more of a civilian mentality than [what you would find with someone in] actual every-day, all-day active duty.

Will you go back into the active army?

No. I'll finish out nine years. By the end of this contract, I'll have my nine years. I'll go back to being a full-time mom. I'll probably go back for my nursing degree.

How old is your child?

I have two amazing, wonderful little boys. I have a five-year-old. His name is Justis. He just lost two teeth last night, his bottom two teeth. Then I have Mickey, four years old. He is my cuddle bug. They are both truly amazing.

Your husband is taking care of them back in Roswell?

Yes, he's taking care of them. He's being Mr. Mom.

Is he enjoying it?

Yes, he's telling me all the stories. He's doing everything I would do if I was back home.

I'm sure you miss your children. But your husband is doing a good job?

I'm pretty sure there are things that I as a mother would do better. But he is doing a good job. He's doing real good. Making sure they are fed three meals a day. Going to school. Going to the park. And everything like that. Doing the doctor's appointments. Everything they need to do. I think he is doing a good job. I'd give my left arm to be home, to be with them. I'll never do this again. I volunteered for this to re-class jobs and everything like that and to come over here. But I'll never do this again. Being a mom is too valuable.

When I first ran into you at the New Mexico Guard Armory in Santa Fe and your company was doing training exercises, I noticed you were carrying the M249.

The M249? The M249 is a light one. It's a squad one. It's only to sustain the squad. And because of the ammunition that is carried, it is the same as the M16. The 240 Bravo—that bad boy is a heavy one. It's in between the .50 cal and the Mark 19. But it's right in there above the SAW, the M249, and the regular .50 cal.

In that training exercise, a simulated ambush, I noticed you were much more aggressive than the male gunner operators.

I put it into my head that it was real. I would want to go home to my kids. It's either [the enemy] or me. I'm not going home in a body bag. I'm going home walking, talking. Alive. So that I can hold my babies. There is no way . . . some people look upon it as a sin if you kill another person. If it's them or me, I'd rather it be them.

When did the 920th get over here?

We got over here on my birthday, June 25. We left Manas over in Kyrgyzstan. We left there on June 25 and got over to the base, Bagram Air Force Base, on my birthday.

Then the company went to O-E? [Orgun-E, a FOB in the department of Paktia in eastern Afghanistan]

Yes.

I understand that you were on a convoy that was ambushed and you were a turret gunner.

I don't remember the exact date, but it was in July. We were doing a convoy. It was a pretty large convoy. They were saying it had been one of the largest convoys that had been able to leave out of that area. On that convoy, one of the gunners got shot in the face. A lot of people got hurt on that convoy. It was out of the RCP, where the gunner had died.

It was one of the Afghan National Army [ANA] gunners?

Negative, it was an American soldier. The RCP is a Route Clearance Patrol. One of our 916s had broken down, and it was about a mile out of the hot zone. It's a sixteen-wheeler with a smaller cab and with a long trailer. Something went wrong, and it locked up. They couldn't get it out of gear. The brakes were frozen. We pulled up. My MRAP [Mine-Resistant Ambush Protected tactical vehicle] was [model] 504. And we pulled up on the left side, I was pulling security on the left side. A five-ton pulled up on the right, which had Sergeant Haines in it and PFC Jonas. And it pulled up on the right side, and we were pulling security for them. And on that 916, we had a blown-up MRAP and we were transporting the MRAP over to Sharana, [Iraq]. They were deciding whether or not to tow it or blow it in place. They were trying to decide because in front of us we had a lot of personnel and they were stuck inside that ambush. I [was] just scanning my left side. They were scanning the right side. They had called for a dump truck to come back and try to unhook the trailer from the 916 truck and try to tow it away. But it wasn't working. We had a convoy coming up behind us, so what ended up happening was that they had a wrecker truck to go ahead and try to recover it. They also had an empty-bed bobtail. We were stuck there for like an hour or so. I couldn't leave my sector of fire. We wanted so bad, everybody inside my truck, we wanted to go forward to go help them. Because you could hear everything on the radio coming through; they were hollering, "Contact Right, Contact Right, Gunner down," and everything like that. You can hear all this stuff over the radio. You wanted to tell your driver, "Just go. Just go. Just go. Let's pick up the personnel and go help them." You feel helpless because you can't go over there to help them. You kind of feel [as though] your child is hurt and you can't take away [that] pain. There is nothing you can do for them. You feel real helpless. Vulnerable. You can't do anything about it. It felt weird. By the time we ended [up] going to Sharana, our vehicle had been hit three times. We didn't even hear it. I guess the armor is too thick and [because of that] we couldn't hear it. And with our headsets on, we couldn't hear anything either—just to know that if the armor was not there, the three bullets would have killed three people. None of them hit the turret. The bad thing is that we have so much gear, yet so much of it is junk. My ammunition was junk for my .50 cal. The round was old. So, it expanded inside my barrel. It cracked my barrel. I think the good Lord was with us, because if we'd gone forward. . . . And had I tried to fire my weapon, I wouldn't have had anything. The only thing I had was my 240 Bravo and my SAW. I would have been throwing bullets from my nine mil at them.

You weren't required to return fire?

No, I wasn't.

Have you been on convoys since then?

No, I've flown everywhere else. There really haven't been any convoys since then.

How do you feel about the experience?

I don't know. I think my anxiety level went up higher than it should have been. I don't know. From my experiences in Iraq and now this, my anxiety level is times ten. It doesn't seem to unwind, even when I try to sleep. It doesn't seem to unwind.

Do you think you have PTSD?

I'm not a doctor. I don't know. I don't know if it's PTSD or just not being able to release [this weight] off of my shoulders.

Do you feel uptight at home?

Like with my children? I don't know. I feel like a little kid all over again. It's a learning experience. I'm learning everything with them all over again. Stuff I forgot in school. I'm learning everything all over again. And it's awesome because I'm getting to relive things I missed out [on] when I was a kid. Do everything all over with my children. I think it's awesome, doing everything I wanted to do with them.

Would you encourage other females to join the military?

I think if they do decide to join the military, they have to be able to bend. They have to be able to forget some of their own personality traits. And be able to pick up and learn from other people's mistakes. They have to be able to learn. They have to want to change for the better. And if they are going down the wrong road in life, I would encourage them to do at least three years [in the military]. It will teach them something. It will point them in the right direction. The military opens a lot of doors. I may regret it now, but I don't know where I'd be right now if I [hadn't] joined the military. I'd probably be in prison instead of working in a prison.

You are working in a state prison now. It's a level-two? And it's all males?

Yes, it's all males.

Do you see any similarities between the males in prison and the males here?

Yes, I do. And I think a lot of the males and a lot of the troops and a lot of soldiers, they join the military in order to change their lives. I think if a lot of them hadn't joined, I'd be having job security all the time.

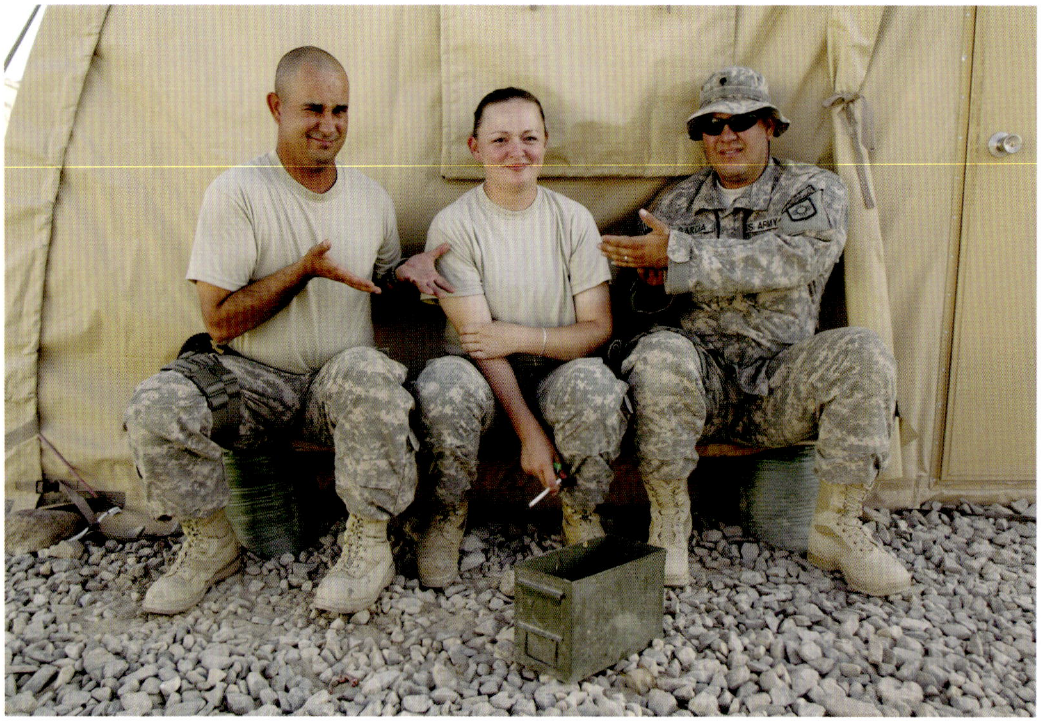

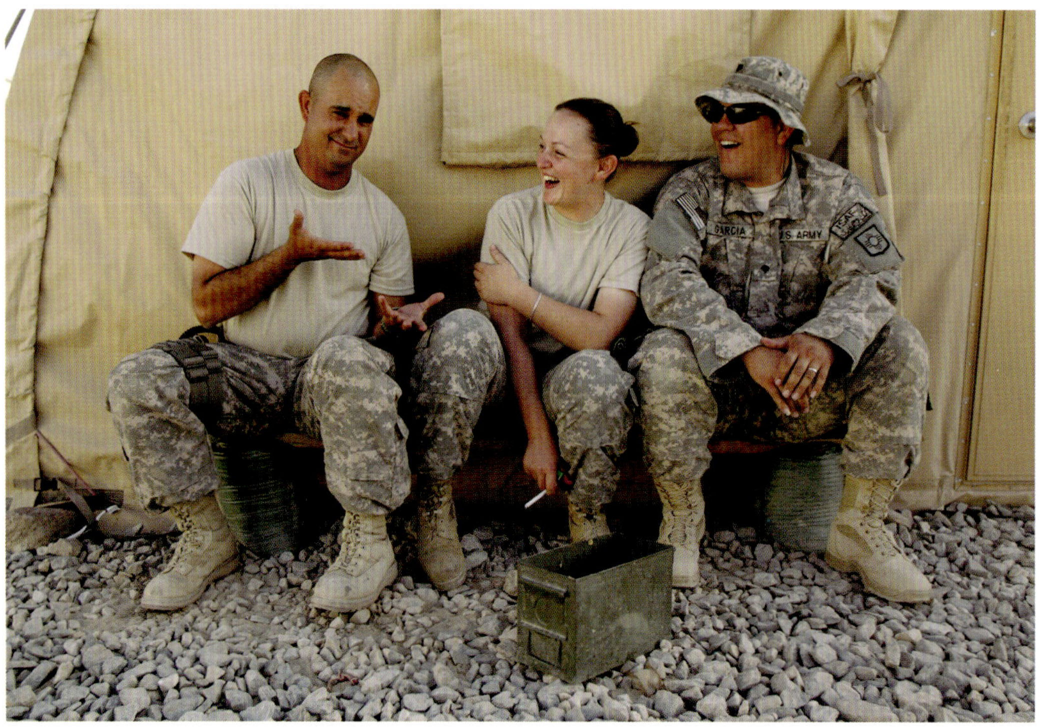

SSG Donald Tackett, SPC Angelina Espinoza, and SPC Mathew (Matt Matt) Garcia goof off in front of their housing tent on FOB Morales-Frazier, Kapisa Province, Afghanistan.

Author's note: As I was interviewing Angelina, SSG Donald Tackett and SPC Mathew (aka Matt Matt) Garcia walked by and wanted to provide this quote:

Females in the military have a tough time with the stigma that a lot of male soldiers put on them. SPC Espinoza was a great asset to us in MF. She took over the ordering of food and cooking for the American side as well as arranged cook-outs with the French. Espinoza also moved dirt along with the rest of the engineers. She was just as tough as any of us and didn't complain about the harsh living conditions (living in an eight-person tent—that leaked—with eleven soldiers, dirt floors, no AC, no water rations for personal hygiene, mortars, no mail, dust storms, [and more].

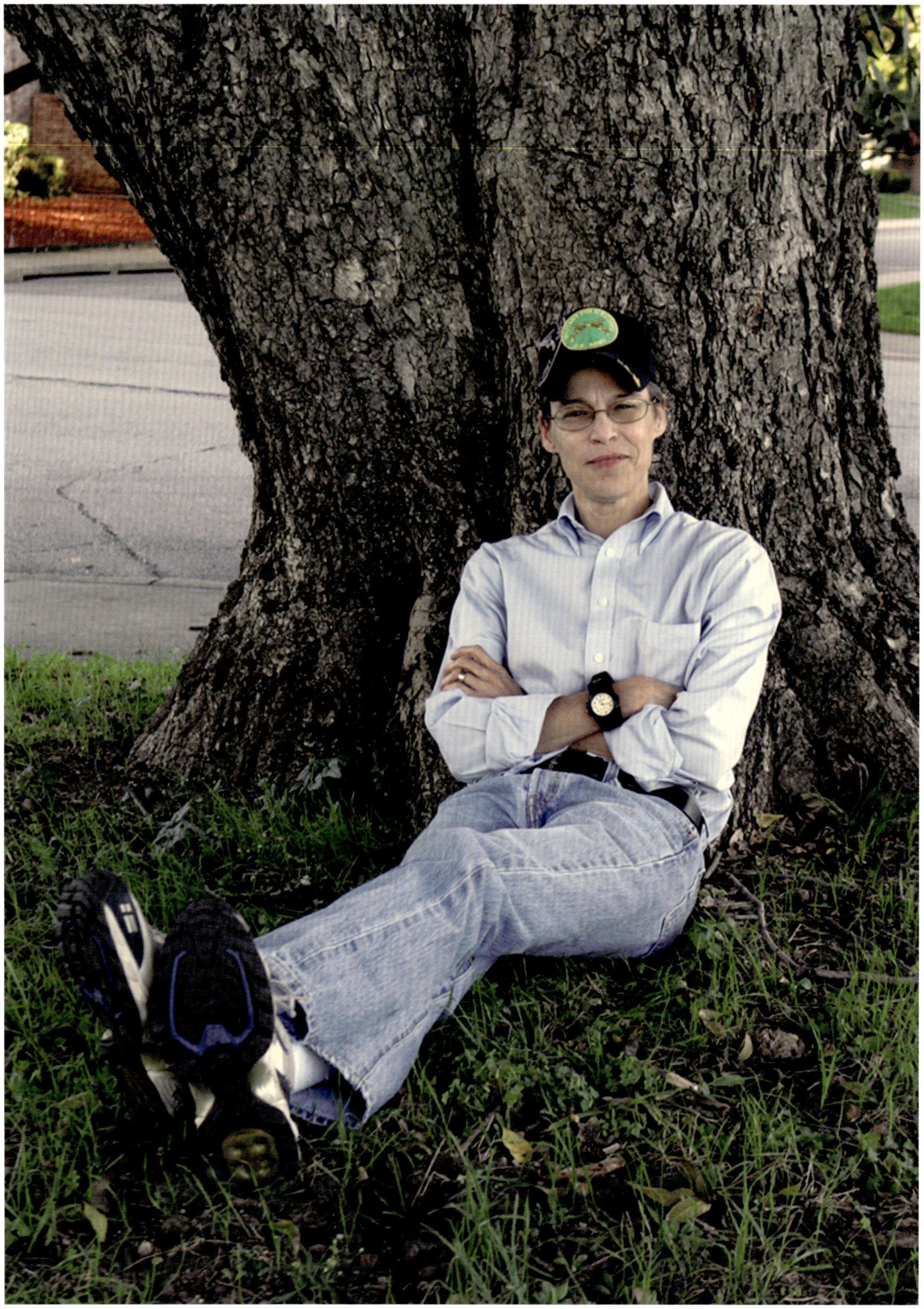

Roselle Graskey leans against a tree near her East Dallas, TX apartment.

Roselle Graskey

Interviewed on October 19, 2012 in Dallas, Texas

Why did you join the army?

It's kind of a sad, funny story. My parents broke up when I was two. My mother made the mistake of telling me around the age of seven or eight that my father had been in the army. All I ever heard was, "You are exactly like your father." At age eight, I thought, "I'm going to join the army at the age of eighteen." I did. I was very fortunate. I had the world's coolest army recruiter. He was honest with all his recruits. He told us exactly what to expect, how hard it was going to be, how hard you could make it on yourself. I had been preparing myself since the age of eight to be in the army. I think I saw every army movie that was made during that time period, in [those] ten years. I had a pretty good idea of what to expect. And I talked to a lot of soldiers, because El Paso is where Fort Bliss is. We had neighbors who were soldiers, and I asked them questions. I was lucky—they were as honest as you can be with a ten-year-old kid. They actually gave me good pointers, too. Basic training was quite an eye-opening experience. I was not sheltered, but I was naïve in a lot of ways.

At this point, was the army open to having females?

It was 1985 and the army was open to having females. It was fully integrated. But there was still the attitude [that] women don't belong in the army. Especially from the older guys. You heard this a lot as a female MP: Women don't belong in the army. Women don't belong in the MP Corps. There were a lot of older senior NCOs who had a very negative view of female MPs. I think everyone has the mental image of MPs clearing up barroom brawls. I've done that. In fact, one of my concussions came from a barroom brawl. And I was stationed overseas. I was actually stationed during my MP years in Germany. The second little town I lived in, Bad Kissingen, was my law enforcement realm of duties. We had engineers and cavalry scouts, and then support personnel. Engineers and cavalry scouts do not like each other. When you mix that intense dislike with copious amounts of German beer, you get bar brawls. And that was part of it.

When the Gulf War began, I was in Lubbock, Texas. I was going to school at Texas Tech. And when I got off active duty, I was out for nine months, and I absolutely missed it. So, I looked around and Lubbock had a reserve unit. I thought, I can't be an MP right now, so I'll just go ahead [and] do civil affairs. And that's how I ended up in the desert. Civil affairs [is] basically when the military goes through and destroys a place, the US government has this tendency to feel like they have to rebuild the place. So, what civil affairs does, they go through and work with the host nation to rebuild the infrastructure. In civil affairs, you have everything from judges to cops, plumbers, carpenters, teachers, guys who can drive bulldozers. So, it's a very eclectic group of people, as opposed to an MP unit where all you have are MPs in support tasks. Since they didn't really know how much Kuwait was needing to rebuild, and by going to Iraq they didn't know at the time how many civil affairs units they would need, they sent everybody. We had a whole bunch of police officers and law enforcement types, so we created a forty-man enemy/prisoner-of-war team. [The people on this team] would be the ones guarding, collecting, and doing the initial questioning of any prisoners that might have been gathered and sent to a prisoner-of-war point. That is what I ended up doing in Desert Storm. We actually had an interpreter attached to our civil affairs unit. His family was in Kuwait City. We went in after the "cessation of hostilities," I think is the way [President] Bush put it. A few days after the ground war stopped, we went to our interpreter's family's house to take them water and MREs because they were starving and met one of the most interesting families. The men of the family were hidden by women. One of the guys—I was actually impressed [because] his ego had taken a major blow. [He had been] a traffic police officer, which in Kuwait was a prestigious occupation for him to have. Usually it's the macho, egotistical guys who get those jobs. And to have to be hidden by the women in the family, it was an eye-opening experience for him. He actually said if any of the women in the family wanted to drive, which is a big thing because women can't drive in Kuwait, that he would protect them the way they had protected him. So, that was kind of cool. This family has pictures floating around somewhere of all the girls sitting in the driver's seat of our truck. It's funny—they were amazed when we stepped out of our vehicle and that particular truck was driven by a female sergeant. [We took] off our helmets and they were like, "Oh my god, they're women and they are soldiers and they are carrying guns. Wow!" I felt like a rock star. It was kind of neat.

The draftees, they couldn't have cared who was guarding them. They were just happy to have food and water and shelter. Apparently, the air strikes were a hell of a lot more impressive than even we thought they would be. The Republican Guard, however, were less impressed. You really had to, as we said in the MP Corps, get their full and undivided attention. I had this one guy we were guarding in a bunch of prisoners at the hospital compound. The doctors had told us no weapons. All [we] had were batons. I am standing guard at this dental unit and they were sitting four or five to a cot, waiting for their turn to go to the dentist. There was this one guy who was obviously different. His uniform was different. I found out later that he was a member of the Republican Guard. He kept standing up and looking around, and the MP kept telling him to sit down. Then he really annoyed me. One of the dental techs came out because they were having a hard time with a generator. She's in her BDUs [Battle Dress Uniform] and her boots. She's not wearing her BDU top, but she's got the brown t-shirt on. And he's, for lack of a better term, ogling her. He's nudging the guy next to him and saying something. I don't know if she was aware of it; she's trying to fix the generator. Finally, after a couple of minutes, I went up to him and the other draftees moved away. I told him very succinctly to sit down, shut up, keep [his] eyes forward. He gave me a look. I grabbed the bottom of the cot and lifted it up, and I knocked him backwards. Put him on his ass. I think he got the message. We righted the cot. The other MP is looking at him, and he's got this look on his face: "I'm not the one you've got to be afraid of." He sat down and his head did not turn. He did not stand up again. I think I made my point.

When I went into the military at the age of eighteen, I didn't know if I was gay or not. I didn't figure it out until much later. I was in the reserves when I figured out I was gay. Or maybe when I admitted to myself that I was gay. But when I was in Germany, no, I wasn't gay. I was engaged, to be married to a guy. For a cav scout, he wasn't too stupid. Honestly, he was a really good guy. Until he came to the States. And then everything he liked about my personality when we were in Germany changed, [like me] being independent. As a gift at one point, he handed me makeup. I'm like, "The only time I've put on makeup on my face is when I was in theater. What makes you think it's going to happen now?" I don't like makeup. I don't like the way it makes your face feel. I just don't wear makeup. Suddenly everything he liked about me when we hit the States was an annoyance. I think it was peer pressure he was feeling. He didn't say that, but that's just kind of the idea I got after a while. We split amicably.

I figured it out that I was gay when I entered the reserves. I really don't believe that for me, there was ever a choice. I just think it took me a while to figure it out and then just kind of accept it. Being gay and knowing it was grounds for a dishonorable discharge, [which] was really weird because overseas, I knew a lot of gay and lesbian soldiers when I was stationed in Germany. Nobody cared. I mean, some people were like, "Oh, I think so and so is gay," [and] commanders would be like, "And the problem is?" Unless the individual was just the world's worst soldier or too out there, nobody did anything. Nobody really said anything. We didn't care. Overseas, what we cared about [was]: Do you have my back? Can you put bullets down range? Can you shoot the bad guy? And if I get hit, can you drag my ass out of there? That's what mattered. Not so-and-so is gay. There was more concern about which spouses people thought were committing adultery.

My nephew, he is out now. Yes. "Out of the military?" I really hate having to make that differentiation. He was a squad leader and he knew which one of his soldiers was gay. He joined a Texas National Guard unit here in the Dallas/Fort Worth area for a short period of time. He thought it was interesting because right after the implementation [of Don't Ask, Don't Tell], he had two or three of his soldiers come to him and say, "This really isn't important, but I thought you should know I was gay." And he said he was very proud to say, "No, I'm cool with that. My aunt is gay." He is one of the most accepting kids I've ever known. For him, an army sergeant, to have the ability to say, "I don't care if you're gay—you're still doing this [badly]. I'm not picking on you because you're gay; I'm picking on you because you are stupid"—it's really kind of cool to see.

Why do you think it's such a big deal in the States, and why do people want to pry?

When you are in a situation where you or your buddy can be killed in the next two minutes, you discover what is important and what is really, really stupid. What I find interesting now is the individuals I've spoken to who still have a problem with gay people being in the military are usually the individuals whose butts have never been overseas and into a war zone. They've never had to face the fact: *I can step outside the wire and die or get seriously hurt.* When you face that, certain things become very apparent. In the case you get hit, you are not going to stop the guy who is dragging [you to safety] to ask, "Hold on a second—do you happen to be gay? OK, put me down and let me bleed to death." A lot of people who are vehemently against gay people in the military, they live in their own little bubble. And the people who are in the military, who have been overseas and who are still anti-gay, I don't have an answer for them. I really don't. I'm not sure what makes them tick. I think the future is bright. Especially when you look at other countries who have [allowed gay people to be in the military]. One of my favorite examples is England, which was one of the most quiet homophobic countries. I've got English friends, and for as much as they like to say they are open and accepting and things like that, their military was quite homophobic and conservative. They spent the first two years saying, "Oh my god, the fabric of the military is going to fall apart," and it's doom and gloom. A couple of years passed by, and they looked around and [said], "Oh. None of that happened. And I think that's exactly what is going to happen to the US military now. They are looking around now and going, "Oh, well, it didn't destroy itself. We are still standing. Maybe we were a little unfounded [with] those fears."

One of the most interesting things I've noticed about gay soldiers is, [they] tend to be the ones who excel. By and large, gay soldiers tend to excel. Almost every gay soldier who I knew was gay was exceptional at what they did, and very, very professional. Even when it was just us gay soldiers, like in my reserve unit, we would tend to congregate together on occasion [and] we rarely talked about our personal lives. [We] didn't do what I've heard so many straight soldiers do—I mean [discussing] details ad nauseam on what was going on in their lives, up to and including their sex lives. It was like, no, no, no, too much information! Please go away—I don't need to know that. It was very interesting how the professionalism of the gay soldiers I knew carried on even when we were by ourselves. So, I honestly think the future is incredibly bright for gay soldiers. The institution hasn't imploded; it hasn't rained cats and dogs.

My only [point] about advising [any] civilian to join the military would be [to say], "Are you sure this is something you want to do?" It's a life [not meant] for everybody. I've heard stories of army families [where couples] have been married ten years and the spouse has been home maybe three years. They've been off in a war zone for [the other] seven. [Mentally and] emotionally, are you ready for that? It's not a life for everybody. It can be a hell of a hard life. Deployments aside, if you're stateside and depending on what your job is, you can be out in the field for six months out of the year. You have to know these things. Do your research.

Have we not touched on anything else you would like to say?

I would join the army all over again, in a heartbeat. I wish they would change the rules so that if you were my age and you wanted to go back in, you could.

Kinga Kiss-Johnson

Interviewed: May 3, 2012 at the Olympic Training Center, Colorado Springs, Colorado

You were in the army?

Yes. I was in the US Army. I'm a retired sergeant.

Where was your base?

I went to basic training at Fort Jackson [in South Carolina] and the AIT in Fort Leonard Wood [in Missouri]. [For my] first duty station directly out of Fort Leonard Wood, I went to Bamberg, Germany and deployed right after my arrival. A few months later I deployed to Afghanistan.

What unit were you with?

I was with 173rd Airborne.

Did you get your wings?

I did not go to jump school. It was just my thought—I am really tall. I am 6 foot 7 inches. They did give us the opportunity to jump, yes, but I came in and right away deployed, so I didn't have the opportunity.

You are not originally from the United States?

I was born and raised in Romania and played basketball in Romania on the Romania National Team, [the] Junior Team. And then I played in Hungary for four years, basketball. They asked me to come to college here in the United States to St. Louis to Hillsboro, [to] Jefferson College in Hillsboro, Missouri. I took the opportunity. Originally, when they asked me to come, I said, "No, I don't speak English," and I didn't think it [was] possible to get a visa because it is such an impossibility to actually get a visa even to visit. For me it was like a dream coming true to actually get my visa and [walk] out of the embassy with the visa. And coming here to play. It was [a] very exciting time for me.

What year was that?

I came in 1998 and I stayed at Hillsboro. I graduated. I got my associate degree from Jefferson College. I was recruited by Southwest Missouri State and I went to [the] NCAA Final Four [tournament] in 2001. And graduated in 2003 from college with my bachelor's degree. During this time, while I was doing my bachelor's degree, 9/11 happened—and all this time, I was thinking fathers, mothers deploying back-to-back. And I really wanted to enlist but I was still on full scholarship, and I think: *If I can [be exchanged for one soldier who] did not have to deploy one more time and keep those parents with their children and then I do my duty and I give something back to this country, that give[s] me an opportunity of a lifetime to actually study and love this freedom you have in the US*. I grew up during communism in Romania. I felt I grew up with the oppression of communism, of not being able to go to the grocery store and just buy what you want. Everything was rationed. Coming to this country where you

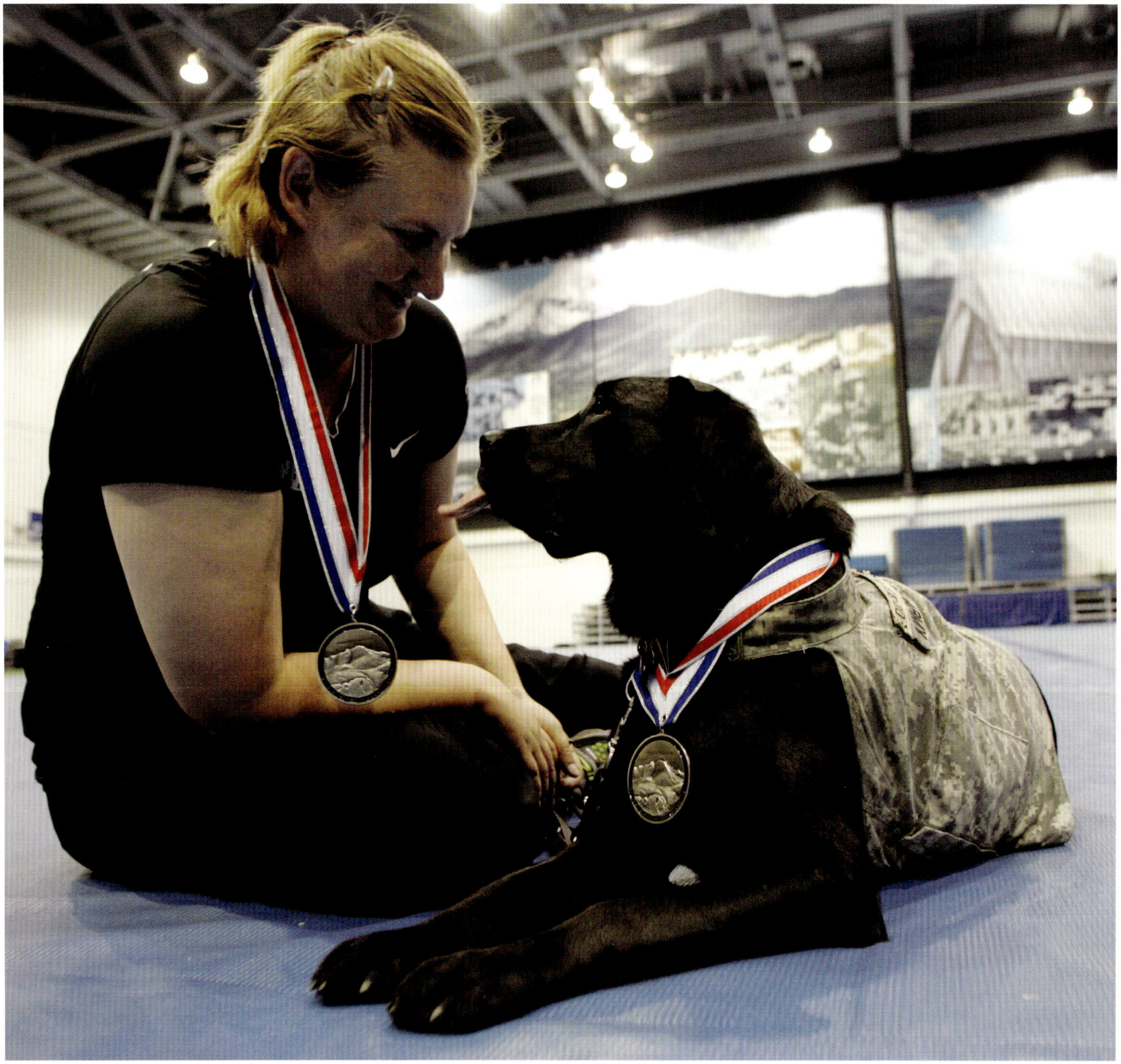

Following the awarding of two silver medals won during archery competition during the 2012 Warrior Games, Kinga Kiss-Johnson sits with her service dog Ba Ho.

have these freedoms, where you can do whatever you want to—you have your freedom of speech, you have everything, everyone our United States ancestors fought for, for so many years—I felt it was my duty to protect that because I was given that opportunity. It was my way of giving back.

So you went to Baghdad?

No, I went to Afghanistan. I was in Afghanistan. I was there in 2007. I was on [an] eighteen-month deployment to Afghanistan. I got injured seven months into my deployment. I was medevaced out to Germany. They kept me in Germany to do all my surgeries, recovery in Germany. And when they got me stable, they got me back to Fort Gordon, Georgia to Eisenhower Medical Center. I retired in 2010. December of 2010.

Can you tell me about your injury?

I really don't like to talk about my injury. I don't like to think about it. But I'm thinking about my recovery; I want to get on with my life from there. A lot of people asked what happened. I'm feeling support from my family and friends and local community. I'm thinking I want to get along with my life. I want to become a productive member of society again. I thought there was no life after injury. Especially as a female veteran, we come back [and] we just become civilians. It's different when you have a veteran who comes back as a male veteran. It's a little bit [of a] different feeling when it comes to job markets and trying to get back to the civilian world. For us female veterans, we don't look like a soldier. We have long hair; we don't look the same. And unless you have a very visual impairment, you just blend in. Which is absolutely great. My family helped me to reach out. I really did not want to reach out. I was closed in, not leaving my house for a long time. But the local community reached out and started to get me back. Doing internships and doing little things like that, getting my life back with one step at a time. That's why I'm here at the Warrior Games, because of the local community. In Augusta, Georgia we have a program they call Champions Made from Adversity. And they are having a wheelchair basketball team and an archery program, and they asked me to come out and participate in wheelchair basketball with my occupational therapist. She was pushing me: "Come on, just play with us. Basketball is your life; try to get back into it." And I was really questioning [whether I was] able to do that. And they pretty much told me, "It's your abilities you [function with alongside] your disability. You become better." Listening to my family, like my husband . . . he has been beside me since [the time I came back] from Afghanistan. Being there every day, pushing me every day. One day I was trying to do everything. I thought the whole world was on my shoulder. He stopped me and he said, "Honey, we are together in this." That's when it got me to this reality that I'm not stuck in this world by myself. And I have to reach out for help and [the] support everyone gives. And it's such an honor to be here at the Warrior Games because you look at all these volunteers out here helping these soldiers compete and have fun. A lot of people forget that this is fun, having actually a little piece of fun, not to worry about our injuries, our hurts. I went home after the Warrior Games last year, tried to recruit some females to come and compete. I actually have one of the ladies I shot archery with all season long and she is going to come and compete next year in archery. Those are the things that give us hope for [the] future and knowing that we are going to be OK. We are going to be OK.

Can you tell me a bit about your service dog?

This is Ba Ho. He has been with me for two and a half years after I got back to Fort Gordon, to Eisenhower Medical Center. America's Vet Dog Foundation, which is [the] sister [organization] of The Guide Dog Foundation, works specifically with veterans injured in Iraq and Afghanistan. They reached out to me. They knew I was housebound. My husband was taking care of me. He was the one driving around. Dressed me. Helping me around. They reached out to me and told me, "Come and train with us, [we'll] get you a service dog to get your life back." I got him in February 2010. It just changed my life. It got my independence back. I'm driving short distances by myself with him. My husband was able to go back to work. He lost his job when we were in Germany just in order to take care of me. A lot of time, spouses don't get that credit, but they have the harder job. And my husband definitely did, and he is not taking any credit for it. He saved my life. And by getting me the service dog, my husband got his independence back too. He was able to go back to work. Now my puppy is helping me out. I go everywhere with him. I feel that little bit of freedom again being by myself. He's been a lifesaver.

It sounds like it was your community, your dog, and your husband that got you out there enjoying your life again.

Yes. If it wasn't for local community and family support, I don't know where I would be today. I don't know what shape I would be [in]. I had a really good unit at Eisenhower. They were really, really supportive of my recovery and helped me to connect with the local community. Before I knew I was retiring and I knew I was getting out of the military, a veterans program helped me connect with the local community to do an internship with them, and it is only veterans working for them. So, it was three of us girls [who] went through the program. It was only seven of us [who] started the program and went through the program, and they finished six months successfully. We started to step back into the civilian world. By doing that program, we got more involved into the local community. I [have also] gotten involved with Habitat for Humanity. We actually dedicated two houses before Christmas. The community has those long arms reaching for us and helping us to get jobs and become part of the community. We could not do that without it. Just like after I finished the Veterans Duration project of six months, I got to do this project with the Dr. Martin Luther King Jr. Center [on a] project digitalizing documents [in partnership with] JPMorgan Chase. That would not be happening without the initiative of JPMorgan because this was specifically for hiring veterans for this project and interns for students. It was not open to [the] civilian world; they wanted specifically veterans. It gives us a chance to give back. It gives us a chance to transition smoothly back into civilian life.

If a young woman were to ask your advice about joining the military, what would you tell her?

I would tell her that . . . it's an experience. It's an honor to go after your dream and know you have done something only 1 percent of [the] United States population would do. It takes a lot of courage to leave your home, to leave your family. Go to total strangers. But you know you have done something for society. You have done something just like doctors and nurses. It takes a lot of courage. You grow. The military teaches certain things [that] in [the] civilian world you do not learn. In [the] civilian world, you would learn [for] years and years. In the military, you learn these skills and life experiences that will help you through the rest of your life. Everything you learn—discipline, management, [any] of those little skills your mom and dad teach you—it will multiply when you go into the military. It makes you a stronger person. We need brave men and women to fight for this country and to be free. And that's the bottom line. I would encourage females to go into the military. We are not any different. We do the same thing. It's not any different, just like the Warrior Games. We are all one team, [in] one fight. It doesn't matter what color we are; we have the abilities to do the same thing.

Is there anything we haven't touched on that you want to discuss?

I really want to thank the community that reaches out to us soldiers. It doesn't matter what branches of service it may be—the local community support [or the] American Legion, all the veteran support groups that are out there. And employers who are trying to get us employed into their business. I want to thank them because [when] we [come] back, we are lost and we need those little directions. You need those little arrows to point us in the right direction, to feel alive again after our injuries. I just want to thank all the staff [who] are supporting us from the day we leave this country to go overseas to the day we come back, and [even during] the years after that, they are supporting us. There [are] not enough words to say thank you for them.

We can't end without mentioning your two medals. Can you tell me about them?

I'm really proud of them because this is the first year that [I got them] as an individual in archery. Last year I came here and missed qualifying by four points. I went home last year really disappointed. And I said, "Well, it is a good reason to shoot and come back; it is a good goal to come back." [I got] silver in individual recurve [archery] and silver in [the] recurve event. I have two more events: basketball and shot put. I'm looking forward to [competing] again. I'm hoping I'm going to give veterans an opportunity, especially female veterans [who] are not involved yet in archery. We can compete; we can be out there competing with the marines or the navy—doesn't matter who they are. We can compete with them. I'm looking forward to it. It's [an] exciting feeling.

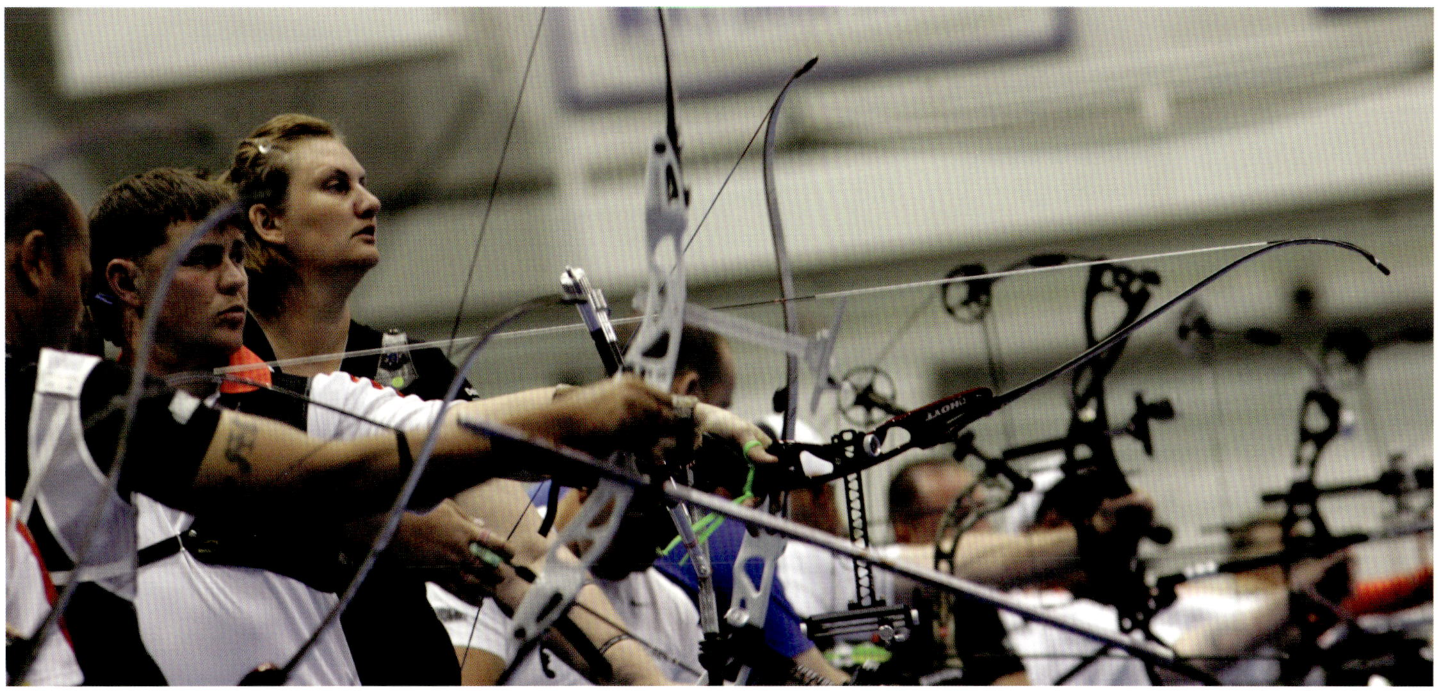

Army archer Kinga Kiss-Johnson stands at the shooting line during the 2012 Warrior Games held in Colorado Springs, CO. The archery events were held at the US Air Force Academy. Kinga won silver medals for individual and team contests.

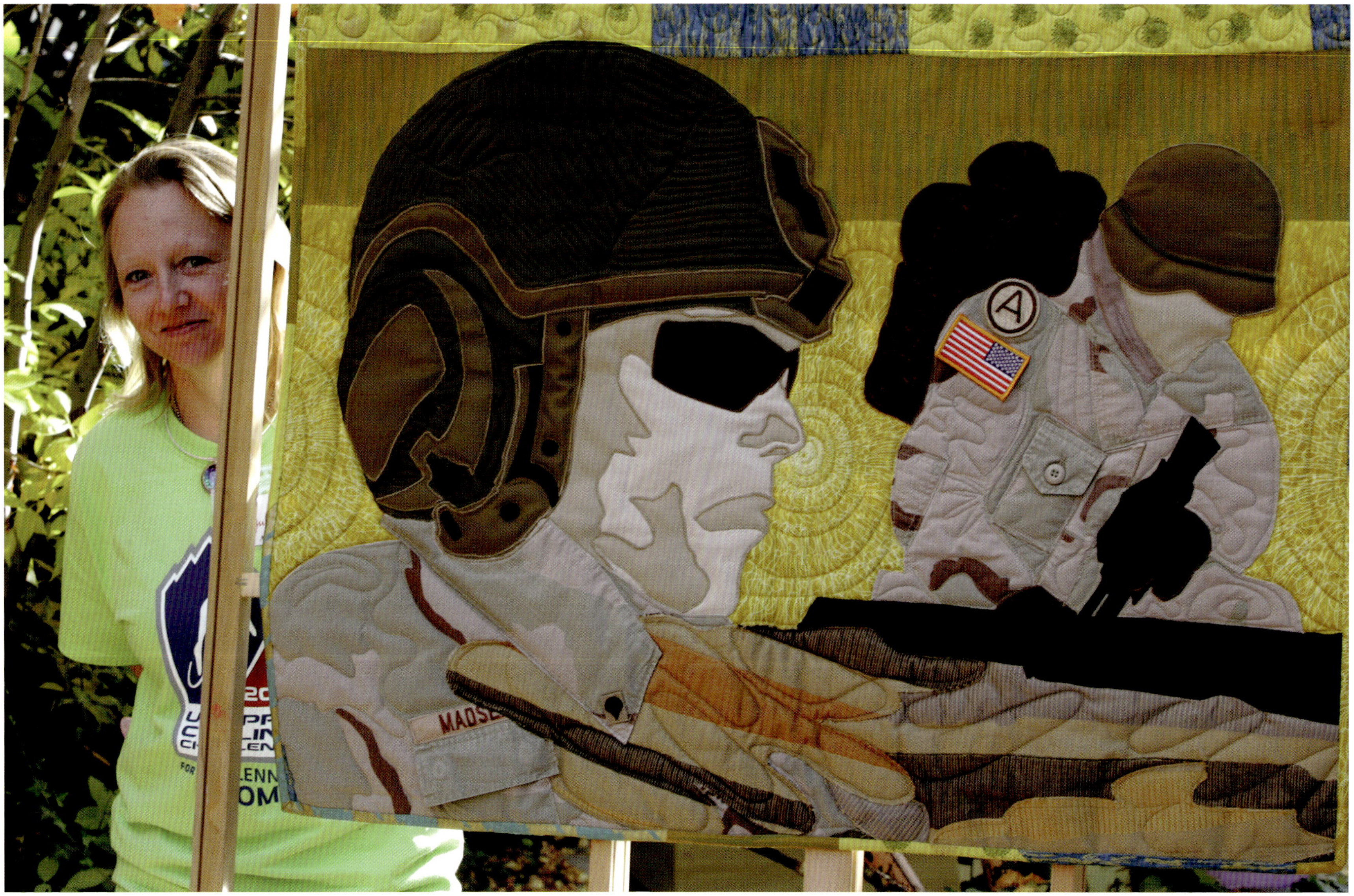

Veteran Juliet Madsen stands next to one of her quilts. Madsen suffered a traumatic brain injury [TBI] during active duty caused by an improvised explosive device [IED]. She also suffers from PTSD. The quilt is on display at an art exhibit showcasing works made by veterans enrolled in a therapy program for PTSD.

Juliet Madsen

Interviewed: October 16, 2011 in Castle Rock, Colorado

My grandfather was in the United States Army Cavalry, World War I. And, actually, every generation of my family had somebody who served in a war. It was always taught to me that you serve your country in some way or another. I grew up volunteering in hospitals and for different places. It was taught to me that you always give back.

I joined halfway through my senior year in high school. I graduated [early]. I had to have my parents' permission to join, and I went to basic training. I was actually sixteen when I signed the paperwork. I still had my braces on.

I ended up doing something for the kitchen staff. I ended up doing something for the chaplain. I just went from job to job, doing whatever I could. I had a really great first sergeant who said, "Learn whatever you can and take whatever classes they give you and don't ever turn anything down." So, I have certificate after certificate. I have a whole slew of them.

I was working at the prison with the prisoners and we had a convoy [traveling within Iraq]. We were transporting a bunch of boxes and stuff. I was sitting in the back of the truck. I had fallen asleep in the back of the truck. The back of the truck filled up with really fine sand. I remember it spinning and the radio going crazy and hearing lots and lots of noise. And staring through the front window because the back of the truck didn't have windows. Military ambulances don't have windows. [I remember] looking out the front window and everything being black and on fire. We eventually got out of the truck and started taking care of patients. We had like nine patients, ten patients. We had five trucks destroyed. Things were blowing up. Apparently, I [got] hurt. I know that while we were working, there were explosions still going on. I had no idea. To this day I have no idea [what hurt me]. I never asked. And I don't want to know. I treated the most critical patients. I triaged the most critical. I farmed out the less critical to the two folks I had left, who had less experience than I did. Called in the medevac. And we got them back to base. It was sometime in the afternoon when it happened. We got back to our unit. People kept saying that I did a good job but [that] I looked funny. I knew I didn't feel good. The commander kept telling me to sit down, but I had work to do. That night we had midnight chow for those of us who worked all day and [hadn't been able to] get away for regular meal hours. Midnight chow was between 10 p.m. and 12 a.m. I went to midnight chow, and I remember saying that I didn't feel good. I started having seizures on the floor of the chow hall.

The next thing I remember is being on the airplane with the guys who I had evacuated from the accident]—which was kind of cheesy because I was on a stretcher, and they weren't. They kept saying, "Hey doc, we're here for you." It was pissing me off. I kept asking them how they were feeling and trying to take care of them. And they kept trying to mother me, which was pissing me off. I got to Kuwait and had another series of seizures. And then of course they really started mothering me, which really pissed me off. We went from there to Germany. Then we really banded together because it's a huge facility. You go from a field hospital environment in Kuwait to [a large hospital in] Germany. The guys really took care of me there. My brain injury is the most significant thing. The strokes left me with some left-sided weakness. I'm great [now] compared to how I was. I had trouble with my speech. I had a lot of trouble with word-finding. My speech is a lot better [now], probably to my husband's dismay. I have short-term memory [issues]. I have lots of holes in my memory. Like if I get stressed out or if I get tired or overwhelmed [it's hard for me to remember things]. I can get overwhelmed really easily. [My brain is] like Swiss cheese.

It's very frustrating to me because Peter and the kids will say something like, "We talked about that three days ago." Well, I don't remember that. Now the brilliant thing is that I can watch a movie fifteen times and it's pretty much a new movie. Or at least I'll see something new every time and others won't. That's a good thing. But it's frustrating because I have to read a paragraph a hundred times before I get the meaning. It's frustrating because I can't work with numbers. It's difficult to read a sentence and actually get the meaning the first time. I have to take seizure medicine. I get migraines. I have PTSD. I have really bad nightmares.

I'm having trouble sleeping, which makes everything so much worse because I don't sleep anyway. That just makes me evil—I [become] a cranky, horrible person. But I still see a neurologist, cardiologist, endocrinologist. We finished with the kidney doctors. We finished with GI doctors because they had to rebuild some of my intestines after that. What else? I still have to see a cardiologist every once in a while. I saw neurology less than a week ago. They are my nemesis.

I did some quilting on my own before any of this. I actually took quilts to Iraq and to Saudi Arabia that I hand-quilted when I was there. But when I got hurt, I lost the ability to do any sewing because I have really bad tremors if I don't take medication now. So, it was recommended to me through the physical therapy department to try and do something like that to work on my fine motor skills. Voc Rehab asked me what I wanted to do because I can't really do a traditional job. They said, "What kind of life-enhancing skills would you like us to help you with?" I said, "I like to sew, so can you help me get a sewing machine?"

But the work I do now is very therapeutic. And somehow, it's kind of morphed. I can't follow patterns because of my brain injury. But I can kind of fall into different designs and layer things and take these little frayed pieces of fabric and make them into what used to be an image in my head. And I now have quilts [displayed] in the Pentagon. I have one in the Library of Congress. And I did have one that was taken to the White House to be in the permanent art collection. I have one that is going to Fort Bliss. I have several in different VAs and military bases. I've been doing a lot of quilts for veterans and for families of veterans who have been killed, where I take their uniforms and build them into my kind of format. So, it's my design but it's their uniforms and I turn them into something the family can keep. They look like my designs and they have their personal effects. They are very hard to do. They only take me a few days, so people think they are easy to do, but they are emotionally draining. What happens is I work on them [and] I kind of become OCD about them. Right now, I'm doing two quilts out of uniforms of a soldier who passed away, for his eight-year-old twin daughters. That includes not only his uniforms, but patches that he wore. I like to incorporate pockets from their uniforms, and in their pockets, I like to put letters that were written to and from the soldier. Most of my quilts that go off to be displayed some place, if they have a pocket, they usually have a letter of mine in them that is laminated so they don't get destroyed. One of my ones that made it to the [US Capitol] building has a letter that I had written to my mother that says, "Everything is fine. I love you. I'll be home soon so don't worry."

So it stays the course. Take it one day at a time. Wake up every morning and put a foot on the floor.

I would encourage women to join the military. I would probably say the same thing that was said to me, which is: Get as much education out of it as you can. Go as many places as you can. Keep your eyes and ears open. Learn as much as you can. Because you will see things that you will never see anywhere else. And that will be the most incredible thing you will ever see. You will never see anything in the world like what you will see here [in the military].

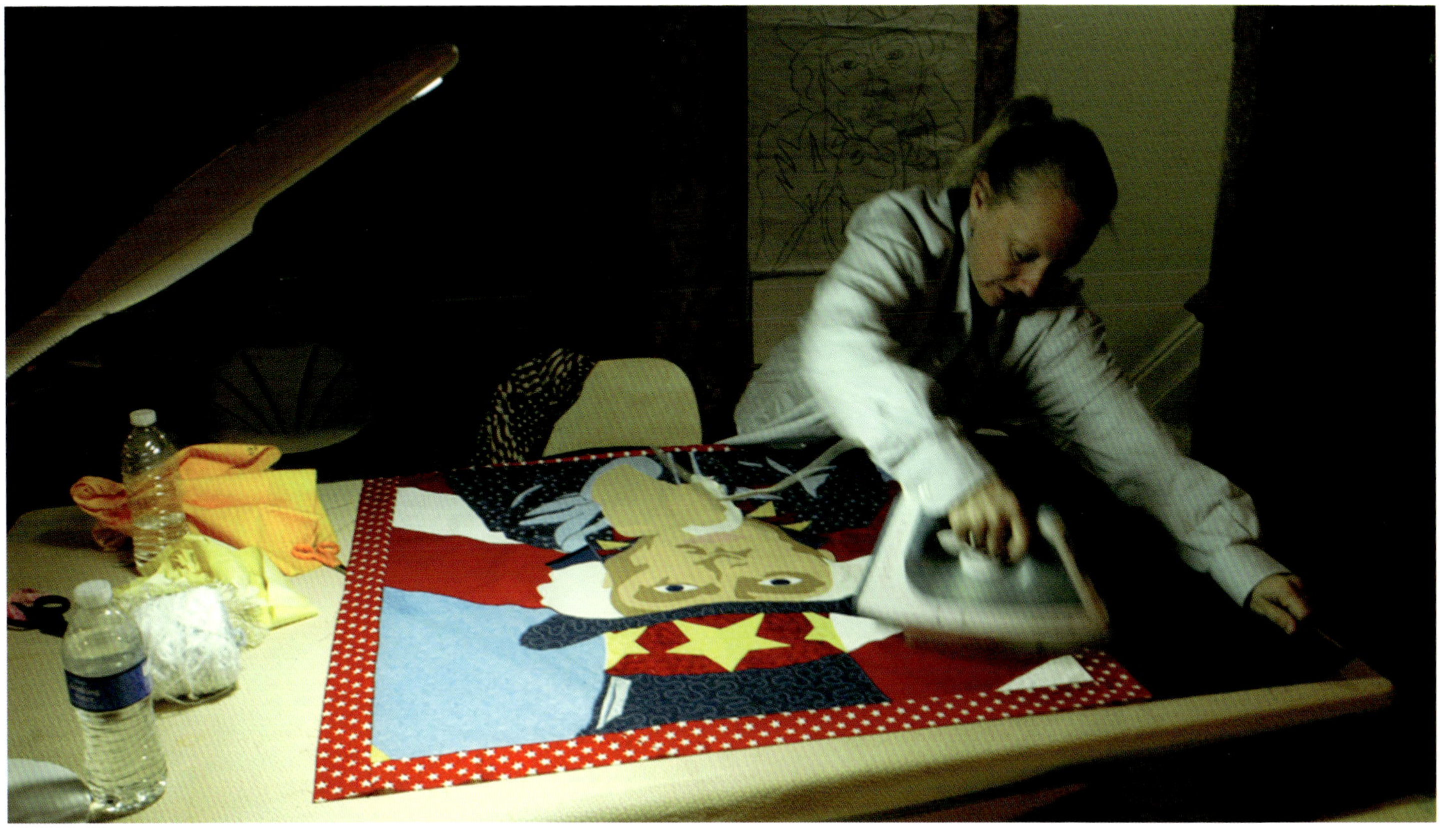

Veteran Juliet Madsen works on a quilt in her basement workshop. Her quilts have become her preferred method of expressing herself about her experiences related to her military duty.

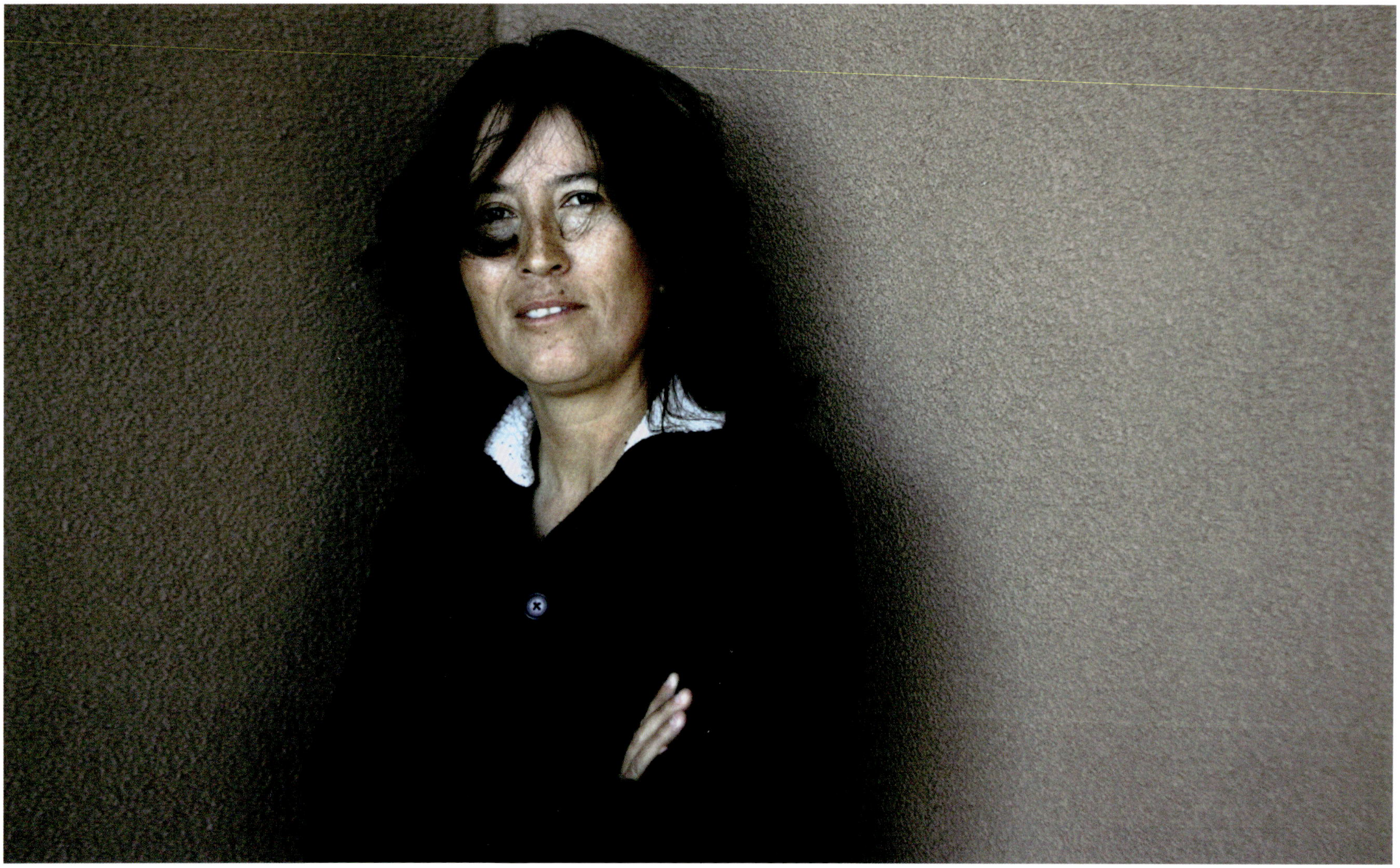

Portrait of Tyra Nakai.

Tyra Nakai

Interviewed: February 8, 2009 in Albuquerque, New Mexico on February 8, 2009

My name in Tyra Nakai. I'm Navajo. I was born in Fort Defiance, Arizona. I had gone to college. I got my associate's degree. I kind of wanted a little bit more of a challenge. The Gulf War had just ended, so I felt like I needed to do something to serve my country. So right after the Gulf War, I decided to join, in 1992. I joined with the reserves when I lived up in South Dakota. I was living up there for a while. I joined up there and ended up transferring back out here to Albuquerque.

I didn't get back into the tradition till about five to seven years ago, just right before my last deployment. My grandparents were full-blooded Navajo. We had just been talking about it and it sounded very intriguing. I don't know my language, and just by the way they talked about the traditions, it was very intriguing. I felt it was [something important for] me to go back to learn my roots and my ancestry. My grandmother would tell me stories, so when she talked to me about it, that kind of inspired me to get back into it. My last deployment [came with] such a short notice, I didn't get to do a ceremony before I left. I had three days' notice. We weren't able to get a hold of a medicine man. I just didn't have enough time. When I came back, though, my grandparents had set it up with a medicine man to come home and get a cleansing ceremony done. To just make sure that I was right mentally, physically, and everything. To help me move on. Do the normalcy of my life after that. Now I've been deployed again [and] we actually had the chance to make arrangements this time. So, I'll go in for prayer protection for [my time during deployment].

The cleansing ceremony, it's pretty intense. My grandfather was sick at the same time. He had just suffered a stroke and so we went through it together. For him, medically; for me, more mentally, for my deployment. It's kind of like a blackening ceremony. [The medicine man and his helpers] build a kiva-type place for you. You go in and you take in the scents of the cedar and everything. They actually do blacken you. I never knew that. They take grease from the sheep and they put it all over your body. And they actually take ashes from the fire. I had to stay like that. It was different. I couldn't sleep. I had to stay up the whole time. That was hard. The entire ceremony lasted two days. It was pretty long. Then they had all the things you could and couldn't do afterwards. But I [can't] go into detail on that.

I had been in contact with my grandmother right after deployment. I was having really bad dreams [and] a lot of anxiety and stress. My grandmother felt like there was something there. Once I did that [ceremony], I felt like a weight was lifted. It did help. At that time, I was given a prayer tree for my grandfather and myself. And you actually go out there with the corn pollen and you pray to the four sacred mountains and to mother earth and everything. I have kept up with that tradition. I am Catholic, but I also keep up with my Navajo culture now.

I did a lot of praying. I think a lot of us did. You know, Navajos, we pray with the corn pollen. And there are certain

SSG Tyra Nakai of the New Mexico National Guard inserts an IV into a vein of fellow guard member SG Tony Garcia during a training class. The class, Combat Life Saving, was given to members of the 920th Engineers to prepare them for deployment to Afghanistan in the summer of 2009. Their anticipated duties were to improve existing roads and build foundations, truck ramps, and other components of Combat Outposts (COPs). The training took place at the Santa Fe Armory.

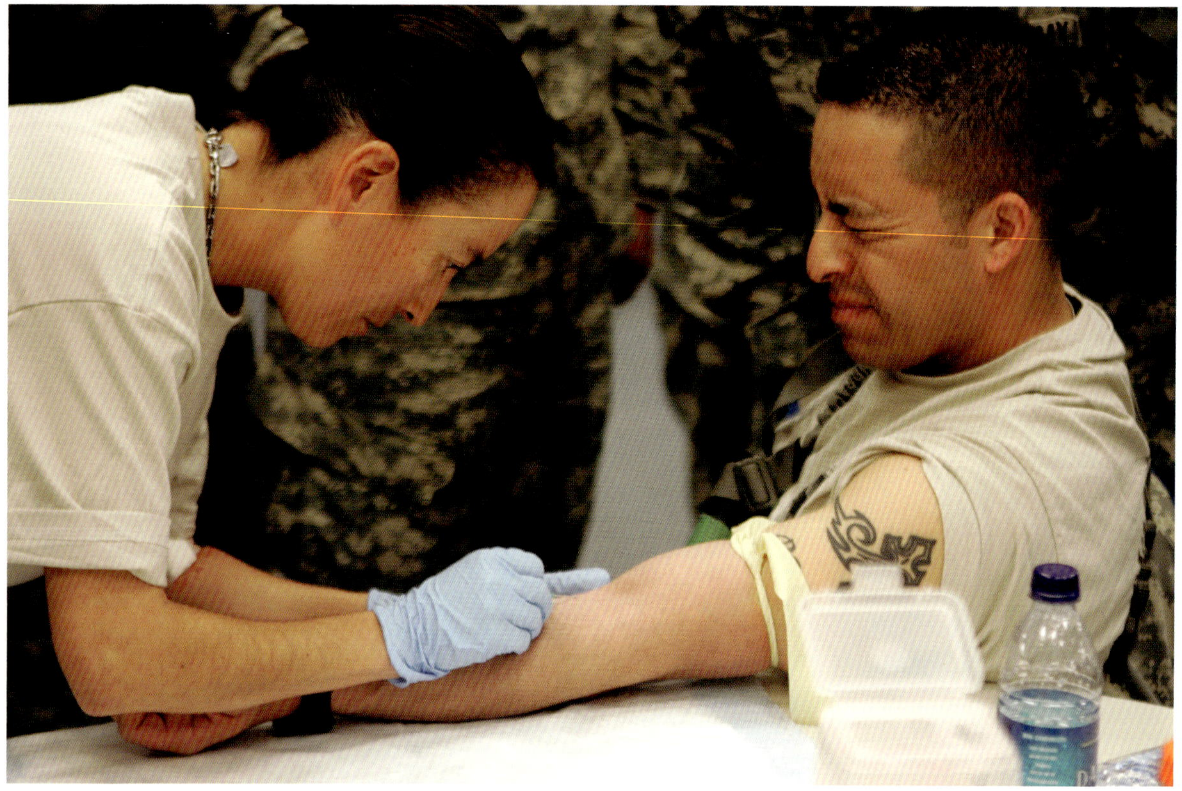

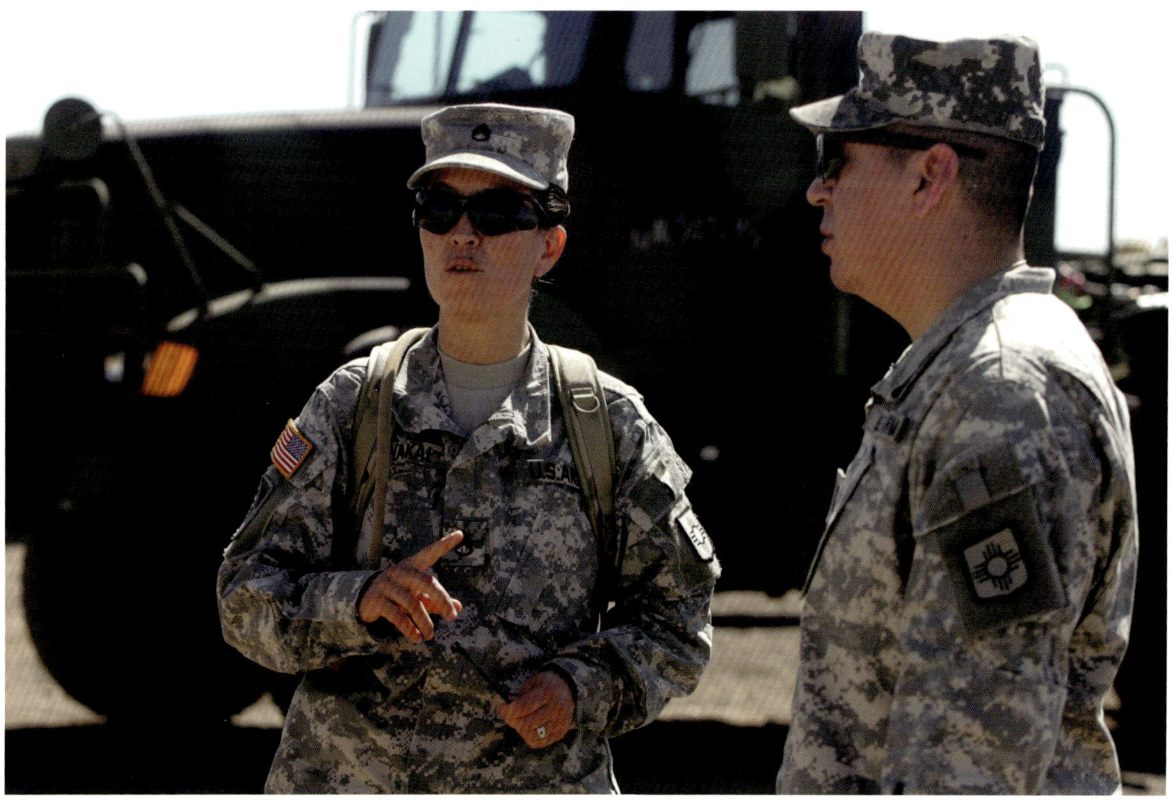

SSG Tyra Nakai talks with another member of the 920th Engineers of the New Mexico National Guard about the upcoming training secession in preparation for their unit's deployment to Afghanistan in 2009.

ways you have to do it. My grandmother had taught me that before I left. Just to make sure, to keep me safe. On top of my regular prayers. You are kind of divided, being Catholic. You can't really choose one over the other. It's hard for me anyways because I believe in both. I believe we all come from the earth. We all had to evolve from somewhere. I also believe there is a higher being.

The unit I'm deploying with right now is probably 95 percent men. I am up there in rank (staff sergeant), which helps. I am the highest-ranking female in our unit, currently. So, I play the role of platoon sergeant, squad leader, you know—just guiding, being friends, counselor to everybody. I believe I have been given a high [level of] respect by a lot of the men here. They know they can confide in me; they can come talk to me. Is it hard? Yes, because I can know all the guys personally, on an intimate level at this [point]. But [if] you go somewhere else and you don't know those men, it's still hard. You have to prove yourself. You still have to prove yourself a lot more.

We have a few Native Americans in the unit. I've seen Native Americans in other units. There is some discrimination. People have their fixed ideas of what Native Americans are. Unfortunately, that stereotype of [Native Americans being alcoholics and poorly educated still exists]. I want to try and break that stereotype.

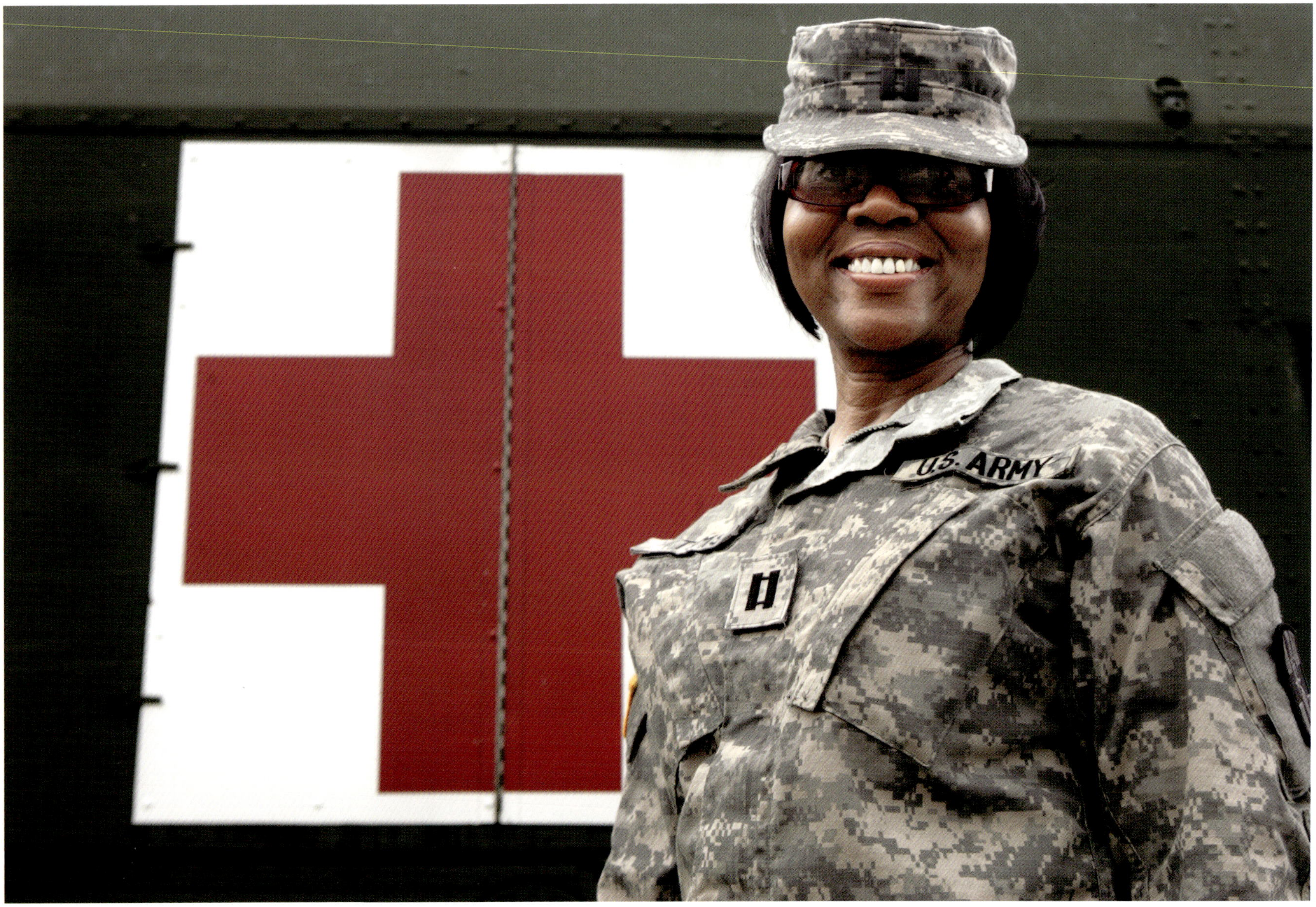

CPT Yvonne Antoinette Tims stands next to a High Mobility Multipurpose Wheeled Vehicle [Humvee] ambulance at the Army Reserve unit of the 341st Multifunctional Medical Battalion [MMB], based at Seagoville, TX.

Yvonne Antoinette Tims

Interviewed: January 12, 2012 in Dallas, Texas

Currently, you're captain in the United States Army Reserves. You deployed to Iraq in November 2010, returned a year later in November 2011. What was your duty there?

I was with Medical Logistics OIC Class VIII, which [handles] the medical supplies that were used to support any ill or wounded soldier in Iraq.

Did you manage to avoid going into the operating rooms while you were there?

On some occasions yes, I did, because I knew what was in there and I didn't think I would be able to handle it. So, I did not go in on a couple of cases because I knew what I was told as far as the soldiers and how they were wounded.

You were up in Mosul?

I went to Mosul. I was there for six months, and from there I went to Tikrit after Mosul, and then I spent a brief period in Al Asad [Airbase in Iraq] when we were at the point of demobilization, coming back to the United States.

What kind of experiences did you have there? Were they routine?

No, in Mosul it was not routine. It was very, very stressful. Going into the country and trying to assimilate [away from] some of the comforts that you know from being home in the States—that transition is hard. You're sent over there with a lot of different personalities. I was sent as a cross level, so I didn't go with my unit, where I knew people. I went with a unit I didn't know. So, I also had that stress of getting to know other people's personalities. And they had to get to know mine. That led to a lot of stress, because I'm a very straightforward person and some people can take me the wrong way when actually I don't mean any harm. I'm a very analytical person. I see and think outside the box. We were mortared over there a lot. That was very, very scary. When I first went there, one place I wouldn't go was on Marez. On the Marez side, there was a lot of bombing. Some of the people I met there and became friends with would go over there and go shopping. For some reason I had [this] fear and I wouldn't go over there. Our chaplain came down; I guess some of the girls I had been spending time with had talked about me. He came and talked to me about my fear of going over to Marez.

This was just the other side of the base, the area where the civilians had shops?

Marez was just on the other side of the base. There were troops on that side too. We were the only ones on our side. We were the combat support hospital set up on our side. There was nothing else over there but us. We had our hospital and our administrative offices. We were right there at the flight line.

When did you join the reserves?

I was twenty-three years old. I joined in 1982. At the time I was at the University of Cincinnati. I was trying to attend college. And I had a little girl. I had moved out. I was used to living the way I had lived with my mother and father. It just wasn't working. I had gotten on public assistance. I was in Section 8 housing. And I was trying to go to school with my daughter, so I wasn't doing so well in college. Because when I went to college, I realized that although I had been one of the smartest young ladies in high school—I was in all the advanced placement classes as I came up—I was ill-equipped for college. So, I was having a hard time. I also didn't like being on welfare. I didn't like living on Section 8 and the area where I was living. I kept my place clean, but I had to fight roaches every day. I said: *Something has got to give. I've got to change something*. And I prayed on it.

I decided initially to join the Marine Corps. My brother had joined the Marine Corps. So I went downtown to the federal building; I did everything you're supposed to. I took the physical, everything for the Marine Corps. When it came to the last day when I was to put my hand up, they said I would have to put my daughter up for adoption. Adoption! That wasn't going to happen. Even if it was putting her up for adoption with a member of my family, I just wasn't going to do that. My initial prayer was to join the army in the first place. I left that office and went across the hall to the army office. Also, the Marine Corps—the job offer they made me was [for] a telephone repair operator because my GT score was pretty high. I went next door and said, "I didn't want to be a telephone operator. What [else] do you have?" They showed me the medical [options]. I got my start in the military in the laboratory. I started the medical laboratory specialist program in the army.

What motivated you to join?

I was motivated to join every time I tried to get off welfare, and this is the honest truth. I'd get a little job and I'd tell [the people at the welfare office]—they would raise the rent. They would take the little money I had from the job. Or they would cut the food stamps. I called one day and I told the lady [at the welfare office], "You're not trying to help people get on their feet—this is a program constructed to keep people down." I said, "How can you expect someone to get on their feet if as they are trying to get on their feet, you take away from them [whatever money they actually start making]?" You know what I'm saying. Every time I tried to go out and get myself a job to get myself to a point to elevate myself, they would cut the food stamps and increase the rent. Well, that meant I had to work more. Which meant [I would not be able to] study as much as I needed to study. So, then I wasn't doing as well in school. I decided I was going to join the military because the army had education incentives. I had no skills. [I thought]: *I have to do something because I have this little baby I have to take care of.* So, when I came back from basic training and my advanced individual training [AIT], I called the welfare office. I was offered a job at the West End Health Center in downtown Cincinnati as a medical lab technician. I was paid $12,500, which was good money, especially compared to the $216 per month welfare check and $100 in food stamps. I was very proud and very happy to get that job, so I called them and I relinquished the welfare check. The army was responsible for helping me do this because I was trained in a skill whereby I was able to get a job.

You continued to go to school?

I continued to go to school. I was a medical lab technician, but I wasn't completely qualified; I didn't have the advanced laboratory [requirements]. The West End Health Center was a stepping stone for me. It was a training ground. I guess I did pretty well there because [a doctor at the] Cincinnati Health Department heard about me [and invited me to apply there for a job]. I got a job at $16,500. So now I increased my income even more.

Is this a private job?

No, this is [through] the Cincinnati Health Department. So, I'm working in the laboratory upstairs . . . then I was still going to school working on that bachelor's degree. Just couldn't seem to get those grades up. Because my mind was torn between taking care of my daughter and trying to work. And then trying to studying for classes where I don't have a clue what they are talking about. I'm trying to learn [the class material] in about two weeks. It is hard to learn material when you never had seen the material before. I had a girlfriend; we were in chemistry together. We had this chemistry professor and he was pretty good and he was very clear and he would explain well and everything. It was only good if you had been exposed to it [before] because the way he was teaching was [in a manner in which] he assumed you had been exposed to it before. So, me and Kim, we are African American, and this one Caucasian girl behind me, she was answering all these questions. People were holding up their hands. I guess I was outspoken back then too. I just turned around and I asked, "Excuse me, but how do y'all know this?" They said they had learned it in high school. This was our second week of college. So, we knew right then we were in trouble. Because the school we went to didn't take us all through this. It was a challenge.

What happened then was I became the first person to go through the contract program. It's a contract program where the military contracts with the university, so they contracted with Cincinnati State Technical College for the advanced laboratories. For this I would actually get a two-year associate degree, instead of an ASVAB [Armed Forces Vocational Aptitude Battery] type military background with the army, which is what the health department would accept.

[They] respected that training; they accepted that because I had been through that initial training through the military. Doctor Suddendorf—he was actually my colonel, who was the man I wanted to swear me in—he was a colonel by the time I graduated. I was the first person to go through that program through the United States military to obtain a two-year degree [to become a] medical lab technician without having to go to Fort Sam Houston and having to spend a year [there]. It allowed me to be home with my daughter. They gave us housing assistance and a check every two weeks. You did have to worry about studying, but you had your study time because you didn't have to work. And you didn't have to worry about money. So, that clears your head to study. So that four-year degree I had been working on at the University of Cincinnati, I still had about two years of classes I needed to complete there. So here I am: I don't have to work. I don't have to worry about how I'm going to pay my rent. I'm not living in those crazy apartments anymore. We weren't on welfare anymore. We had moved up. I decided I was going to finish my four-year degree at the same time [I was] going to finish my associate's degree, since the military was going to take advantage of it. [I thought:] *How I'm going to do it, I don't know.* I had to go to school during the day for the associate's degree and I went to the night school at the University of Cincinnati every night except for Thursday night. So, I ended up taking twenty-seven credit hours per quarter. I used the Franklin planner. I was introduced to the Franklin planner. I planned and documented everything out. [Such as] how many hours I needed to study to get a decent grade. Every Friday, my daughter knew that I was not going to pick up a book until Sunday night. Those days were hers.

That time was devoted to your daughter?

She knew that on Friday after we got home, she could have a sleepover; we could go to the movies. The next day I would get a bunch of her friends together. The next day I would take them to the park. We would get ice cream, we would go to McDonald's, we might go skating. So, she knew those were her days. I didn't have the quantity, but I tried to make the quality at that time.

Somehow you were a good mother and a student at the same time?

I had to make sure I succeeded at Cincinnati State Technical College because Doctor Suddendorf told me if I didn't make it, they would shut the program down because I was the pilot. I was like the guinea pig. The military paid for that—they paid for books; they paid for everything. I graduated with my Medical Lab Technician [MLT] associate's and my bachelor's [degrees] at the same time. And then my professor at Cincinnati State, she said, "I knew you were doing something else." I guess that in my mind I was really, really focused.

No one was aware of your working on two degrees at the same time?

I didn't tell anybody. The army didn't know. I knew I had to succeed. No, they weren't paying for [the bachelor's degree]. They were only paying for Cincinnati State.

You were also doing the reserves?

No, I wasn't doing the reserves while I was doing the two-year program. I was considered active duty. That was an option we could go into if we wanted. But we didn't have to because we weren't going to be paid anything extra.

You were being paid to be a full-time student?

[I was] getting paid just like [I was] on active duty, but my job was to go to school because even today, there aren't a lot of lab technicians. I applied for a job. I [was] able to work as a medical technologist. So [then I] tripled my income. A medical lab technologist is a clinical lab scientist, which is what I am today.

Your brother, who was in the Marine Corps, didn't really encourage you to go into the military. You didn't have anyone else in the family who had ever been in the military?

Yes, my father. He had been in when he was young. I was looking for a way to make my life situation better, and the only thing I could think of where I could get a skill was in the military. Like I said, initially I tried to do the Marine Corps. I ended up in the army because you only had to get guardianship papers with the army, which my parents and my daughter's father's mother had no problem signing. But the adoption thing—I thought that was a little bit much.

You were able to study and be in the full-time reserves, and you made it up to the ranking of staff sergeant?

Yes, I made it up to staff sergeant. And I had put my packet in for sergeant first class. But initially you asked me what made me decide to become an officer. I actually wanted to become an officer when I was much younger. I was told incorrectly, I was basically lied to and told, that I was too old. That I couldn't become an officer. I said, "I have a bachelor's degree." And I remember the person sitting down with me [to review my paperwork] and [he said,] "It says biology." I said, "It's a bachelor of science degree." [I thought at first I wouldn't be able to become an officer] because he was the one who was in charge of the paperwork. Well, we had a nurse [who] had just gotten commissioned. She was a second lieutenant. And I said, "How did she get a commission?" I found out she had a two-year RN degree. I said, "Wait a minute. How is it somebody who has a two-year RN degree can get a commission, and here I have a four-year bachelor of science degree, and I was told I couldn't get a commission?" I looked into it further and I found an outside recruiter. She did all my paperwork and everything. Her name was Leslie Gibbs. I'll never forget [her]. And I didn't tell anybody, not one person, because I didn't want anybody standing in my way or creating obstacles. The only person I told was the nurse, Major Fitzwater, who had to sign my paperwork, authorizing that it was OK for me to apply to become an officer. That took six or seven months. And then I get a call one day. And I go to the phone and they say, "May I speak to Lieutenant Tims?" And of course, I lose my mind, in the front yard. I started screaming. I was so happy. The next drill they had my ceremony. I invited my boyfriend, my fiancé at the time. My parents came and all my people that I was in drill with—they were wondering what was going on. They probably thought I was getting promoted to sergeant first class and my parents were there. They called me up to put my hand up because I was getting commissioned as an officer in the United States Army. After it was over, it was so beautiful. Everybody ran to me and said, "What! You became an officer!" I said, "I wasn't going to tell any of you!" I had remembered what had happened to me when I was told that I was too old. So, I didn't want anybody manipulating my paperwork or not sending a piece of paper up or something like that.

You didn't have to go to officer candidate school?

I got a direct commission. That means you have the credentials to be commissioned in the service. Even though I was prior enlisted, I still had to go to a three-month how-to-be-an-officer course, which is called "Officer Basic Course." And then they have other courses that you have to take throughout your career as an officer. You have to complete those. For instance, I am up for major, but I haven't taken the second half of the captain's course, and I won't be able to do it. First of all, I have to get into a unit. When I came back, my unit that I was with was the 145th; they became the 176th. When they became the 176th, I lost my job. And by losing my job and my space when I came back from Iraq, I [no longer had] a slot. Right now, I'm trying to get into the 341st Medlog Battalion in Dallas. I spoke to the major two days ago, and then I talked to his sergeant first class about the paperwork that I need so I can get transferred into the unit. We are in the process of that right now. Once I get in there, I'll probably be going to drill next month and finalizing my paperwork. And then I'll be working on doing what I need to do to get registered into the captain's career course, the second half of it, and get to learn whatever job they'll have me do in this unit.

After that you'll try for major?

All I have to do is take the captain's career course because I was up for major this year. I'll be a major. I would have been a major coming up in two months, if I had been able to take the captain's career course. But I will tell you, I didn't take the captain's career course—I took the first part, but I didn't take the other. I wanted to be deployed. When I came in, I was a 70 Bravo. I went to 70 Kilo school, which is a health materials service officer, which is logistics in all phases. Well, I wanted to be efficient and proficient in it, so initially I took the first correspondence course of the 70 Kilo course. Then I got sick with Graves' disease. I was supposed to be the commander for the 427th in Georgia as the medical logistics officer in Qatar, in 2006. But I got sick with Graves' disease. First, they had to find out what was wrong with me, and [then] I had to get myself and my body back to a point where I could function. [Then] I took my PT test, and I was able to pass them because I [was] getting my muscle mass back. I said I wanted to be deployed. I'm going on thirty years. I did not want to be in the military for thirty years and have never been deployed. So, I went out to the Seagoville unit here in Dallas. I asked my commanders if they could send me to all the schools I need, so that I can become a proficient 70 Kilo. And they did, they signed me up. Major Morton, he was my mentor. He was the best mentor in the world. I miss him. He guided me through a lot and he put his foot down on me too. He let me know I wouldn't get away with nothin.'

So, you were ready to be deployed?

There aren't many 70 Kilos in the military. Period. Even when I talked to major the day before yesterday. I said I was told he had some 70 Kilo positions. He said the position that he had was a 70 Kilo, but it is for force protection. And it's for a major. I'm still a captain. And he only had two captain positions that were 70 Kilo. I said, "I'll take it. I'll take the 70 Kilo. They are not going to get anybody to take that 70 Kilo in force protection as a major." So, when I get my promotion—I mean when I get through the captain's career course and I become a major. . . . That's what we talked about. He'll put me into that position because he himself said, "You guys are very rare and you are very hard to find." And we are. Our job is stressful. When I was a property book officer at this unit in Seagoville, [it was] hard. People hate you in the beginning. They thought I was a B-I-T-C-H because I would say, "You need to do this, you need to do that." I was always in their face until the end. When the commanders are trying to leave and they are doing that inventory and they have lost equipment, now they have an FLI that's over a half a million dollars. An FLI is a Financial Liability Investigation. Now they want to be your friend.

Because you saved their butts?

No, I did not save their butts. They wouldn't listen to me. They didn't want to hear what I had to say. Now they wanted to hear what I had to say. I saved one guy $247,000 because we did find [some missing items]. He had $500,000 worth of missing equipment. He had a $313,000 piece of equipment that people said they [helped him look for]. Now, I did find that [piece of equipment] for him because all I did was, I used critical thinking. I saved him $313,000. Of course, the responsibility would have been shared. He would have been the main person to be responsible because he was the commander; he is the one who signed the hand receipts for it. If he does the inventory the way he is supposed to and he puts his eyes and hands on what he is supposed to, he doesn't have to worry. But if something is missing, you can annotate that it was missing from a previous officer who handed it over [so] that doesn't make you liable for that. Because you could say that you looked for it: "I'm the new kid on the block, but it's not here, so I don't want this [error] put under me."

What does your family back in Cincinnati think of your career?

They are very, very proud of me. Especially my father. My mother is too. My mother, she thinks I am the sharpest woman on the planet earth. Her daughter is sharp. She has seen me come up from enlisted to officer. My father he is just very, very proud.

Do you keep in touch with your friends from high school? What do they think?

They know I am an officer. You know how women are. And men—they are very impressed.

Do you think they are intimidated?

Yes. Maybe that's why I can't get married. I don't like military men. No, not to marry, because they travel too much. And that leads too much [to the opportunity of] infidelity. And I don't want to hurt anybody.

Considering how good the military has been to you, what kind of advice would you give to a young woman who approached you and asked about joining the military?

I would say that if she was struggling like I was struggling, and if she has any inkling of a little bit of determination to making it, I feel the military can be a good stepping stone, something to help to elevate your life. If you use the system of the military and you use it the right way, take advantage of the opportunities and benefits that they give you, [you can go a long way]. I mean, look at me—I have a master's in biomedical science. I did not think that I was going to continue with the military because I was trying to go to med school. But that was the year I got sick with Graves' disease, when I graduated. I did not have the military pay for my master's, but I could have had the military pay for my master's. I got my bachelor's and my associate and the military paid for [those degrees]. I paid for my master's. I can tell you this: I wanted to go to medical school. I was trying to figure out how in the heck [to do it]. This has always been a dream of mine; when I was in school with the young baby, that's what I was going to school for. That's when I realized that [my classmates and I] were ill-prepared. We didn't have the chemistry; we didn't have the physics. We didn't have what the other schools had. [After] 9/11, [the military] pays [for my] housing and they pay 60 percent of my tuition for any school I go to. And I deployed out of Texas. I deployed as a state-of-Texas resident, even though I deployed out of Ohio because I was cross-leveled. They call it cross level when they have to pool [people]. They pooled me and my colonel from Dallas, Texas. And they pooled a lab tech. I told you there weren't many lab techs in the military either. They pooled a guy from [Dallas also], and we went to Twinsberg, Ohio. They had to search for us because we are rare. It's amazing. I can use the Hazelwood Act after I have exhausted my post-9/11 benefits and I can go to medical school for free.

Do you intend to do this while you are still in the reserves?

Yes. Yes. Yes. Yes. Because I can get a letter—I know there are ways you don't have to completely get out of the military if you are in medical school. They might require that I do some correspondence courses to get some points so I have a good year. They can use my classes. I know all the things that can be done. I don't want to retire my commission because I want to retire a lieutenant colonel. Age-wise I don't think I can make full bird. But I want to be a psychiatrist and being over in Iraq, the military needs some psychiatrists. They need them bad. I [could provide psychiatric services] through the VA, do it for some of the vets there; I would like to do it for some of the soldiers because [there are] too many suicides. It's just ridiculous. And the signs. The signs are there. I know the signs from just being around [soldiers with trauma]. It's just little things. You just know. We had these suicide programs. Every year we have to watch these videos and we have to sign off on it. So, we're supposed to be battle buddies for our battle buddies. If we're battle buddies for our battle buddies, how come our battle buddies keep killing themselves?

We spoke about this earlier—how does your PTSD affect you?

I don't have the patience that I used to have because of what I've seen and heard, and [because of] some of the dealings I had when I was overseas with people. Now, since I'm home, I have a keen sense of people not appreciating [things]. I don't know; it's not for me to govern that people appreciate what we have over here. I don't know what we have over here. [Civilians] don't have any idea of what goes on over there. Don't look at the soldiers like [they're at fault]. I mean, the [soldiers] who went [overseas to fight], everyone agrees with it: our presidents started it. We [soldiers] may not agree [with] what's going on. We rose our hand [so that] we would defend the Constitution no matter what. That's our duty, to defend our freedom. I had a few people who had problems, who said things like, "Why are you over there?" I had some friends say we were baby killers. And I would say, "What! What are you talking about!" Some people wanted to bring in the Black thing, [that the military is] killing people of color. I'm like, "Try telling me when I'm out there in a bunker, and I'm saying, 'These people are trying to kill me. These people are really trying to kill me!'" Oh my god! One night, they bombed us till 2:30, 3 o'clock in the morning. No sooner than [we heard], "All clear," no sooner than you take your shoes off, here it comes again. So anyway, I just noticed that I'm really, really hyper and I cry real easy. I don't know why I'm crying. I don't even know what triggers it. But it just keeps coming. It comes and it goes. I don't know what it is. I don't know if someone should hypnotize me and find out why. I don't know.

Have you talked to a psychiatrist?

I talked to one before I left Iraq. I'm now just getting all my stuff together for the VA. I just got my appointment yesterday and I went to my OEF [Operation Enduring Freedom] screen [the] day before yesterday. There are so many little things you've got to do. You've got to register for this, register for that. Sign up for this, sign up for that. They are pretty thorough about it, though. The VA people there are pretty nice. Some people don't know their jobs; they are just there for the paycheck. I was already in the system as a non-combat vet, a service-connected vet. The first time when I went to the booth, the man said, "You're already in the system." And so, I'm like, "But something isn't right." I got that feeling. So, I go to another area and they say, "No, go back to him. You are in as an 8, a non-service-connected vet. You need to be changed to a combat-service vet." I was in as an 8 and I needed to be changed to a 6. So, I went back and had to wait in this long line. But that's OK because I do have coping strategies and that's why I probably haven't flipped out. I noticed I have a temper—it's short. It's short. It's like I'm correcting people. And I thought to myself this morning, "You definitely aren't going to get a husband!" because I was on the phone with this lady and she got a little short with me. And I just lost it. I said, "Hold on a minute, lady. I said I need you to be patient with me." I said, "Look, I just came from Iraq and I'm trying to get this information. I don't like the way you are talking to me." I said, "My name is Yvonne, Y-V-O-. . . ." I said, "Is there anything else that you need?" Then, she changed. She was nice.

Was this a civilian matter?

Yes. I told her I [had just come] from Iraq and I could feel myself [grinding] my teeth [and thinking], *Girl, if you don't do your job the way you're supposed to do your job—you're not supposed to impose whatever went on in your house this morning or whatever got you feeling like you got to talk to me short! You got to leave it at the door because we are on the phone and we are trying to handle my business.*

That straightened her out?

Yes. Next thing I know, she paused and was real quiet for a minute. And I didn't know if she'd hung up on me or not. I said, "Are you still there?" And she said, "Yes, I'm just looking up your information." I was OK after that. I've noticed if you are out of order, I kind of snap. If you're not right, I just noticed I'm kind of—of—real quick. One of my girlfriends noticed it too. I had called her. She said, "Hold on Yvonne, hold on, slow down." She said, "What have you had to drink today? How many cups of coffee have you had today?" I said, "I haven't had any coffee." I don't know what's wrong with me.

Is there anything else you would like to say?

I've been saying so much. I can say that it is a blessing that I've been in the military. I've learned a lot. I've seen a lot. I've interacted with a lot of people. I do feel that being in the military and being in the reserves, working in the civilian population and being around civilians, the mindset is different. A lot of times in the civilian world, people don't understand how we [in the military] think; in my opinion, we think differently. At least those who actually do try to think. We think different from the civilian perspective because we see things different. In the military, change is all the time. But in the civilian job [world], if we change computer programs, people really get bent out of shape. In the military, things can change ten times in one day. I've learned to deal with change. I think the military has allowed me to be more resilient than the average person. I'm proud to have served. I'm really proud that I did do my deployment even if it wasn't like a party. But I'm proud that I served. There is something about being over there and then coming back. I appreciate America.

And your family and friends.

Yep.

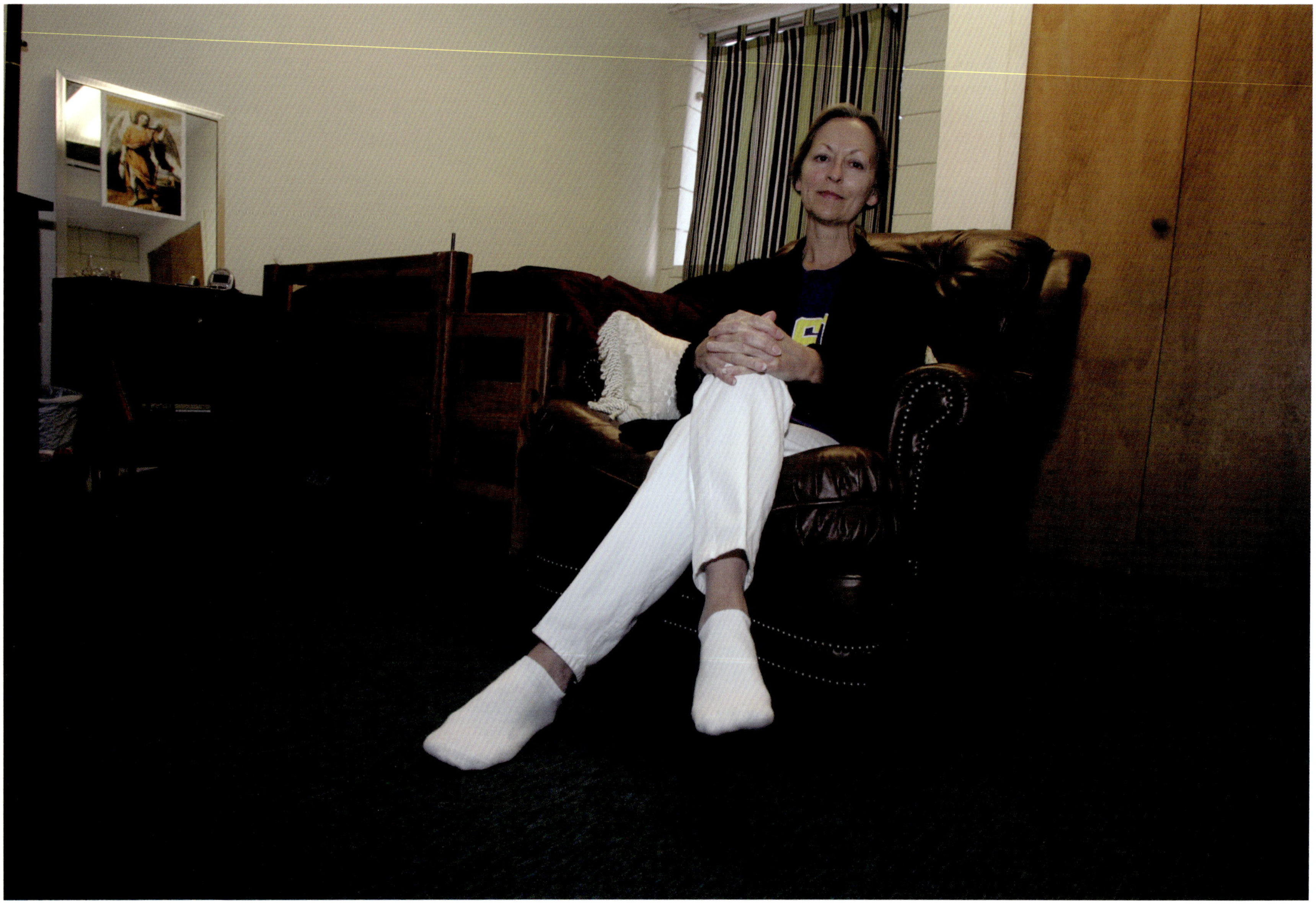

Homeless veteran Ruth Utera sits inside the one room reserved for female veterans at the Crawford House, a shelter located in Colorado Springs, CO for veterans struggling with homelessness and substance abuse. The Crawford House closed in 2022.

Ruth Utera

Interviewed: November 7, 2011 at Crawford House in Colorado Springs, Colorado

You were a German national?

I was born in 1955 [of] German parents, from Cologne, Germany. My father still lives in Cologne, still a German citizen. My mother and I came to this country in 1960. We were sponsored by her older sister, who was a war bride. We became naturalized citizens in 1969.

I guess in postwar Germany you must have been aware of what had happened?

We have the stories from my mother. My mother was ten years old when World War II ended. Her two sisters were older teenagers, and as I said they were war brides. My mother to this day—her stories are quite interesting. Disturbing. I don't think she ever recovered from what happened to her as a child when the war ended. The way she suffered.

Did you have any relatives who were in the military?

My brother did. My older brother. He was reared in Germany. He's now an Australian citizen. But that was mandatory. My older brother, he is a year and a half older than I am. I believe when he was in his late teens, he served the required two years of all young German men. We were not reared together. He was raised with my father in Germany and I was brought up in America with my mother. So, ten years prior to when I went into the US military, he served in the German Army for two years.

His service never affected you?

I didn't see my brother again. We left, my mother and I, in 1960. And we saw each other as adults. I was nineteen, he was twenty-one. From 1960 to . . . fifteen years we didn't see each other. There were letters. Phone calls were far too expensive at that time. My mother kept in touch with my brother through letter-writing correspondence. When we met, I spoke English and very little German, and he spoke very little English. We spoke [a lot through gestures].

Was there any military background in your family that affected you?

My stepfather. My mother remarried in 1961 [when I was six years old]. He was in the air force. He retired from the air force after twenty-three years. My family was all through the years, as I can remember, very patriotic. All I've known is the military life.

You traveled around a lot as a child?

Not so much with the air force as a child. Langley Air Force Base in Virginia. Clark Air Force Base in the Philippines as a teenager, which was very interesting. It was a wonderful experience. By the time I graduated from high school, I had lived on three continents.

You've benefited from the military life in that regard.

Absolutely. Travel is such a privilege for us. [For] most of us, it was difficult. For me it wasn't a novelty.

I guess that most military kids feel that way?

Take it for granted. Right.

How old were you when you joined the military?

I was twenty-eight years old. I was in the midst of a difficult marriage and I needed to support my child, who was four years old at the time. I was working as a secretary, and it wasn't going to pay my living expenses. So, after talking with a good friend of ten or twelve years [I decided to join]. She had done the same thing when she had two young children to take care of and her marriage was failing. So, I did it. I was terrified and thought, "Not me at all," but I did it.

Did you find a lot of support in the military?

Absolutely. Absolutely, I did. My brother went into the air force the same year I went in the army. I wanted to go into the air force first. I was twenty-eight. They couldn't get me active duty before my twenty-eighth birthday, so I went into the army. Because the army and the navy would take you up till thirty-five at that time. They told me a few days after my twenty-eighth birthday that it wasn't going to work. No grace period, nothing. You could not be twenty-eight. You could not have reached your twenty-eighth birthday. So, me: army? I grew up in an air force family. I couldn't fathom the army, but I did. It was survival for me. I had to take care of my child.

The patriotism you were exposed to growing up in the states—did it have any reason for your joining?

[I joined] as soon as I processed the necessity of going into the military. It was second nature. It became second nature to me, the military lifestyle, once I got out of basic training.

What was your MOS?

I started as a 26 Yankee, satellite communications. I tested well, but I had difficulty with the troubleshooting. So, they reclassified me into telecommunications. My background was secretarial and office.

Where were you based?

My first duty assignment was Berlin. At the time, that was 1985. For me: '85 till the summer of '86 before the wall came down. Of course, it was three to four years before the wall came down. Terrorism was something we had to learn to live with, which was extremely difficult to deal with [especially as] a mother watching my first child going on a school bus. He was in the first grade [when I would watch] him board the school bus with our armed machine gunners following the school buses. And hearing in the news about the bombings in Frankfurt. Family members being at risk. I think as a woman it was much, much harder. As a mother it was much, much harder. It was an elite assignment. But in no time, Gaddafi and whoever—I don't remember clearly—I deliberately did not keep up with that. I was pleased to hear that Gaddafi is no longer here. I don't want to remember any of that.

I know that he was behind the bombing of the discotheque.

I knew them. I worked with them. The bombing of the discotheque [in] Berlin. One was a coworker and lost his hearing. Another was severely injured. I didn't know as well.

That would be shocking to have comrades fall.

It doesn't sound like real war. It didn't then. Berlin still isn't [considered during that time period] as a combat zone. . . . But we received the medal before we left Berlin. It was an occupied city. It had the dates. Pearl Harbor [is] on one side of the medal. Army of occupation. It showed Europe on the other, 1945. I don't understand why those who served during the Cold War don't quite have the same benefits. We couldn't go to work in uniform. Traveling freely in our off-duty time was very tense. My husband was stationed in Kaiserslautern. When I went on pilgrimage to Bosnia, I read that that was just as bad as the experience of civilians in World War II, during the war and post-war of World War II. Bosnia, the same. During the attacks [on] Sarajevo, for instance. Of course in [Bosnia-Herzegovina], that was ethnic cleansing. [In] Berlin it was not so obvious. It was—I don't have the words to describe the terrorist threat that was hovering over us. It was a constant unease.

That was the Baader-Meinhof Gang behind the bombings?

You know more about that than I do, Steven. I do recall the neo-Nazis being highly visible. Gaddafi was in another country, and we were not safe. We simply were not safe. It looked ordinary. But we were not safe, the whole time we were there.

Was the military accommodating with your having a child?

Not at all. Not at all. My child had a difficult time adapting and adjusting. I remarried. I married a service member. And while I was in training, before I arrived in Berlin, my child was with my mother in the States. My husband, we had married in 1984, a year after I enlisted. He was stationed in Okinawa. For the first year, he had his duty station in Okinawa. I was in training at Fort Gordon, Georgia and Fort Huachuca in Arizona. I went through extensive training for the first year I was in the military because I was in a long MOS in telecom. [My] mother brought my son a month after I arrived [in Berlin]. He had problems immediately. The services available for the children were excellent; however, I was encouraged to send him back to the States, to my mother. And that was the very reason I did get out of the military. My mother was not willing to care for him. He was a very bright child. He had serious problems adjusting to this life in Germany with me and his stepfather. My NCO recommended that I have him institutionalized. And at that point my mother was not amenable to taking care of him; she was on disability, and she was right. I thought no, that's it. So, I got out on a dependency discharge.

Had you up to that point considered making the military a career?

I had absolutely wanted to. Yes. If there had been greater understanding in the army. We experienced totally different situations in the air force. I remember my mother when I was a child, talking about a friend or neighbor who had a child with special needs, whatever they may have been. In the air force they tend to keep you in one place longer. They were more family-oriented than the army. And I knew that. But I didn't know my child would develop behavioral problems.

I'm sure it's a tremendous stress to go be engulfed in another culture, not that he had to go to German schools.

It's interesting too because no one knew; I didn't know and my former husband didn't know that these problems were temporary. This child was fine. By the time we were back in the States, I was out of the military. How much of that was because I was home full-time for him, I don't know. But this child was fine by the time he was ten years old. This difficult period from the age of seven to ten—I don't know. I wouldn't be here today if I'd served twenty years. I wouldn't be here at the Crawford House today. But my child is whole and he is fine.

What happened after the military?

I was a full-time homemaker. My former husband served for twelve years: US Army Space Command. He did quite well. He was in satellite communications. He separated from the army in 1994. He chose Colorado Springs. He went to work [on] contracts with Peterson and NORAD and did quite well. He earned three times the money that he earned in the service. And he knew that, so we had a very good life as civilians. It was because he was in the military and received such excellent training. We had a good life at the very end.

You've been in the Colorado Springs area since 1994?

Yes. 1994.

Your marriage dissolved?

My marriage ended after twenty-one years. It ended seven years ago.

How did you end up here, in the Crawford House?

As I said earlier, my former husband made a very good living. It was because my older child did so well when I did get out of the army. [The] army was wonderful. It allowed me to take care of my child for a few years. I remarried. A dual military couple with a young child—it didn't work very well. Not only for myself, but for a few of my friends [who] had the same difficulty. But we are speaking of my experience. I had a very good life for ten years from 1994 to 2004 taking care of my family. My husband didn't want me to work. We put the [family] first. We wanted a traditional family. He went through a midlife crisis. He was younger than I was. He struggled with alcoholism. He left the family and the marriage. I had been doing volunteer work for ten years with a local nonprofit organization for women in crisis. Since I had been a homemaker, I didn't have a career. That was my career, and then working as a volunteer for the nonprofit organization. When my marriage ended in 2004, I needed a home. I needed a job. My former husband took radical steps. He abandoned the family. He met someone in a pub and left the States. I lost my home. I lost my vehicle. My priest friend offered me a job, which was in his [former] family home. He was a lay vocation priest. He was a dear friend of mine. And he knew [my] family. I thought I would do that till I retired. My priest friend developed Alzheimer's a few years ago, and the house had to be closed and he moved to a retirement home. I thought my children and I would be fine. I had a nontraditional career now working for a home for unwed mothers; I did that till 2009, until it got to the point the organization had to close here and moved to Omaha, Nebraska. New board members. My children were still in school, one of them, and did not want to go to Omaha. [T]his was their home. So, I started to look [around for work]. The economy, as we all know, by 2009, was difficult. So, I'm looking for traditional work for the first time since I was in the military. I had a difficult time finding a job. I enrolled in Pikes Peak Community College full-time. My son came to live with me. His father decided that Zachary needed to stay here with me and near my older son because he would be beginning high school. He was fourteen at the time. So, I began to look for a job in the private sector. It took a long time. I worked for a company that outsources Verizon [services], from December '09 until June this year when I was laid off. I had my apartment for two years. I lost my apartment and couldn't find work.

Your story is like that of so many other Americans—it was the economy.

The economy because I never [before] had a difficult time finding a job. Now I'm older, so there is that additional challenge. We know there is not supposed to be age discrimination, but there is. There is. If they can hire someone the age of my children—they're quicker, they are more enthusiastic, they are probably going to stay a little longer. Someone like me is going to take the first decent job that comes up. So, McDonald's, Walmart, and the likes have not been options for me. And I've certainly tried.

How long have you been here, in the Crawford House?

I've been here for two weeks today.

Before that, were you out on the streets?

No. I had a few options. None of them were good options: temporary solutions, staying with friends for a few weeks. Perhaps another friend with a young child. Two or three options that were just terrible. Thankfully, the Crawford House had one opening. I had the eviction notice. I had to be out by late October. It was exactly one week before I had to be out of my apartment. Homeless Veterans Office called me and said that the Crawford House had a room. I had never been in this type of situation before. Couldn't imagine it. The story I'm telling you now . . . that happened to other people. We would read a newspaper article or see a story on television [about homeless and struggling veterans]. That was out there. That couldn't touch us, my circle of family and friends.

Are you going out and looking for jobs?

I'm working with Ron, the VA employment counselor. He works [in particular] with homeless veterans. I have met with him twice, in-depth sessions. And I will be going on two interviews on Wednesday; Ron will be taking me. This is new to me. I am told that the employers in the private sector that hire veterans receive some type of tax breaks. I had heard about it vaguely, [a program] that Obama created. It's much better than me looking on my own, what Ron is doing.

So being in the military has paid off?

I'm so grateful. Absolutely. Absolutely. I would be on someone's sofa if it had not been for my service.

How many residents are there in the Crawford House?

Presently? [There have been] a few comings and goings over the last few days. And there are between fifteen and eighteen [residents] I think at the present time. The accommodations for female veterans—there is one room, two beds.

Is there another female veteran here?

We were expecting one woman possibly today. She may come, unless she has resolved her situation. So, I might have a roommate.

Regarding the other veterans here, do you think they are here for the same reason—the economy?

I was talking with two of my family members about this over the weekend. I don't have the exact numbers. Possibly 5 percent, 10 percent of the veterans have been in need for a while. Perhaps years. Destitute. Most of the veterans I've seen are no different from you or I. Enjoyed comfortable lives. A few here [had] lives of privilege. I know one of the managers here was [once] making over $100,000 a year and came here homeless before he was offered the job as a manager. Another gentleman is a West Point graduate. One man was living on the streets for eighteen years.

To boil it all down, you are the victim of a man going through a midlife crisis and the economy.

Yes, that's right.

And your two children—where are they now?

My younger two children with my former husband are here. My twenty-three-year-old son and fifteen-year-old son live here in Colorado Springs. Obviously, I can't take care of my fifteen-year-old son. My twenty-three-year-old son married last year and bought a house. So that is where my youngest son is. Going to the same school district as his older brothers went to. So, he has stability.

You have three sons?

I have three sons: My thirty-two-year-old son was in the army. He lives in Tennessee. He was a son from my previous marriage. He was the reason I enlisted in the military. My thirty-two-year-old son, I had to support him.

How do you feel things are going to turn out?

I'm very optimistic. I am receiving a lot of help with the veterans programs. The programs here at the Crawford House work . . . closely . . . with the staff at the VA clinic on the residents' behalf. The employment counselors, they—as they tell us, "You have a very large team working for you and with you." To get back to being independent, employed. Or some of the residents here are working on disability claims. Either employment or disability claims.

Does the federal government pay for any of this?

Miss Vicky, the program director, could answer those questions.

I know that there are a lot of nonprofit groups that help out.

I just received a coat this morning. A gentleman—I didn't see him, but one of the residents brought me into the office this morning and said, "There was a coat here that might fit you." My [own] coat, my heavy coat that would look appropriate over a suit for a job interview on a cold day, was lost when I was in school a few years ago. I didn't have a warm coat. This morning a gentleman in a suit came and brought us some coats, and that coat was exactly what I needed. So, I received a sporty warm jacket from someone who donated a large amount of clothing the first week I was here. A lighter jacket [too]. I consider them all blessings.

America's Women Down Range

Returning Home

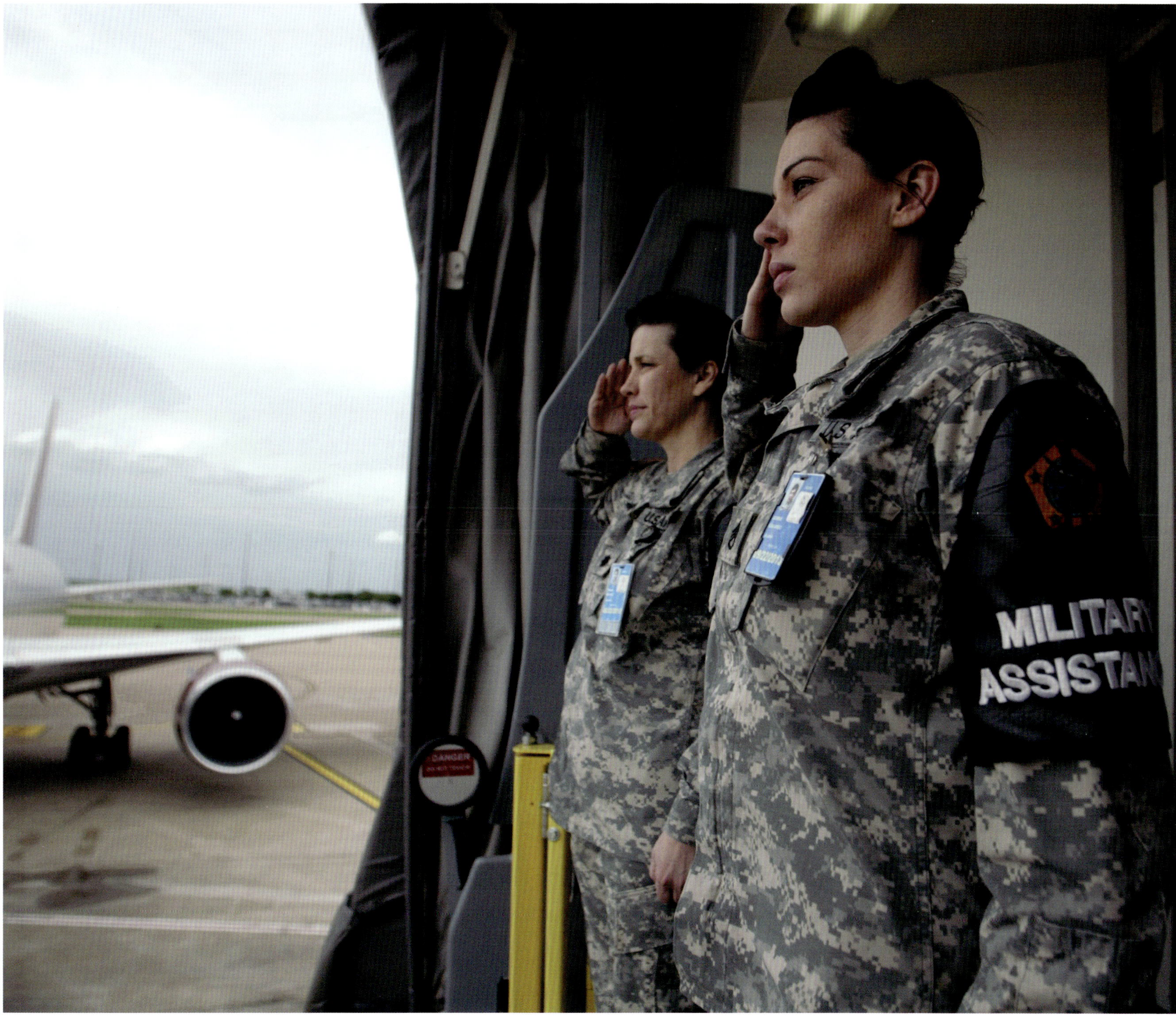

LTC Trisha McAfee, left, and SSG Jasmine Guajardo salute a chartered jetliner taking troops back to their deployment bases from Dallas/Fort Worth International Airport [DFW] to Kuwait.

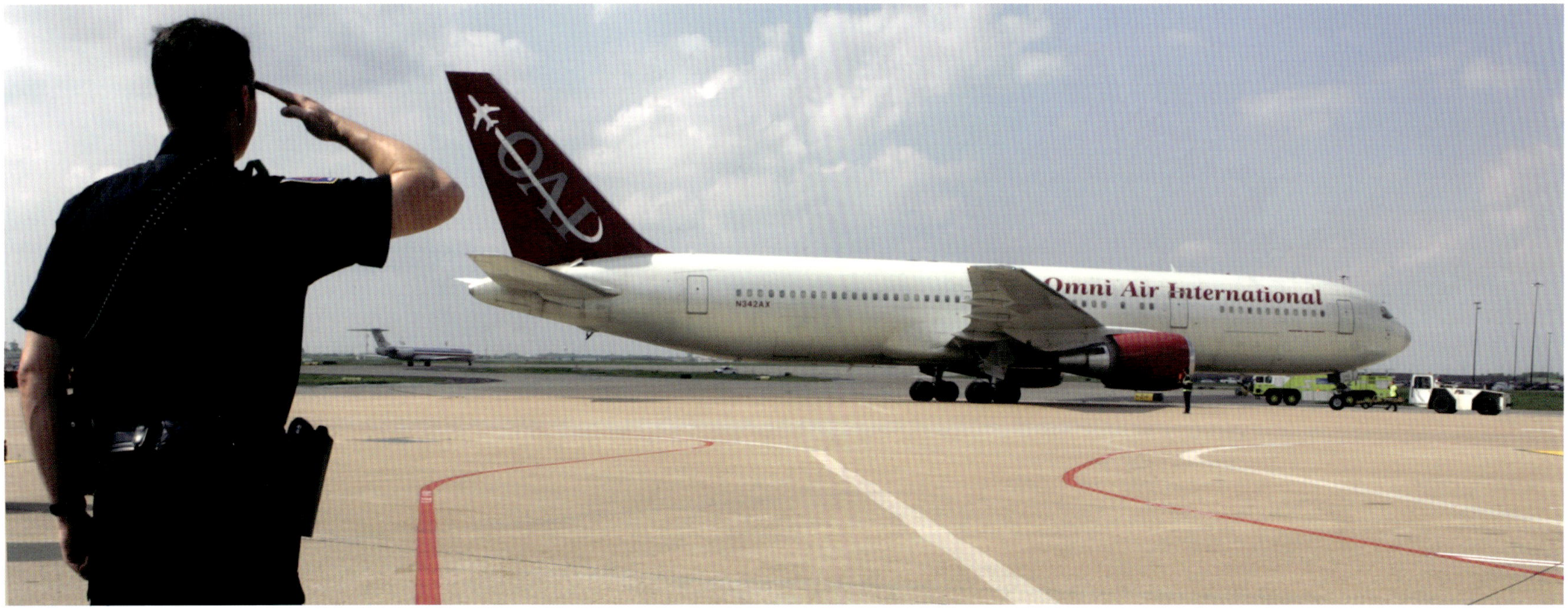

A DFW Airport officer salutes the final flight returning troops to their deployments in Kuwait and Afghanistan.

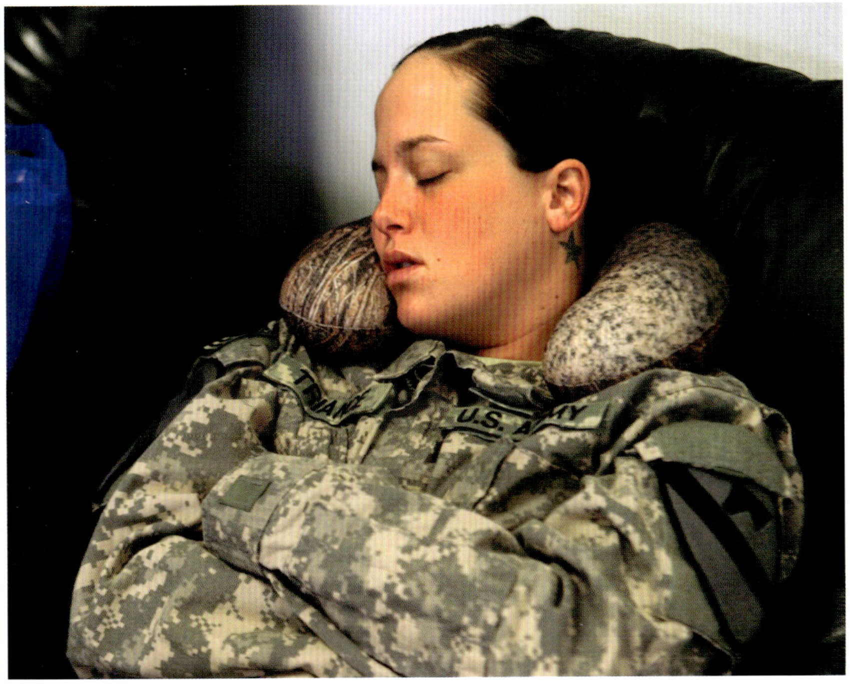

A soldier naps while waiting for a flight to take her back to her deployment post. SPC Jennifer Triance is returning to Kuwait following a two-week R&R leave. When asked how she felt about returning to Kuwait, she replied, "I've got to do what I've got to do."

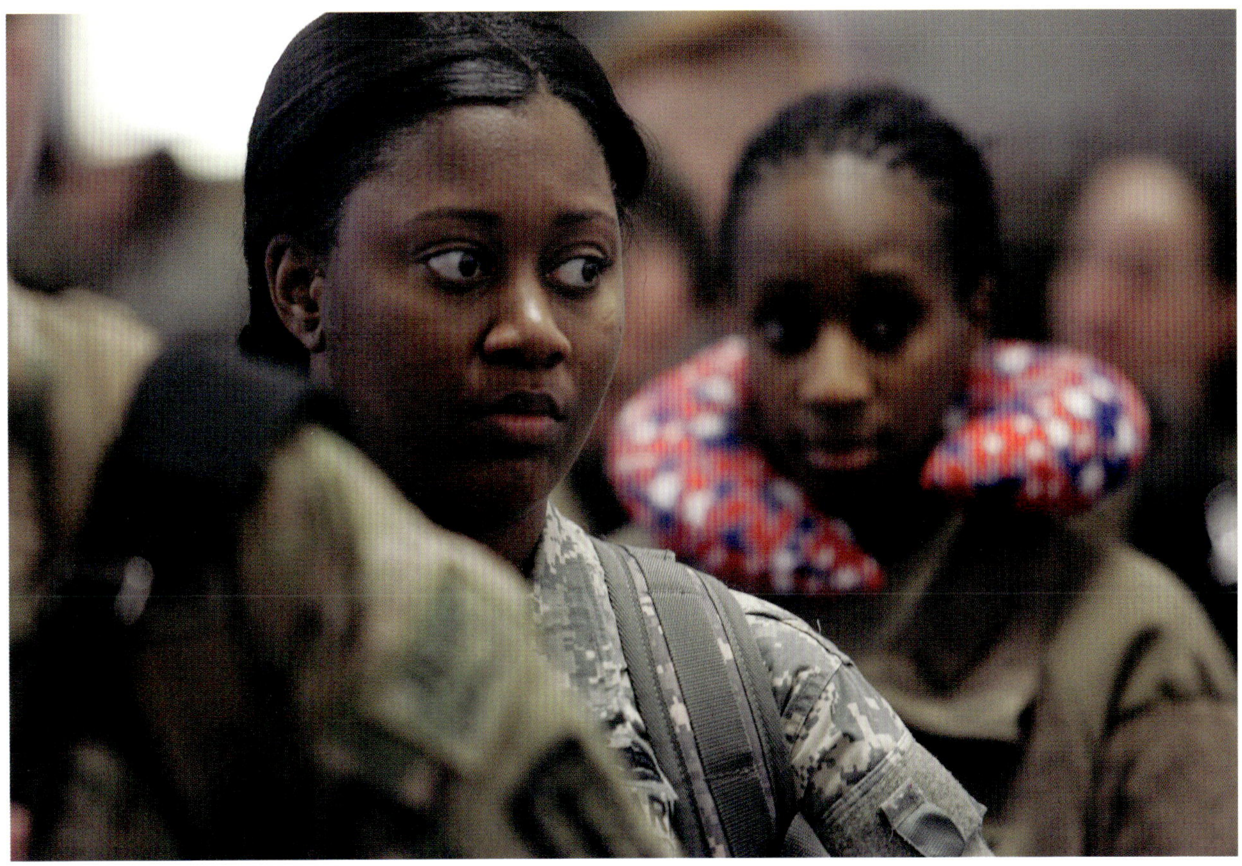

An unknown soldier waits to board a flight to Kuwait following her two-week R&R leave.

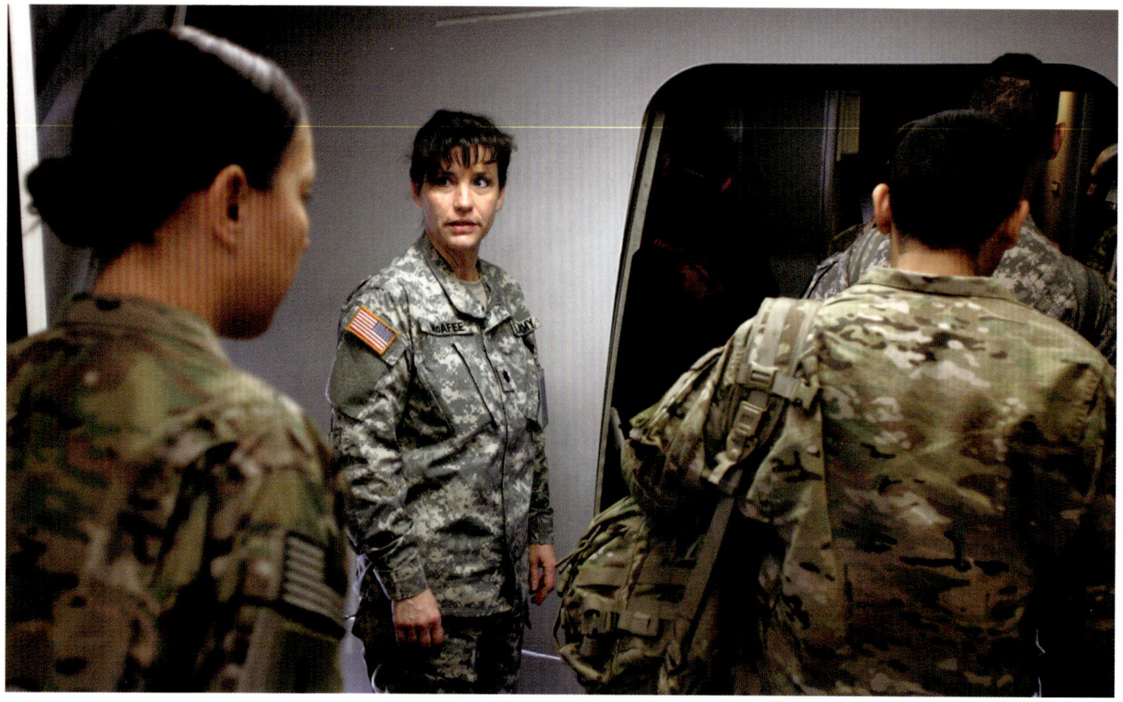

LTC Trisha McAfee, commanding officer of the Military Assistance unit at DFW Airport, stands by the door of a military charter jet while troops file on board. The troops are returning to their deployment bases following a two-week R&R leave.

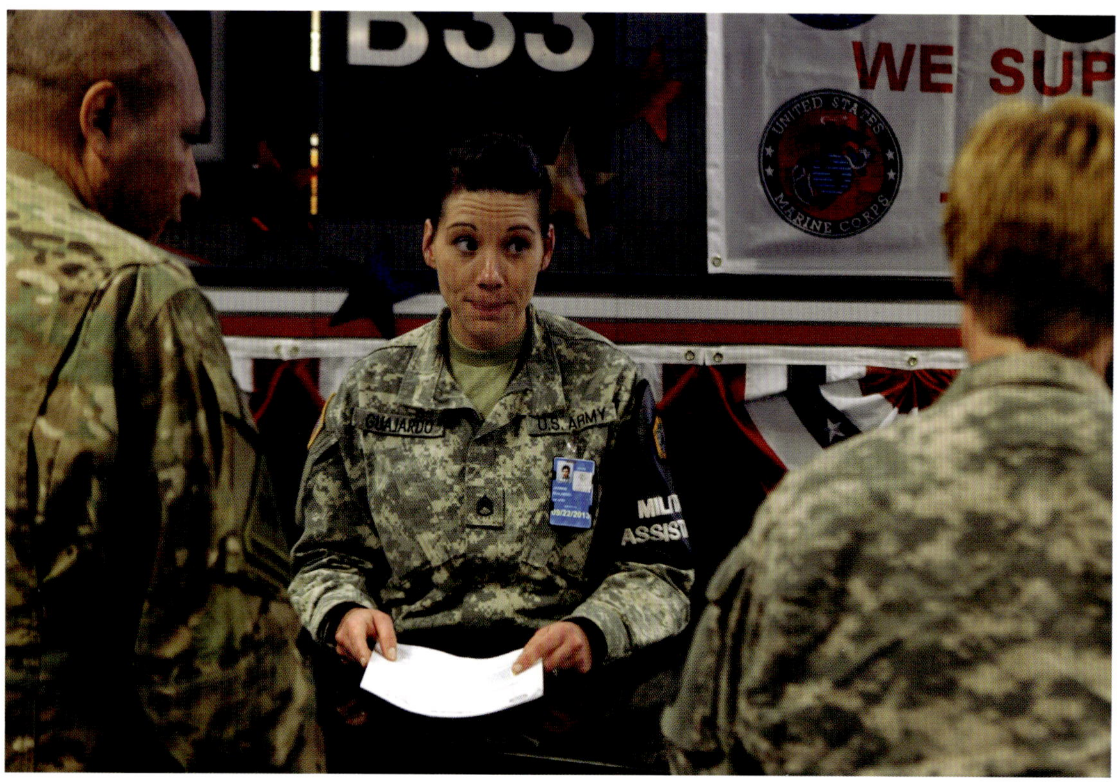

SSG Jasmine Guajardo reviews paperwork with officers who will be traveling on a flight for troops returning to their deployment bases after their two-week R&R leave. The flight is leaving from DFW Airport for Kuwait. Guajardo is part of a Military Assistance unit stationed at the airport.

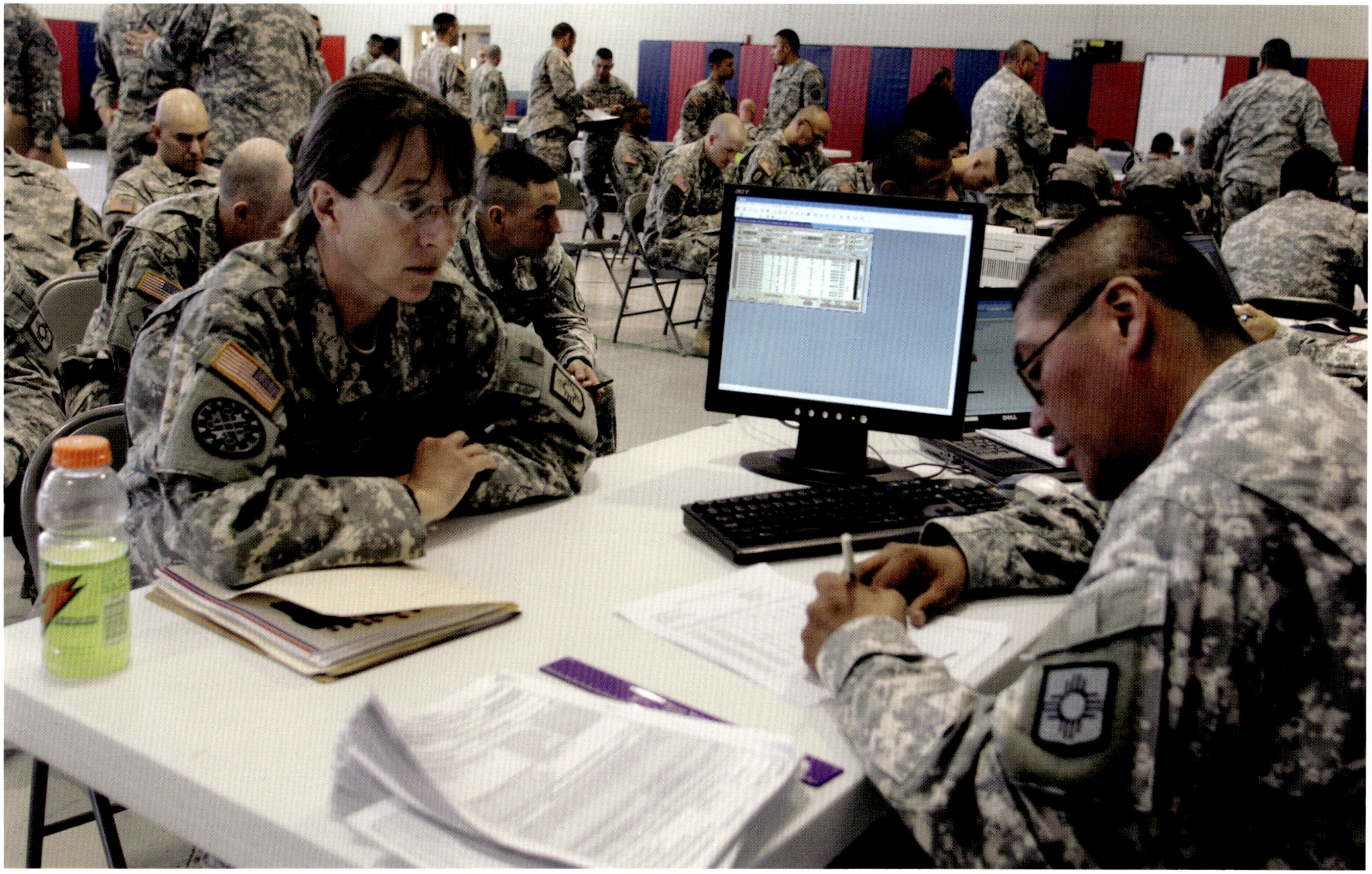

SPC Daylene Marsh of Farmington, NM does paperwork to end her deployment to Iraq.

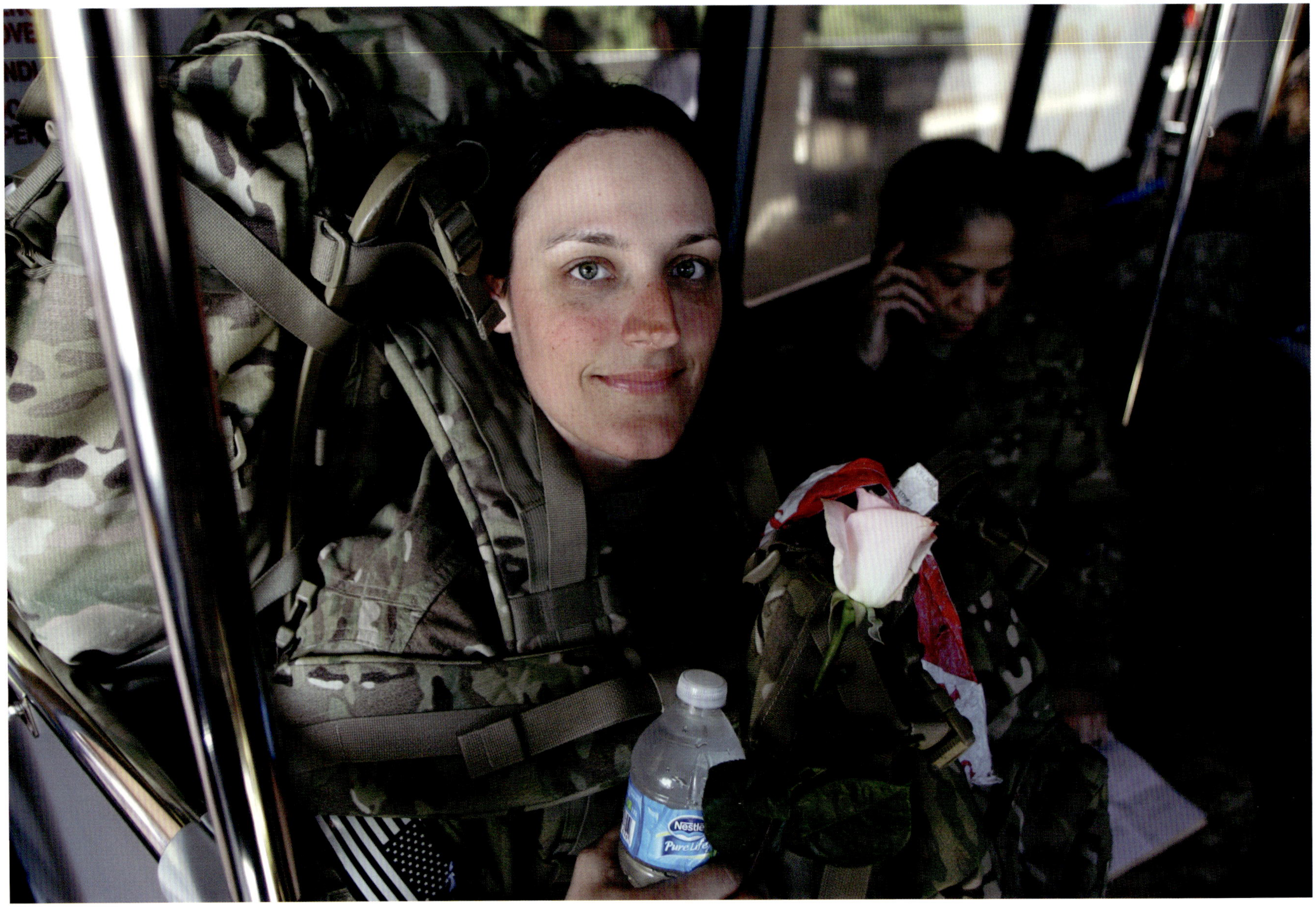

Holding a rose given to her by a WWII veteran greeter, SPC Jenni Garva waits on an airport bus in order to catch her connecting flight home. Garva and the others on the bus were part of a group of ninety-seven soldiers arriving at DFW Airport for R&R leave from their posts in Afghanistan and Kuwait.

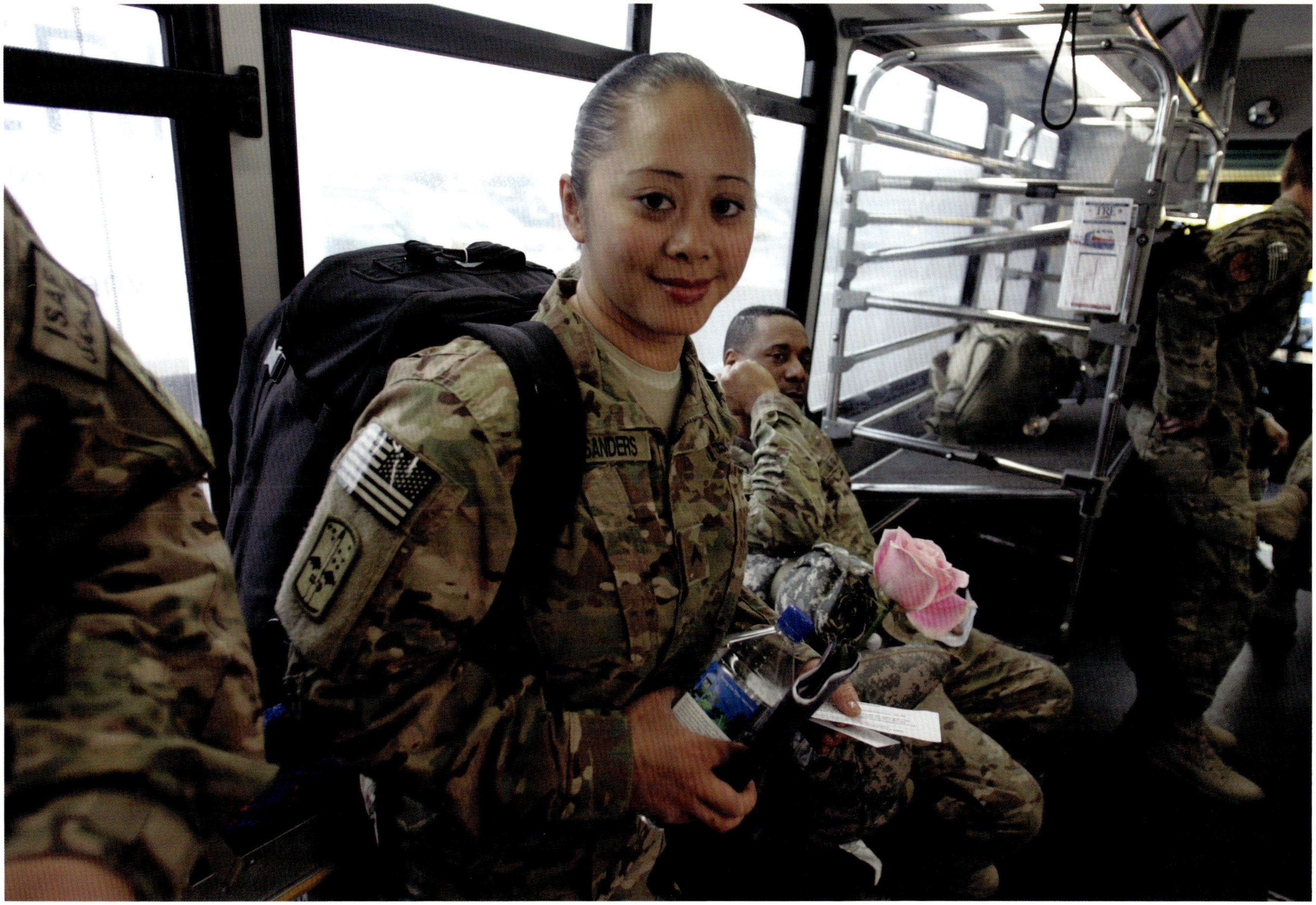

A recently arrived soldier on her two-week R&R leave sits on a DFW Airport bus that will transfer her to a connecting flight. She holds a flower given to her by an official greeter.

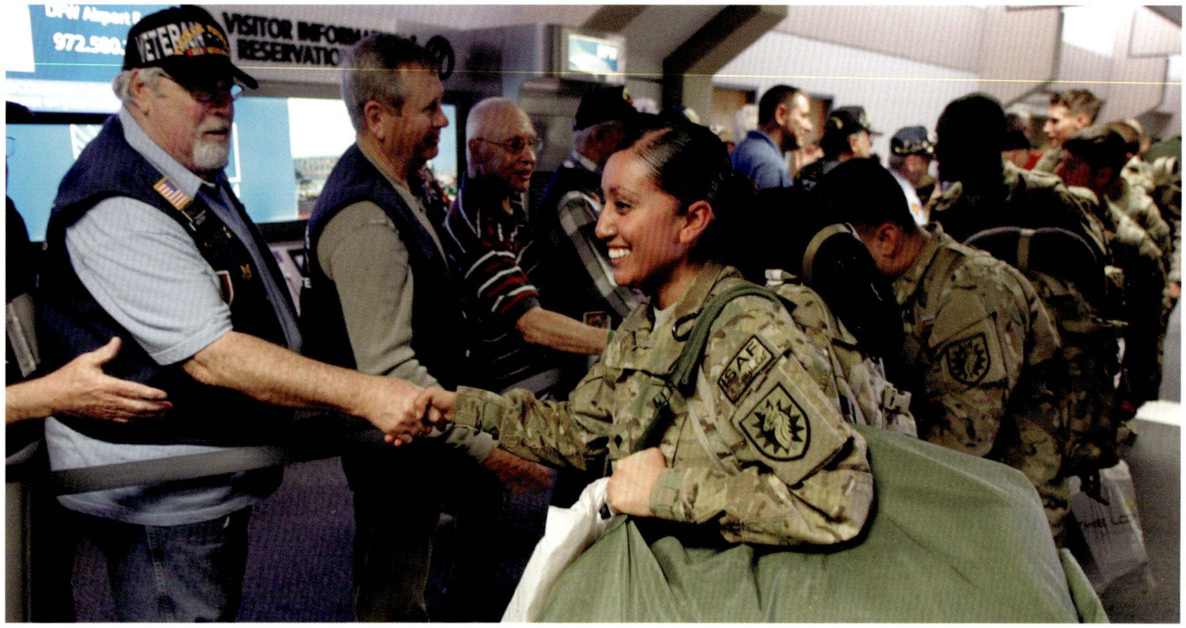

SPC Monse Ramirez shakes hands with military veteran greeters after arriving at DFW Airport. Ramirez was part of a group of ninety-seven soldiers arriving for R&R leave from their posts in Afghanistan and Kuwait. The troops were met by regular greeters and many school children. The R&R flights, which began in 2003, ended on March 14, 2012.

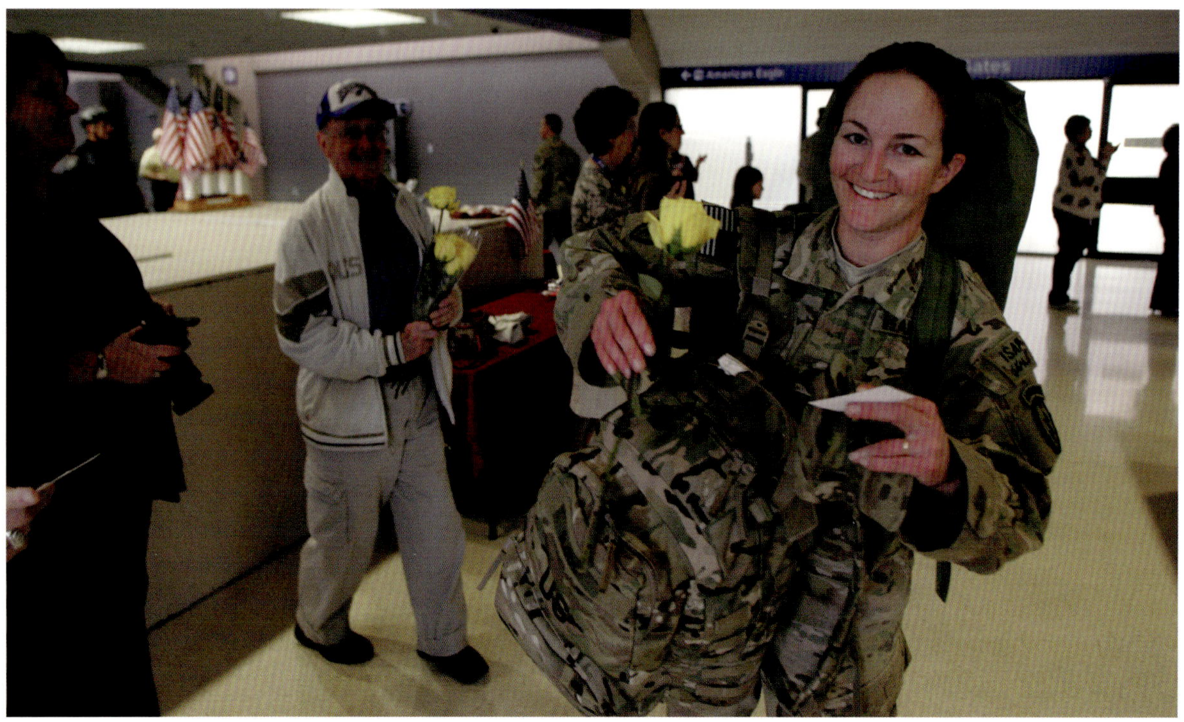

A soldier arrives at DFW Airport for her two-week leave. One member of a contingent of greeters has given her a flower as a welcoming gesture.

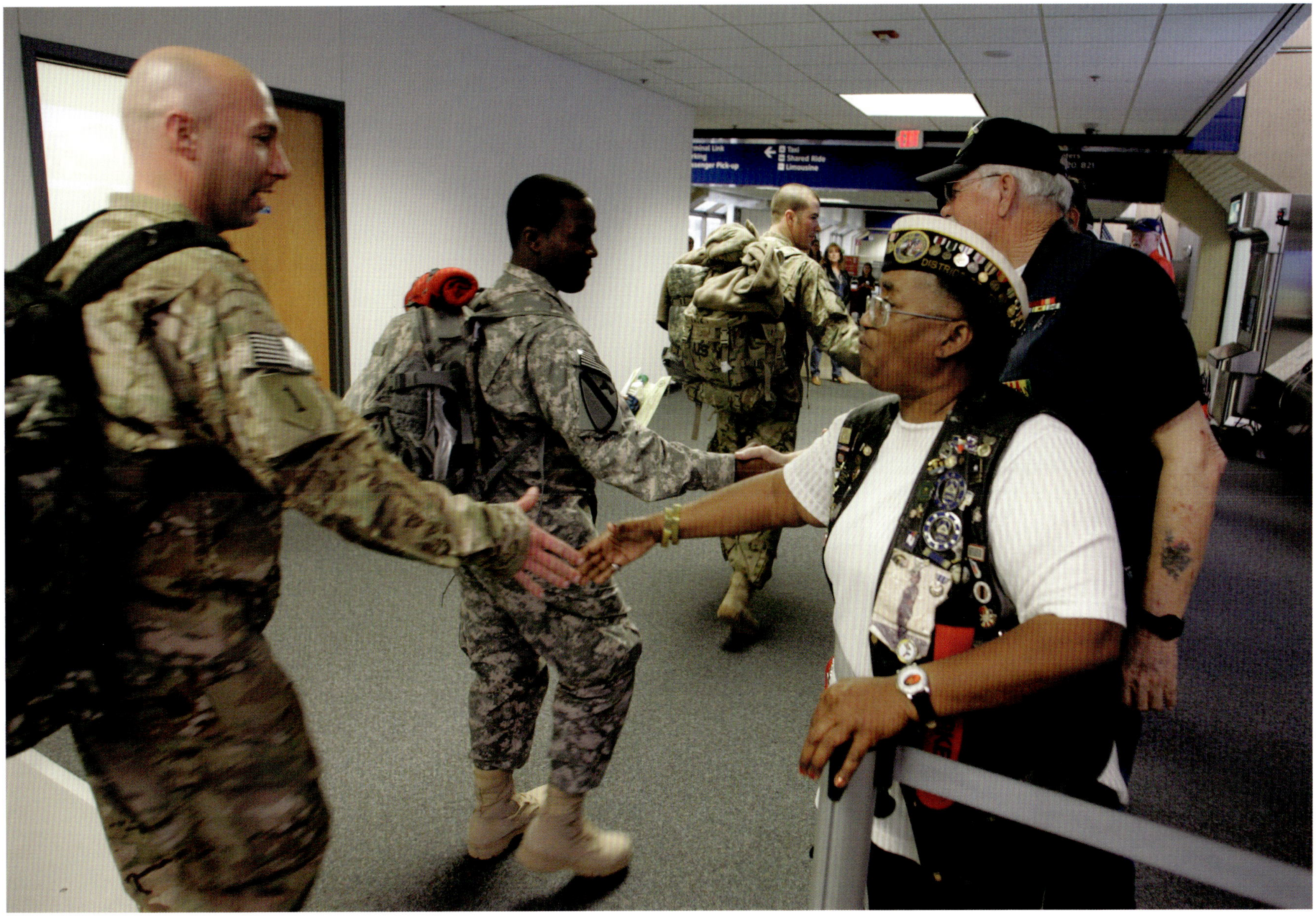

Army Veteran SSG Cynthia Burks welcomes soldiers arriving for their rest and recuperation [R&R] leave at DFW Airport. Burks, a Gulf War veteran who suffers from Gulf War syndrome, served as a medic from 1974 to 1993.

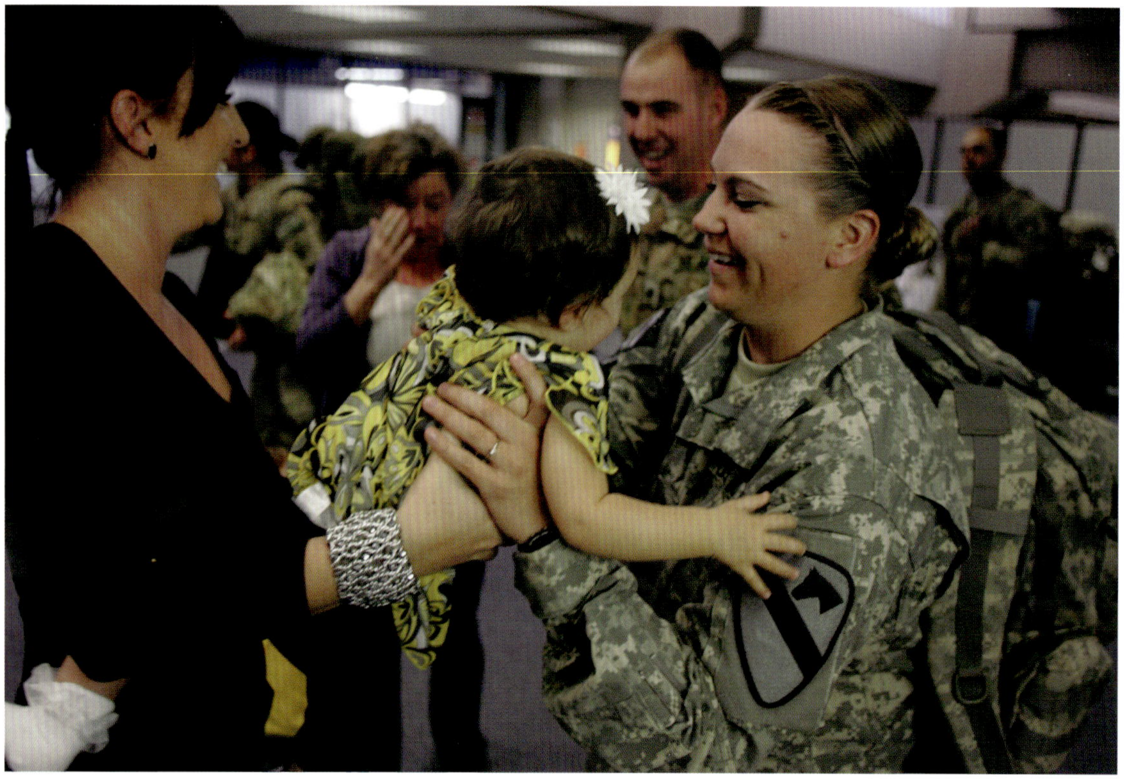

A female soldier reaches for the child of a relative. The soldier has traveled from Afghanistan to Dallas for her two-week R&R leave.

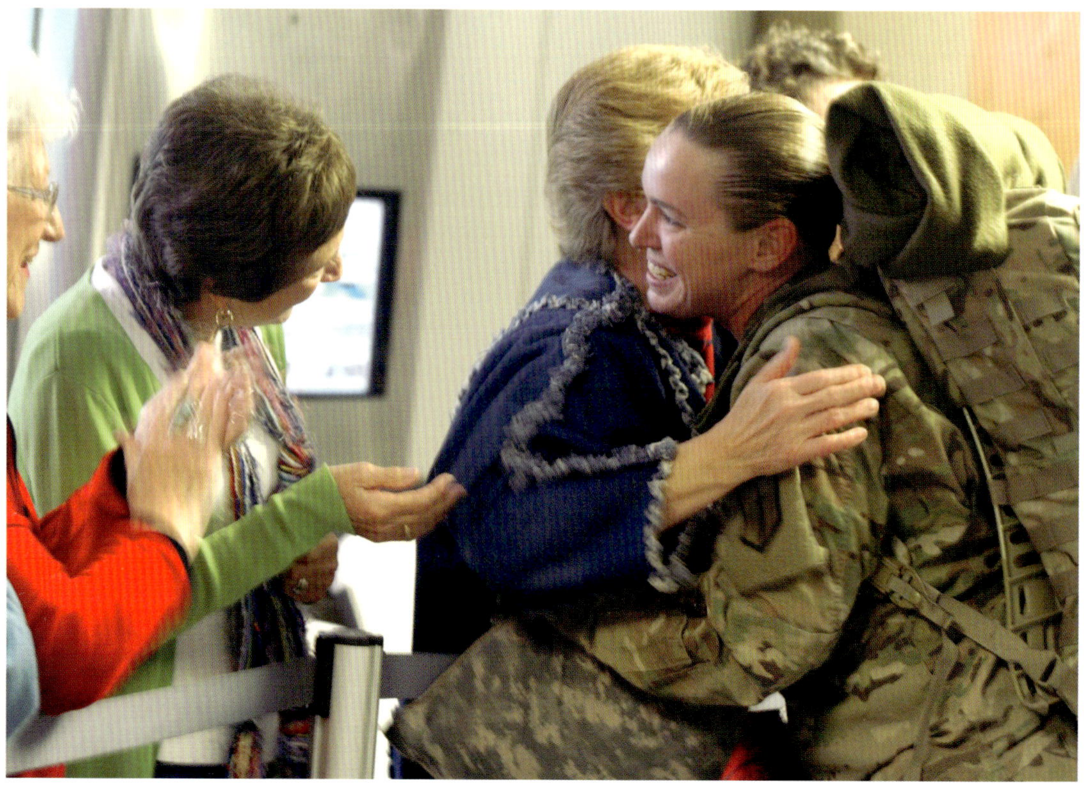

A returning soldier is greeted at DFW Airport. She had just arrived on a charter aircraft from Kuwait.

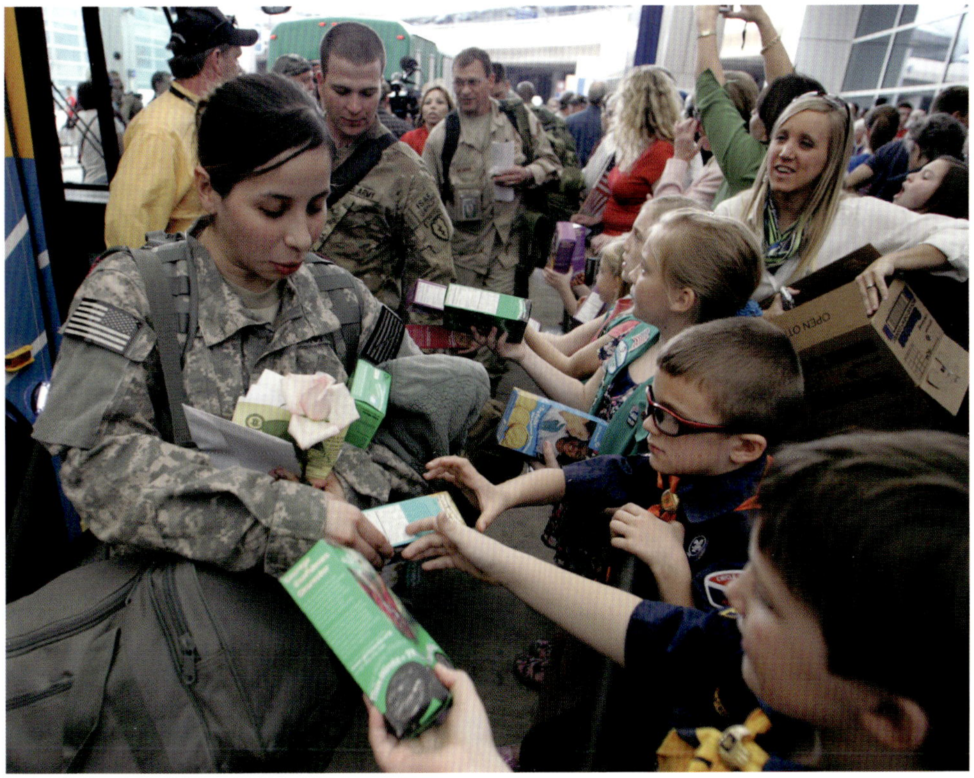

Navy E-5 medic Star Schelnetty passes by Cub Scouts at the DFA Airport. Schelnetty is on her way to a two-week R&R leave from her deployment in Kuwait. This day, March 14, 2012, was the last flight into DFW by the military for the purpose of delivering troops to connecting flights to their hometowns. An estimated two thousand flights have taken place since they began in 2004. During that time, a dedicated group of volunteers and veterans have met each flight with boisterous greetings, snacks, and information about connecting flights. An estimated seven hundred greeters showed up for this final arrival.

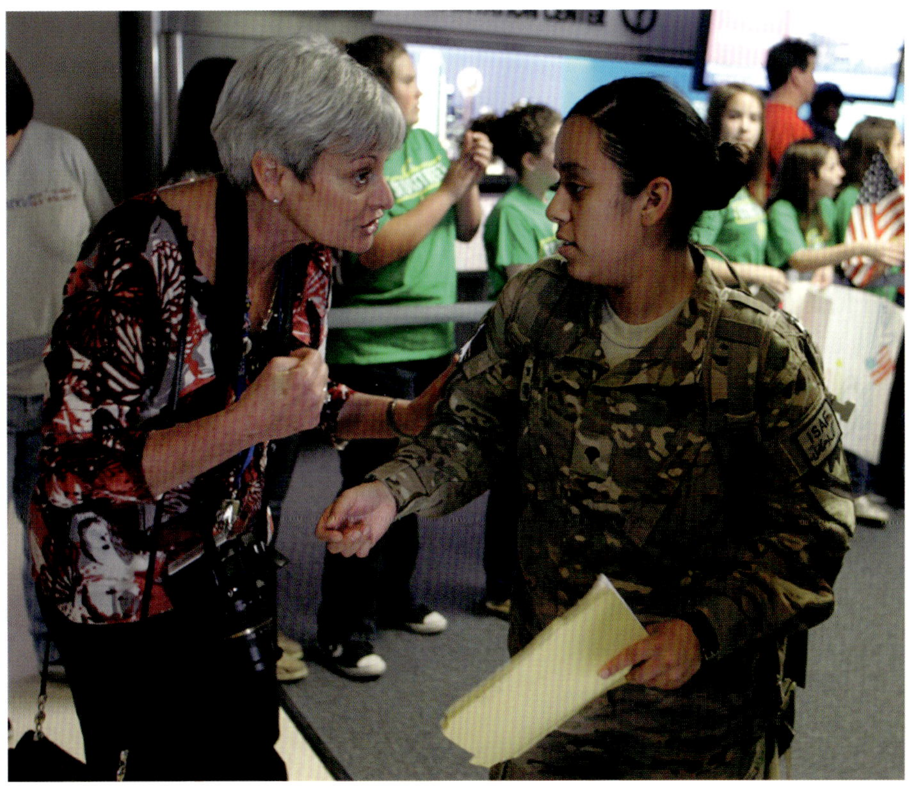

Donna Cranston assists a female soldier in finding her connecting flight from DFW Airport to her home. Cranston is the founder of Welcome Home A Hero, a dedicated group of volunteers who since 2004 have been meeting arriving flights carrying troops from deployments in Kuwait and Afghanistan to their homes.

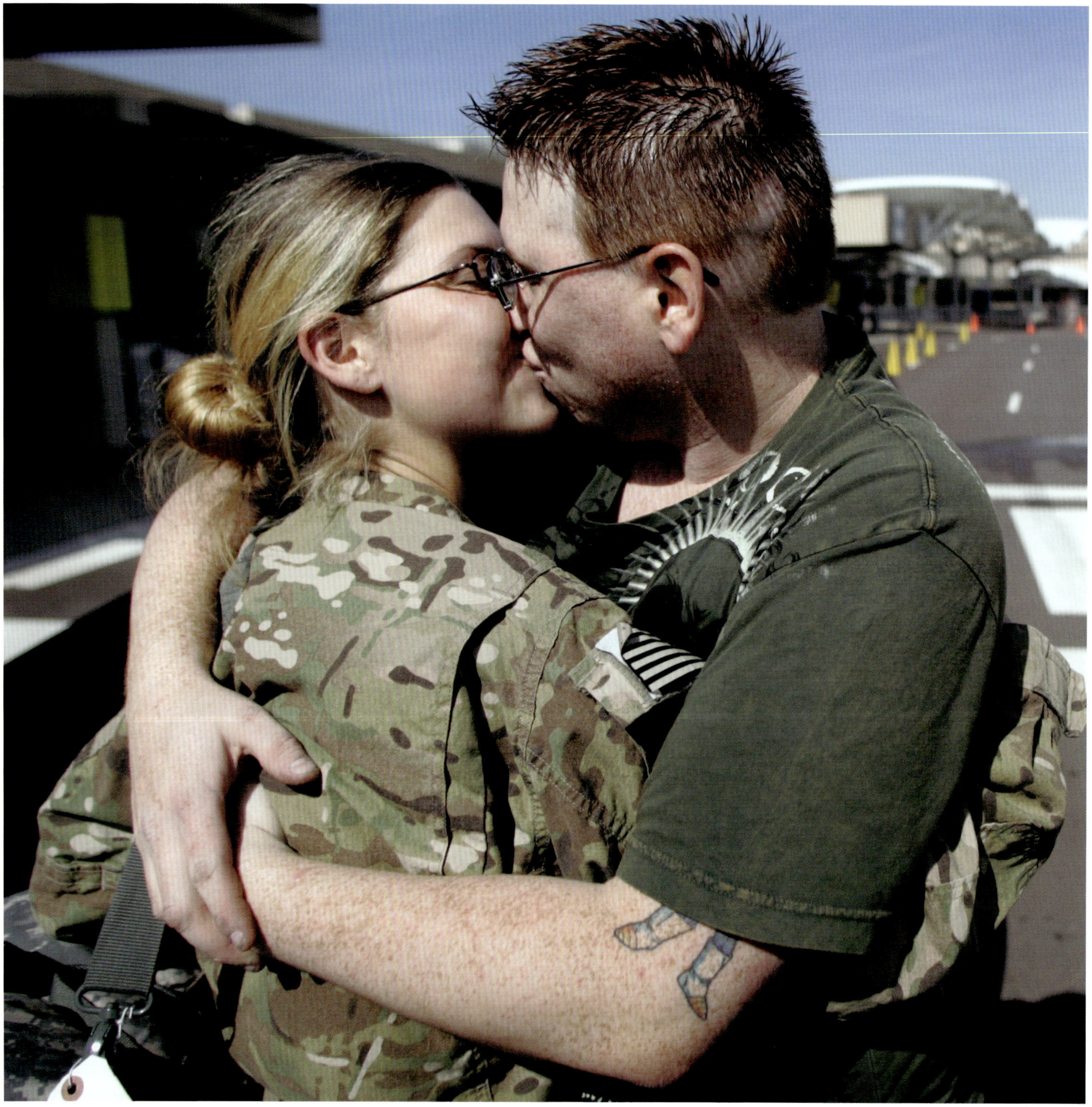

SPC Christina Clausen kisses her husband. Clausen had just arrived at DFW Airport from her duty station in Kuwait for her two-week R&R leave.

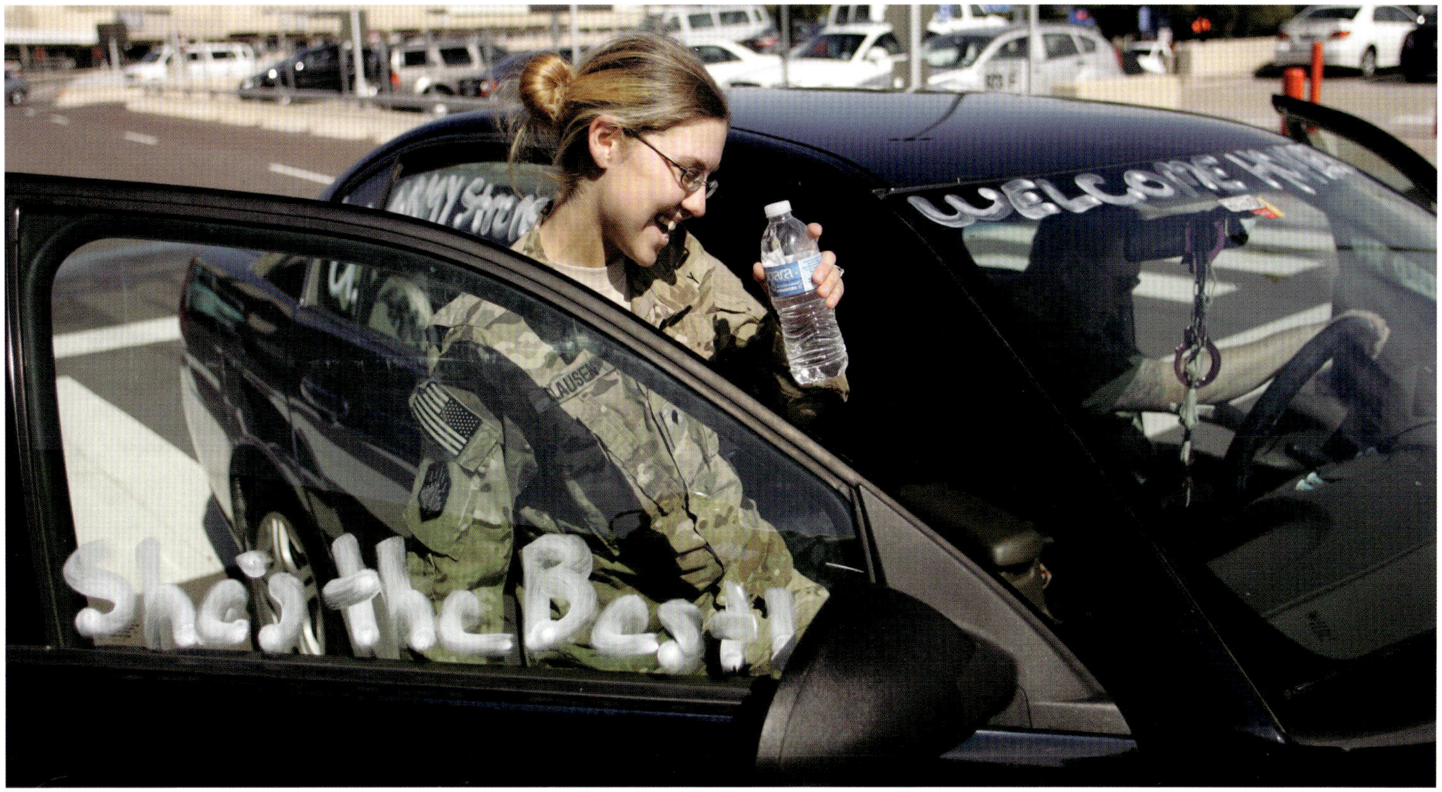

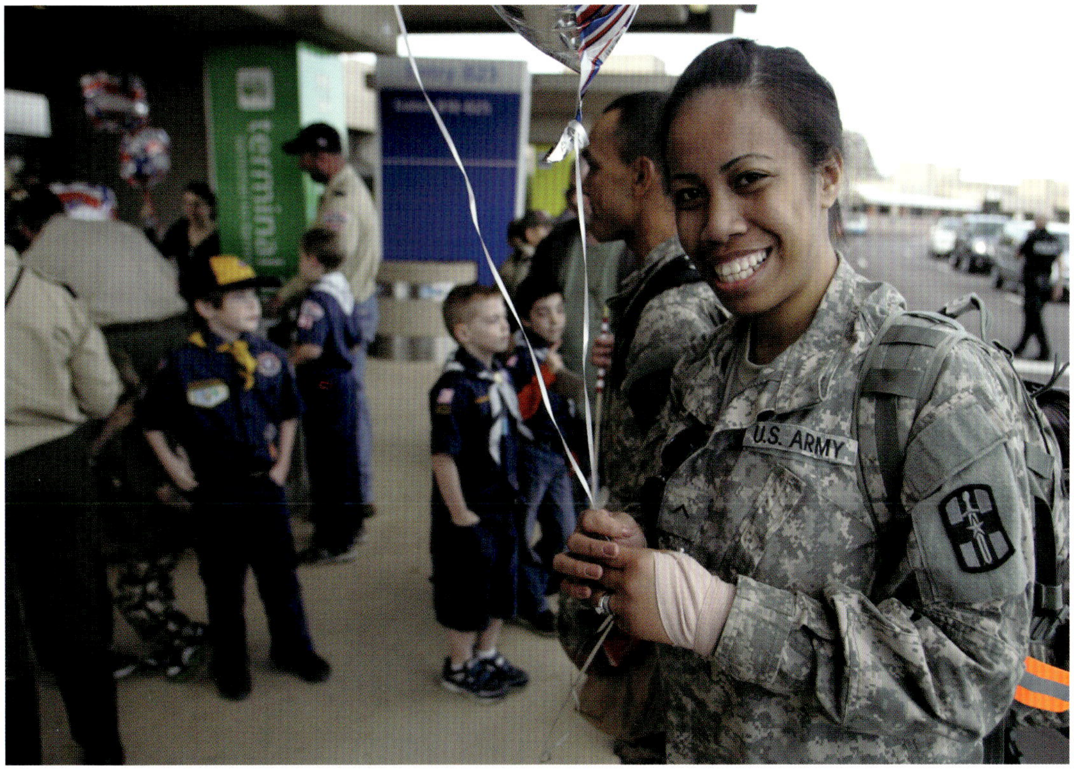

above: SPC Christina Clausen slips into a car being driven by her husband. The mother of two young boys, Clausen had been in the army for two years, with one year left on her contract. She joined the army after struggling financially.

left: *CPL Mary Tauiliili returning to America for her R&R leave and meeting with a contingent of greeters at the DFW Airport. Tauiliili was heading home from her deployment station in Kuwait.*

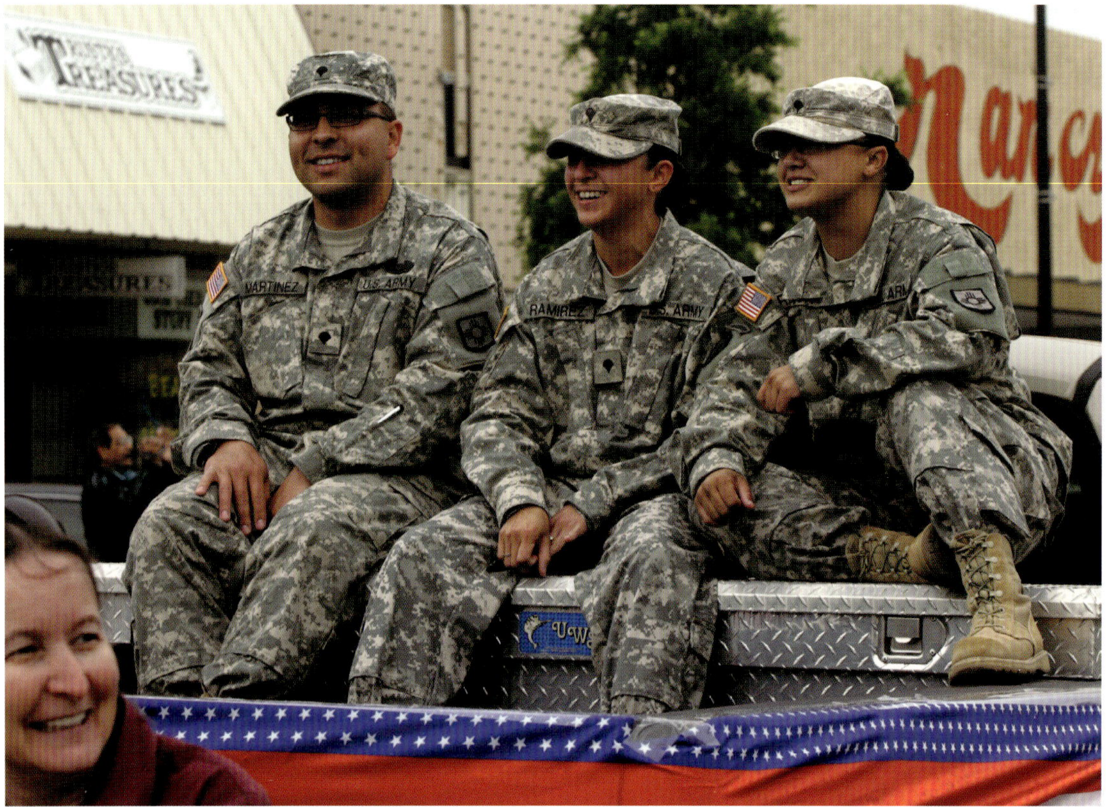

Members of the 920th New Mexico National Guard ride in the rear of a pickup truck in a parade welcoming them home from a year-long deployment to Afghanistan. The parade took place in Roswell, NM.

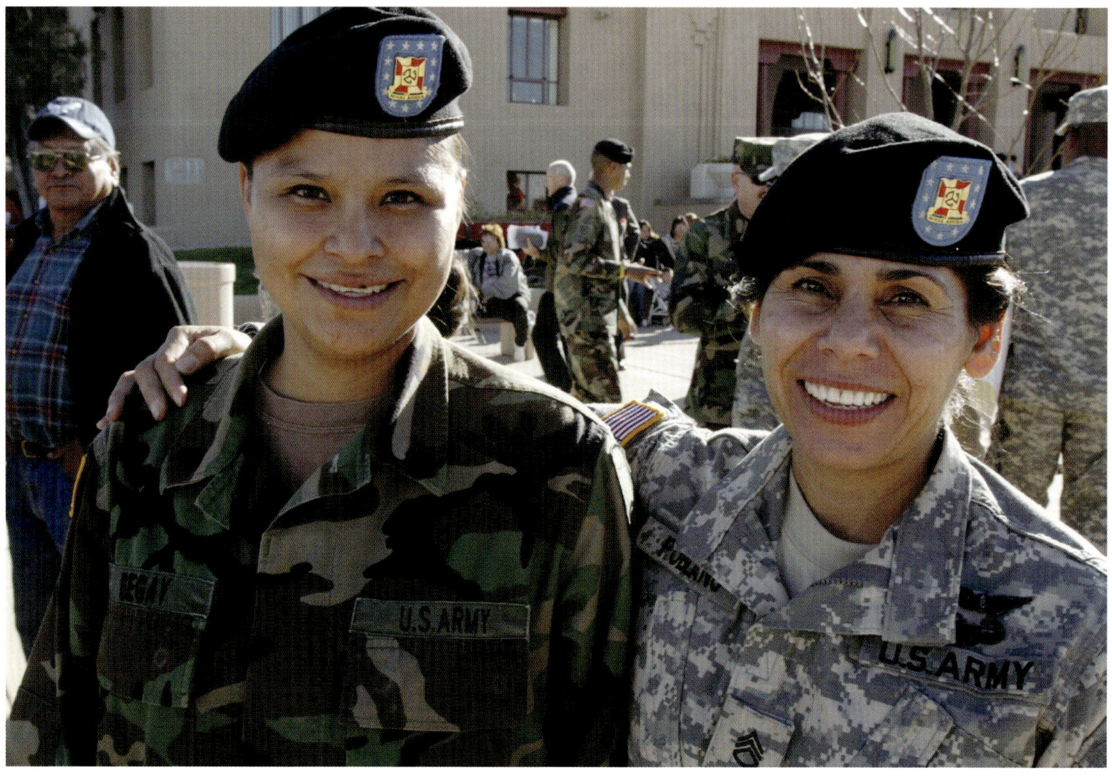

Two Navajo New Mexico Guard members in Gallup at a homecoming event in 2006. Left: Private Phoebe Begay. Right: SSG Dora Poblano.

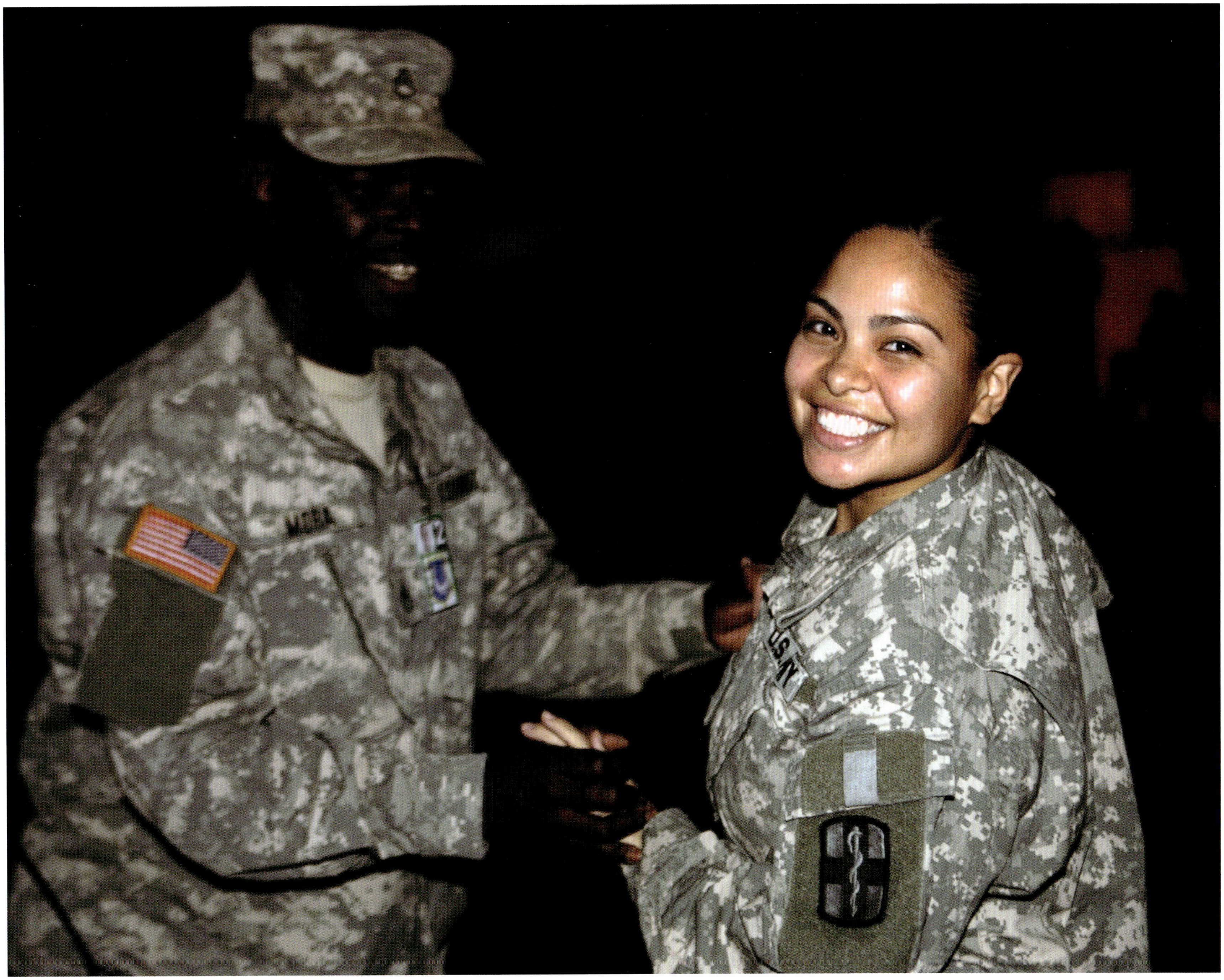

Two soldiers celebrate New Year's Eve at an outdoor dance held at Camp Striker in the Victory Base Complex in Iraq.

Life After Active Duty

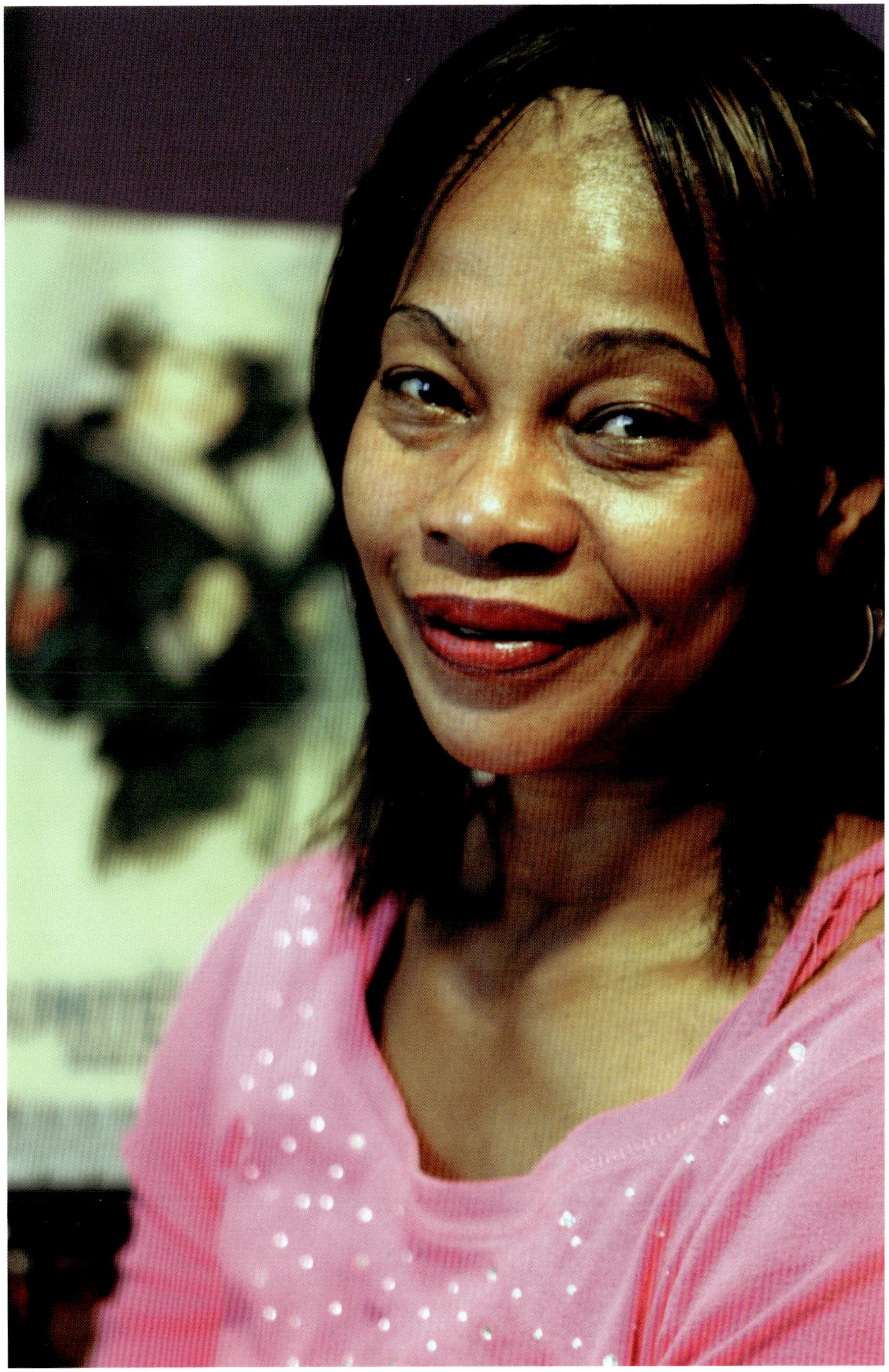

US Navy veteran Daisy Norman poses in front of a WWI navy recruiting poster.

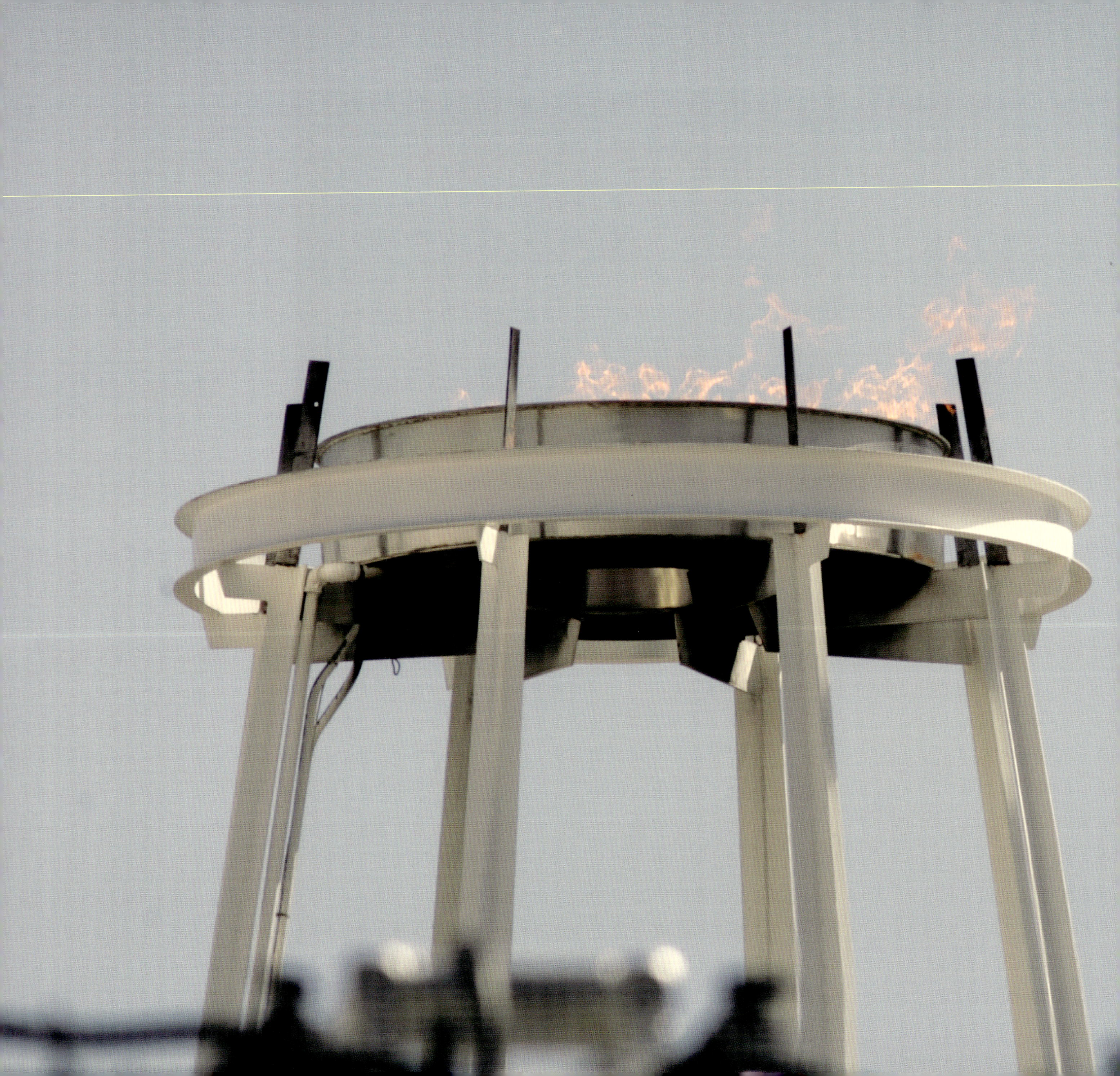

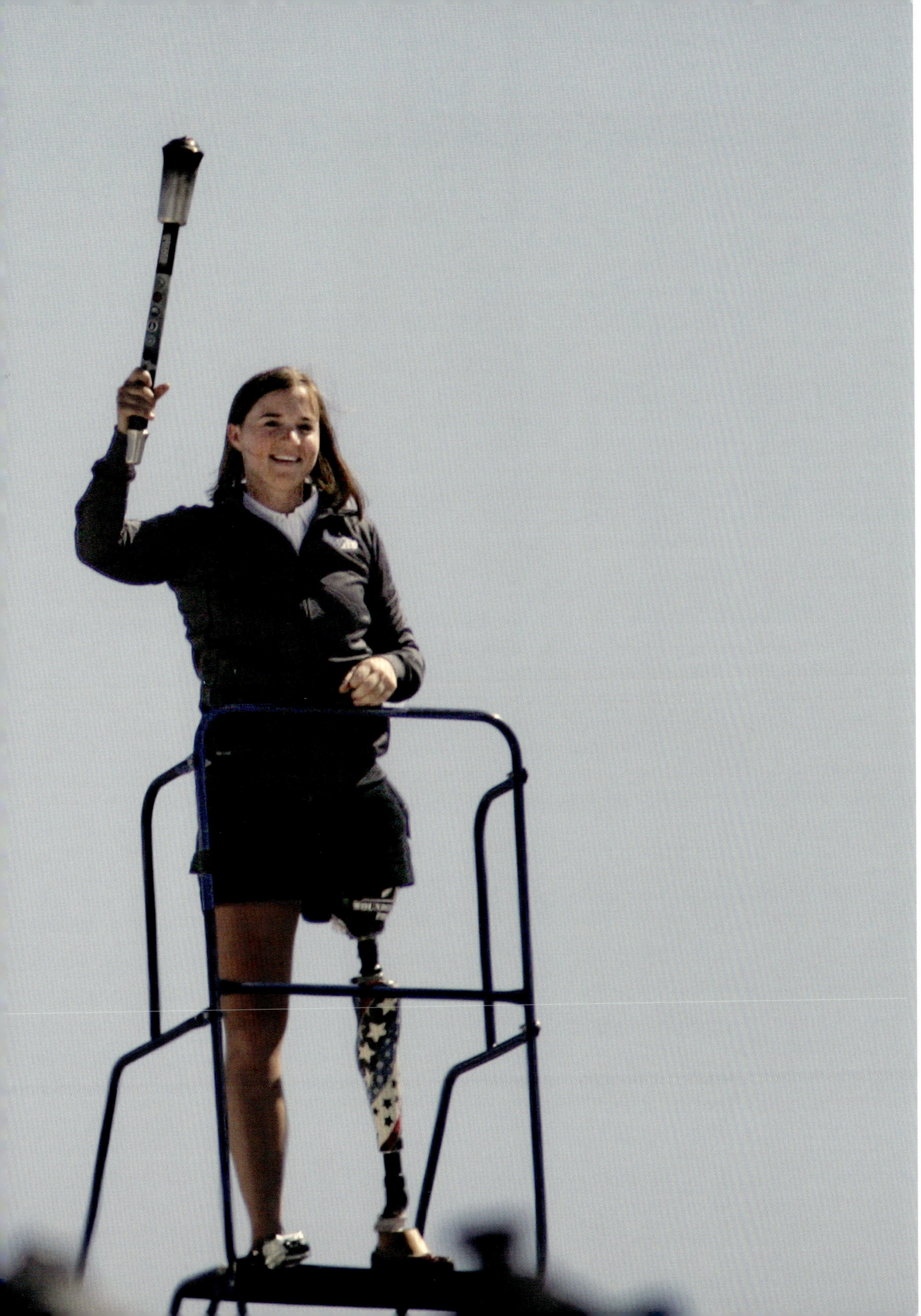

US Army veteran Melissa Stockwell lights the Olympic torch on April 30, 2012 during the opening ceremonies for the Warrior Games held in Colorado Springs, CO.

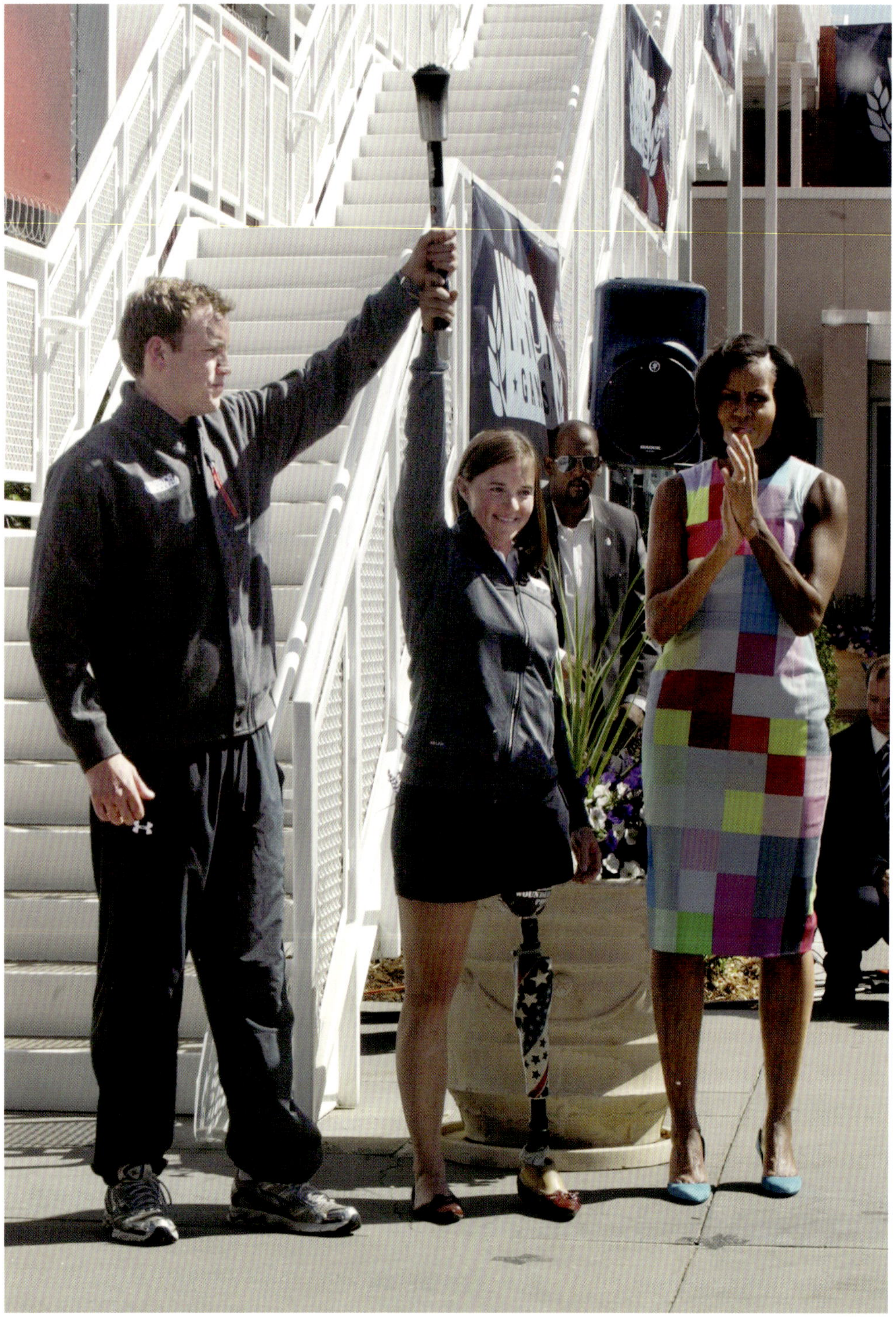

The honorary torch bearers Melissa Stockwell, US Army veteran and paralympian, and Captain Simon Maxwell of the British Armed Forces, hold the Olympic torch as First Lady Michelle Obama looks on during the opening ceremonies for the Warrior Games on April 30, 2012 held in Colorado Springs, CO.

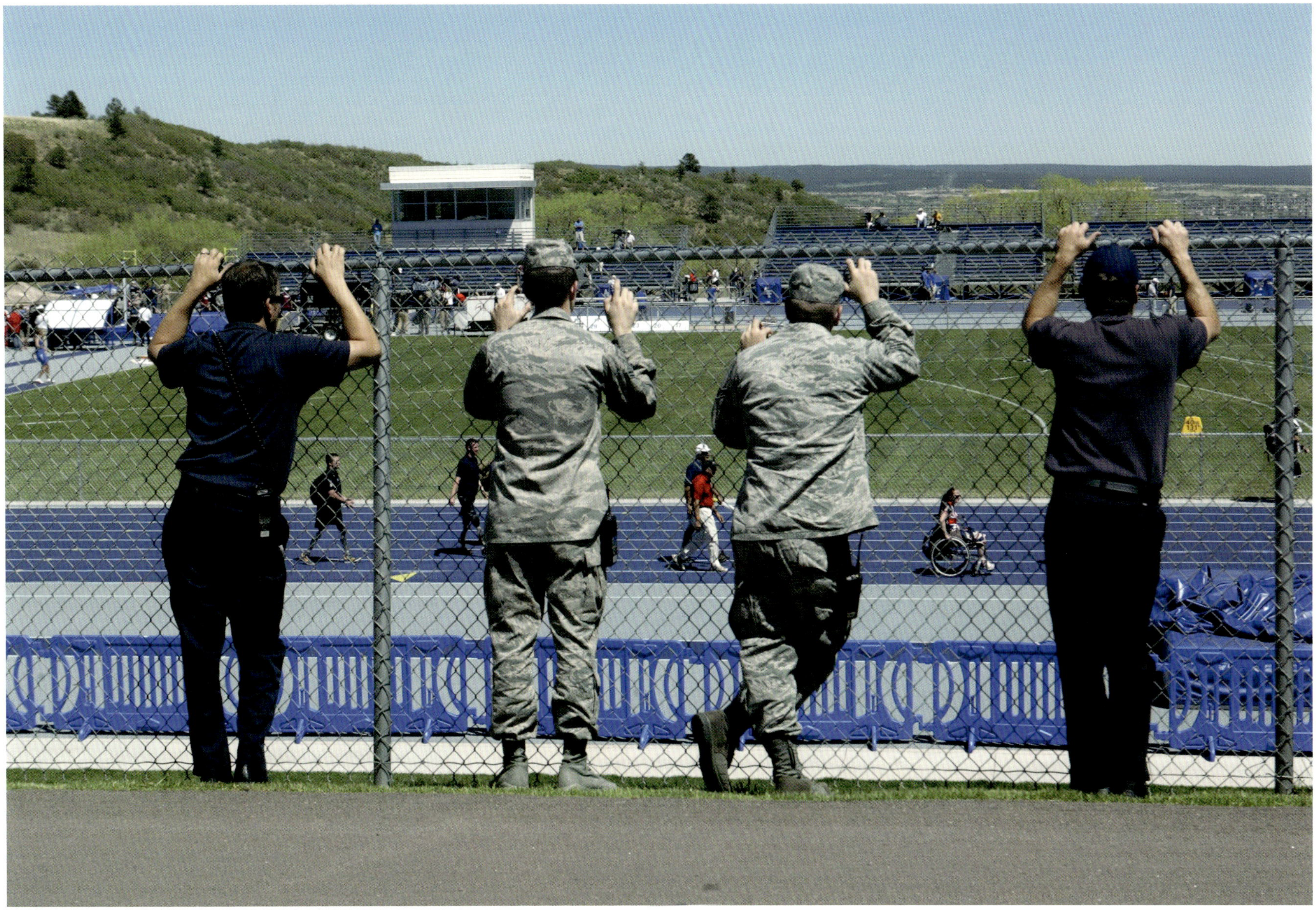

Spectators watch the wrap-up of the Warrior Games being held on the field track at the US Air Force Academy.

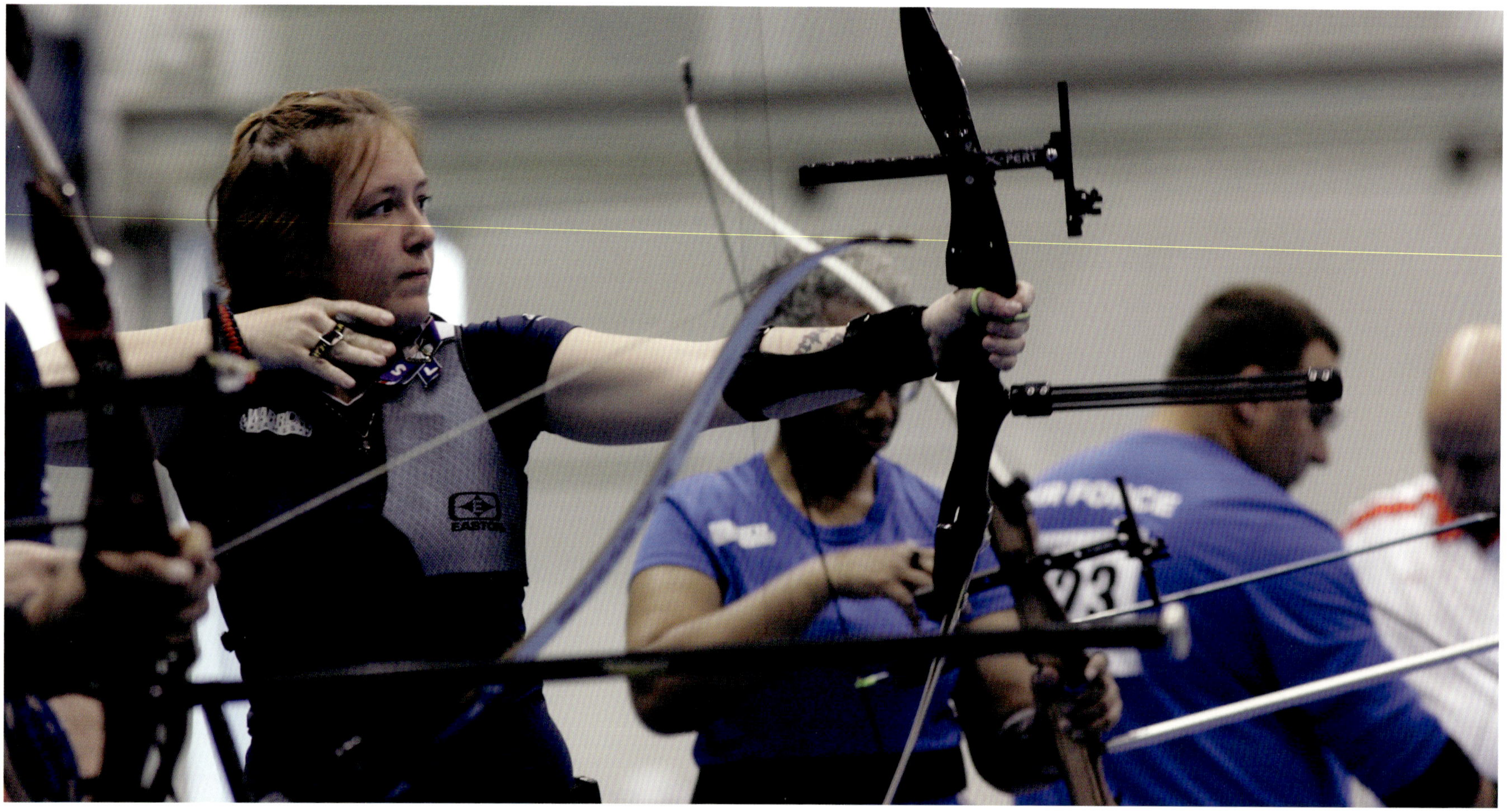

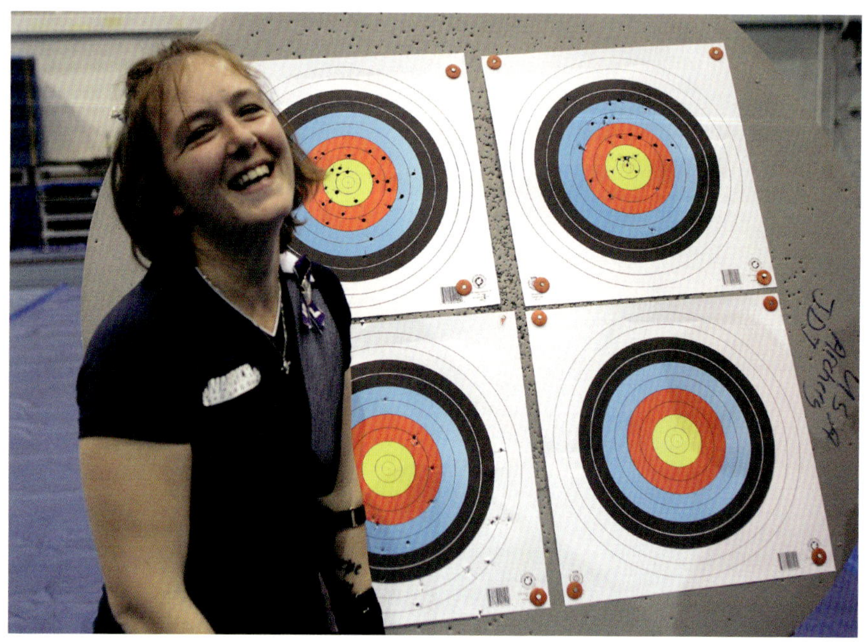

above: US Navy archer Judi Boyce releases an arrow during the Warrior Games in 2012 held at the US Air Force Academy. Having suffered a stroke, Boyce has undergone two brain surgeries.

right: US Navy archer Judi Boyce stands in front of her target during the 2012 Warrior Games held at the US Air Force Academy. She won a bronze medal as part of the Navy archery team.

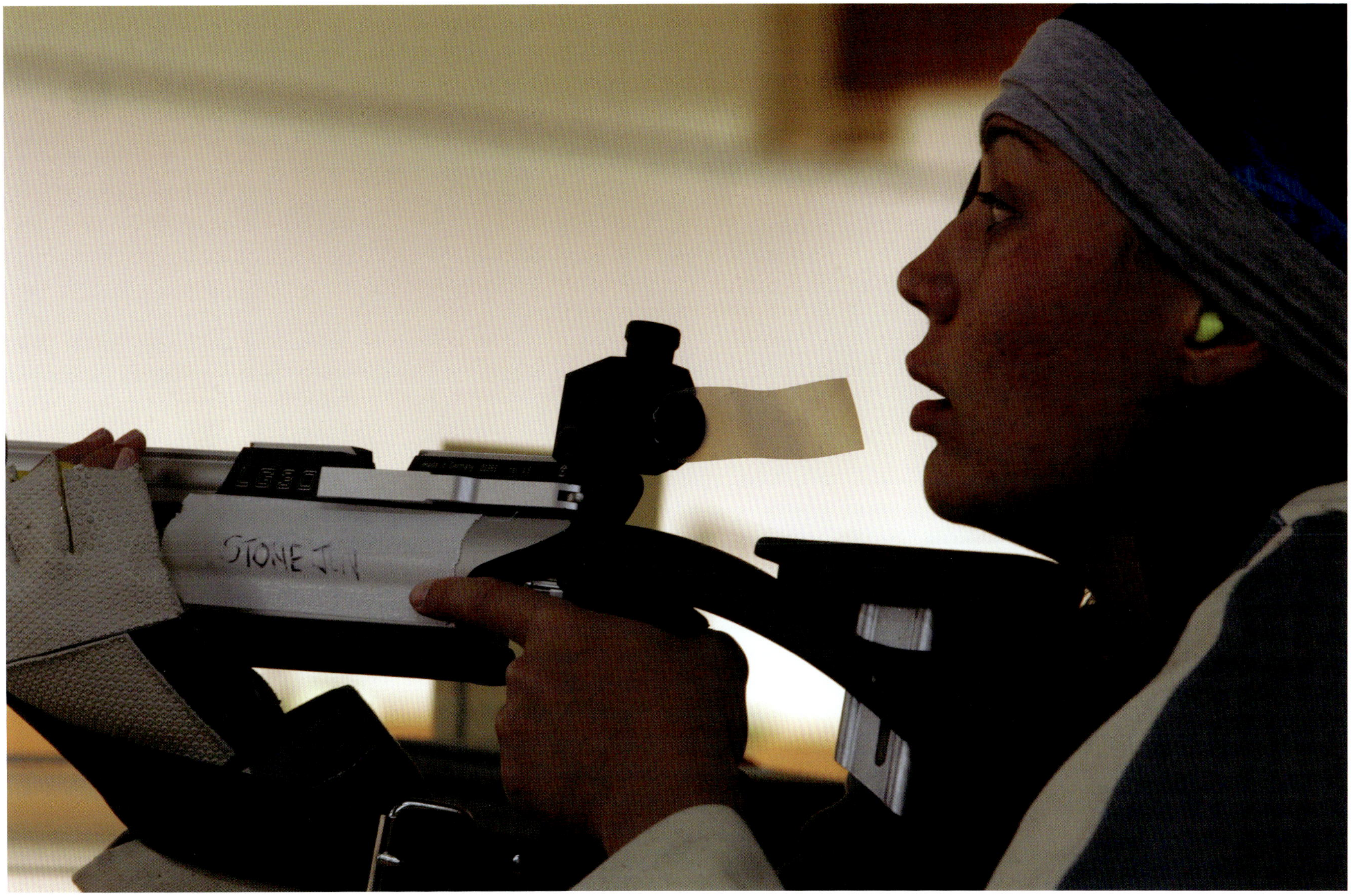

E-4 SrA Jennifer Stone, representing the US Air Force at the 2012 Warrior Games, checks her target during the air rifle shooting competition.

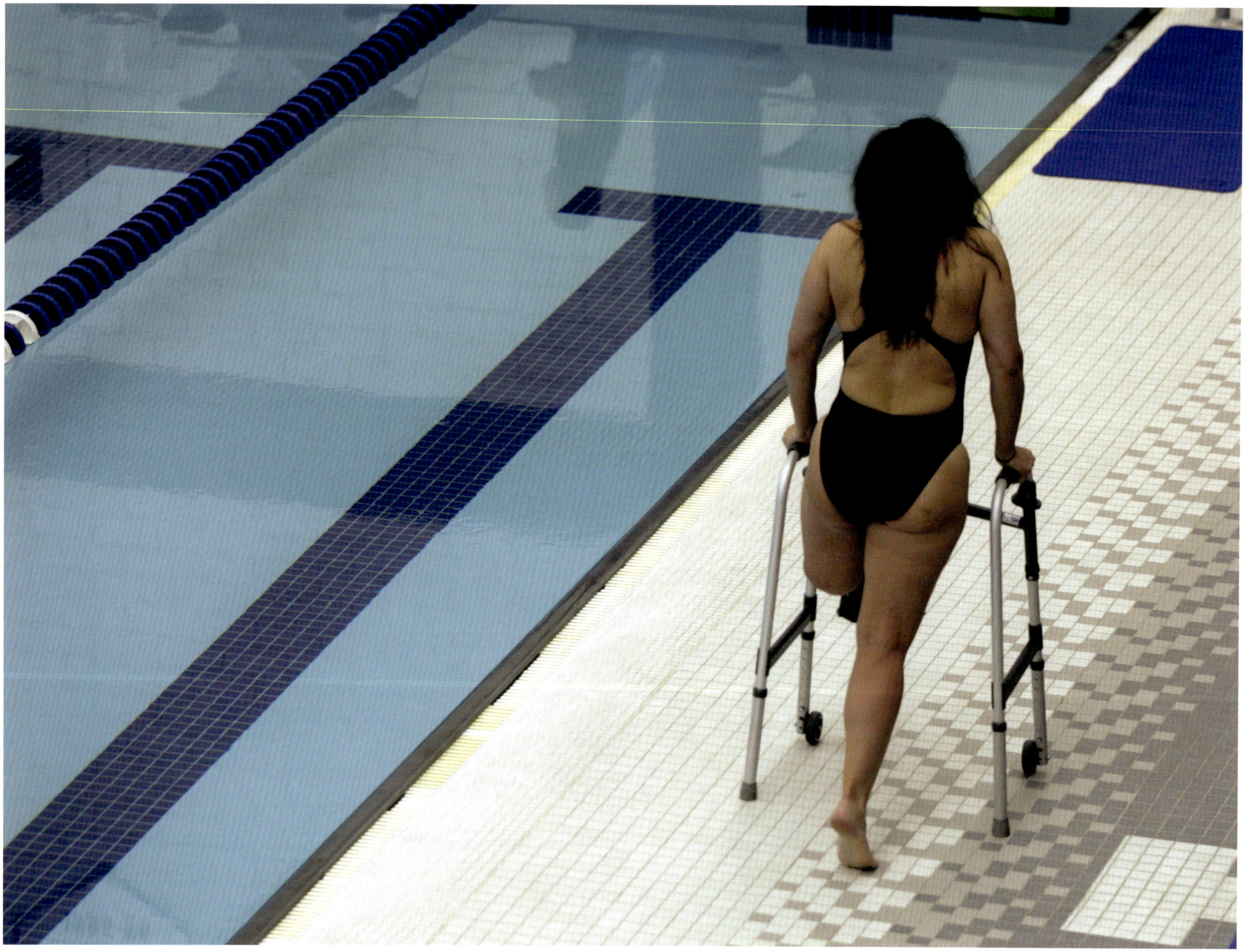

An amputee swimmer approaches the starting point for her race. On the final day of the Warrior Games in 2012, swimming events took place at the US Air Force Academy. More than two hundred athletes attended the competition.

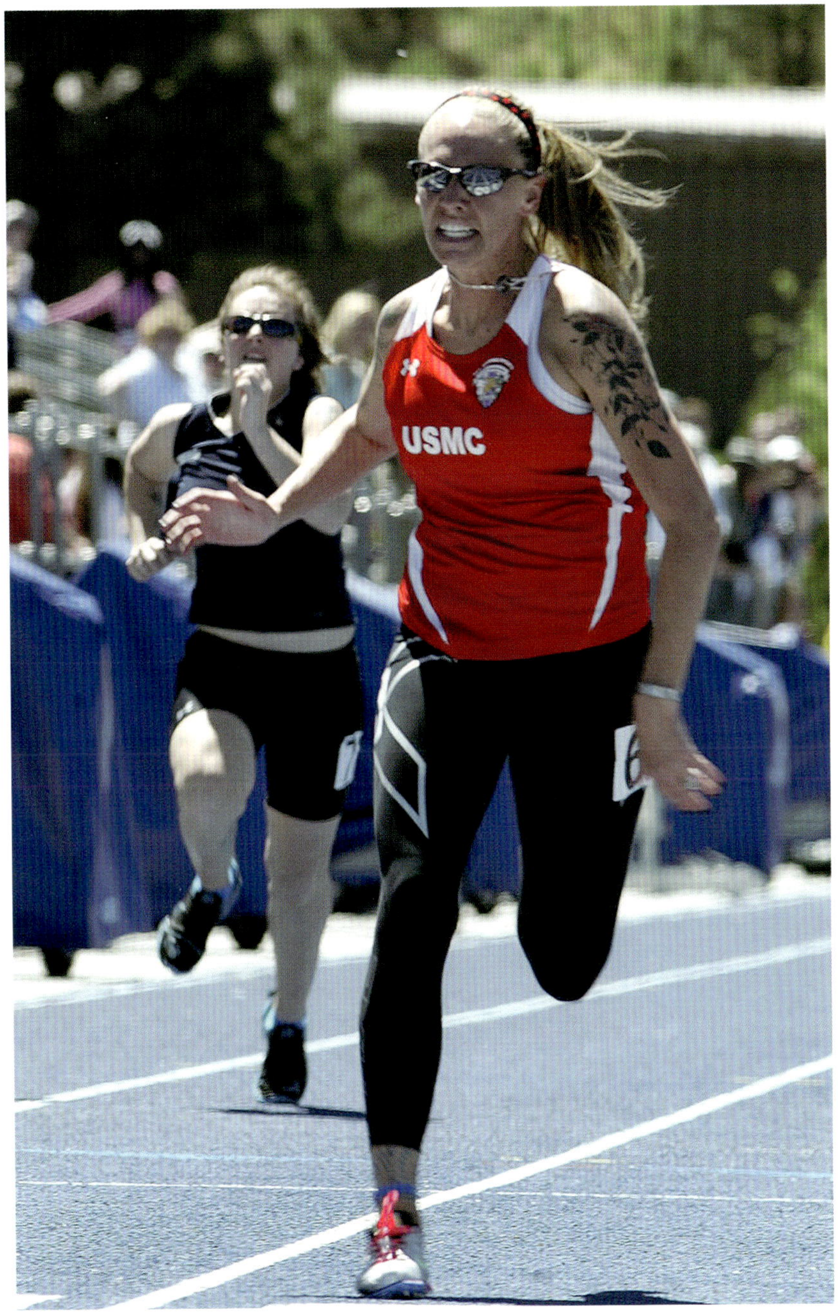

US Marine GySgt Nicole Adams pushes herself to victory during the 2012 Warrior Games held at the US Air Force Academy. Adams won three medals in the track events.

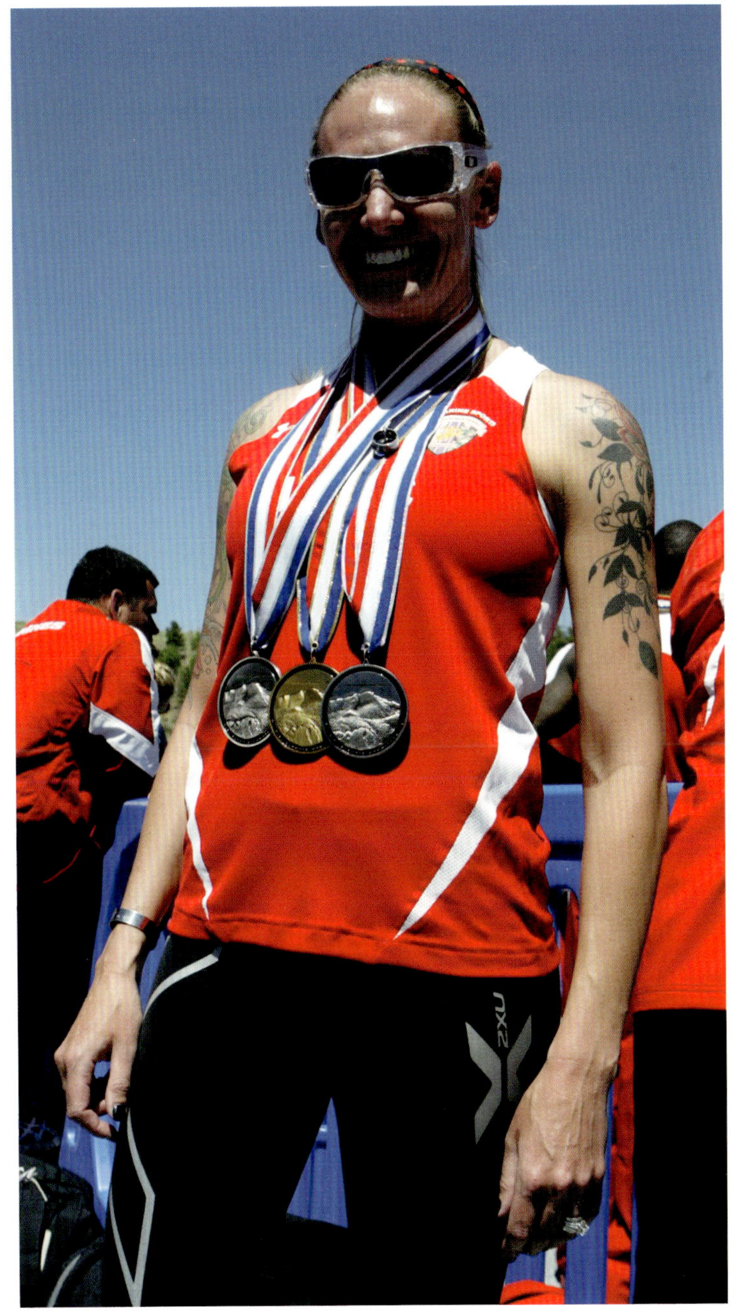

US Marine GySgt Nicole Adams displays her three medals won during the 2012 Warrior Games held at the US Air Force Academy. More than two hundred athletes competed in the games.

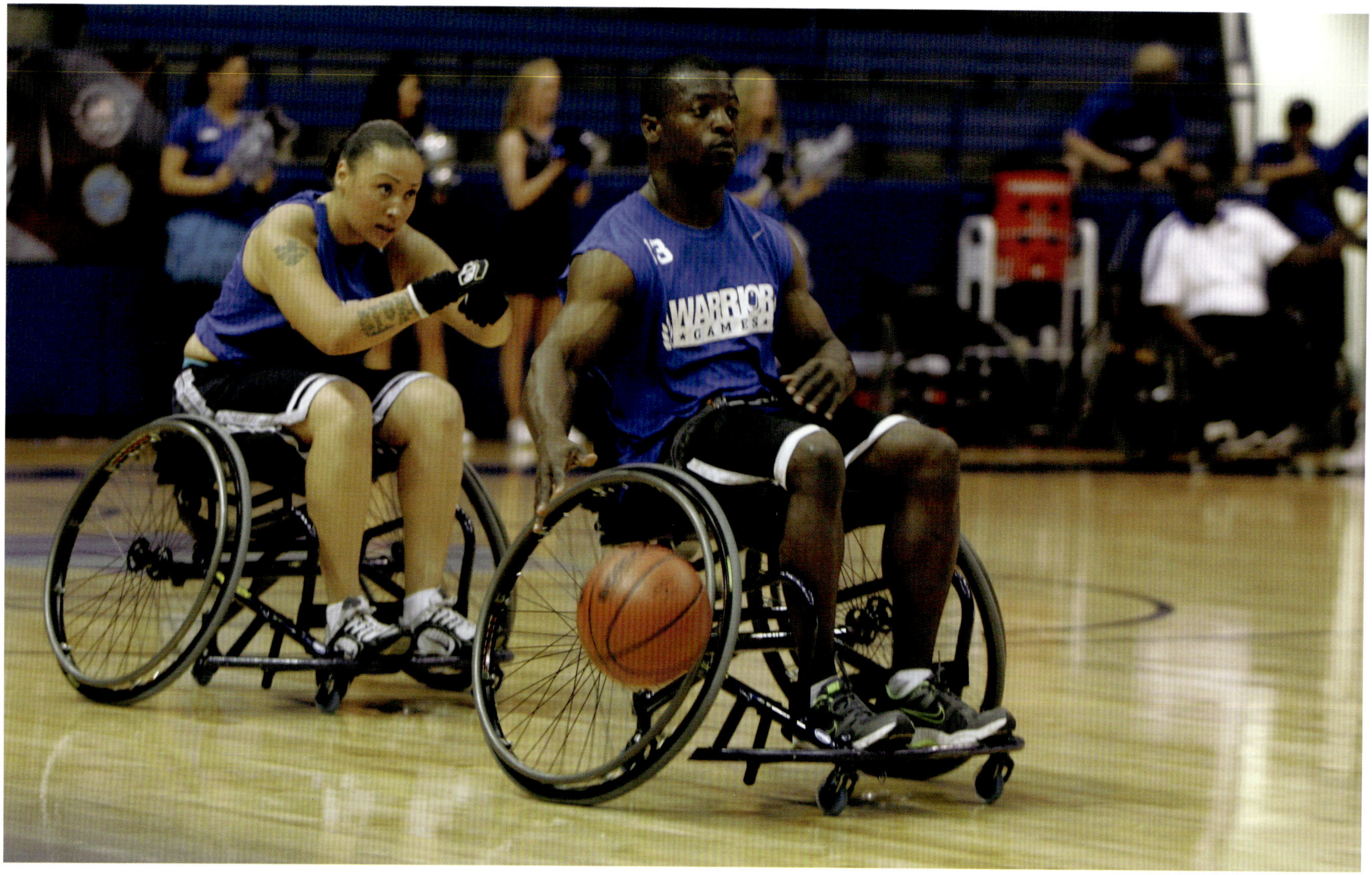

E-4 SrA and basketball player Jennifer Stone follows a team member downcourt during an informal match. Stone is one of more than two hundred athletes who competed in the 2012 Warrior Games played at the US Air Force Academy in Colorado Springs, CO.

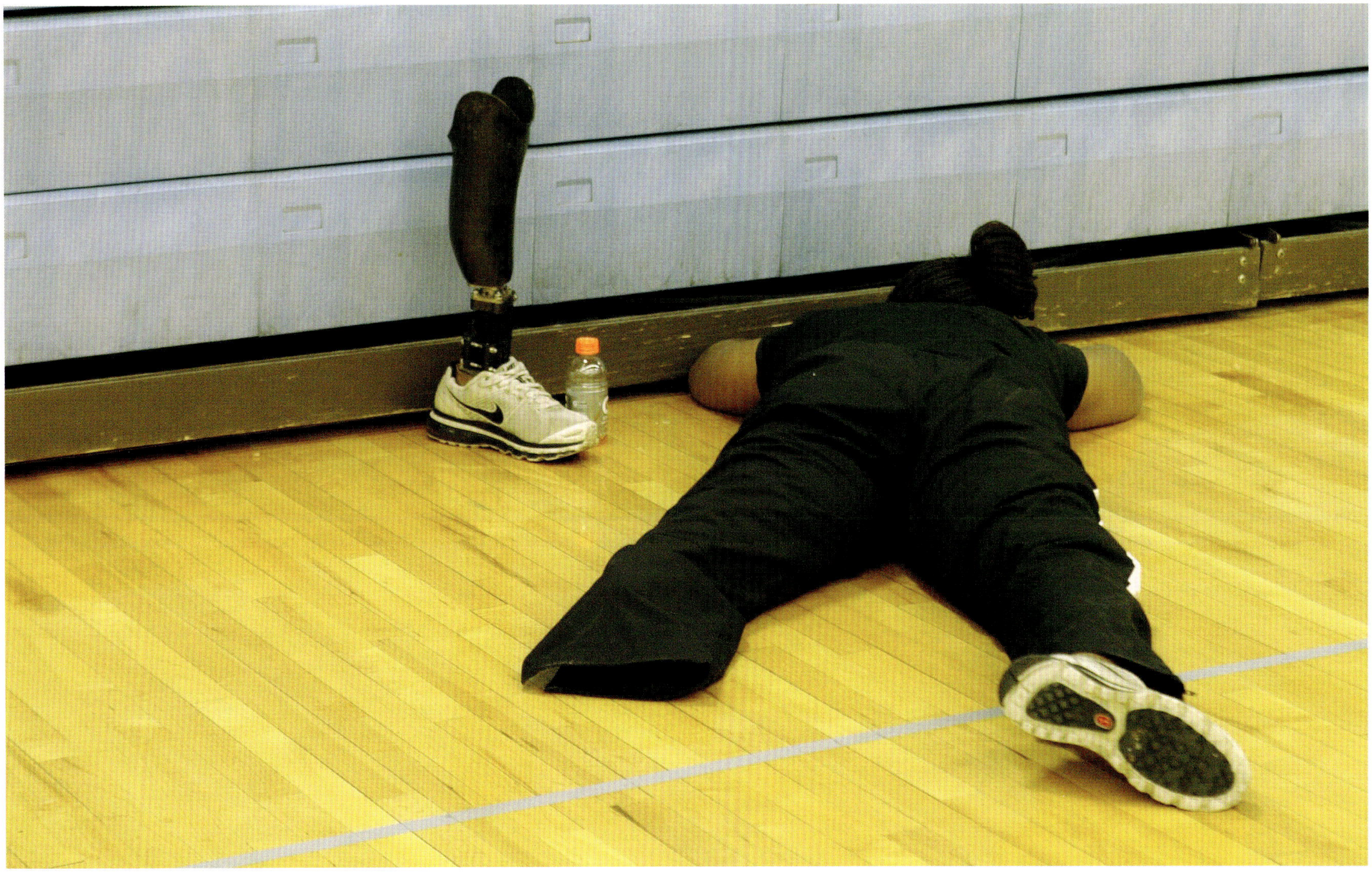

Having removed her prosthetic leg for comfort, a female athlete rests before returning to watch swimming events on the final day of competition. The 2012 Warrior Games lasted from April 30 through May 5. More than two hundred athletes participated in the third annual Warrior Games, held at the Olympic Training Center and the US Air Force Academy in Colorado Springs, CO.

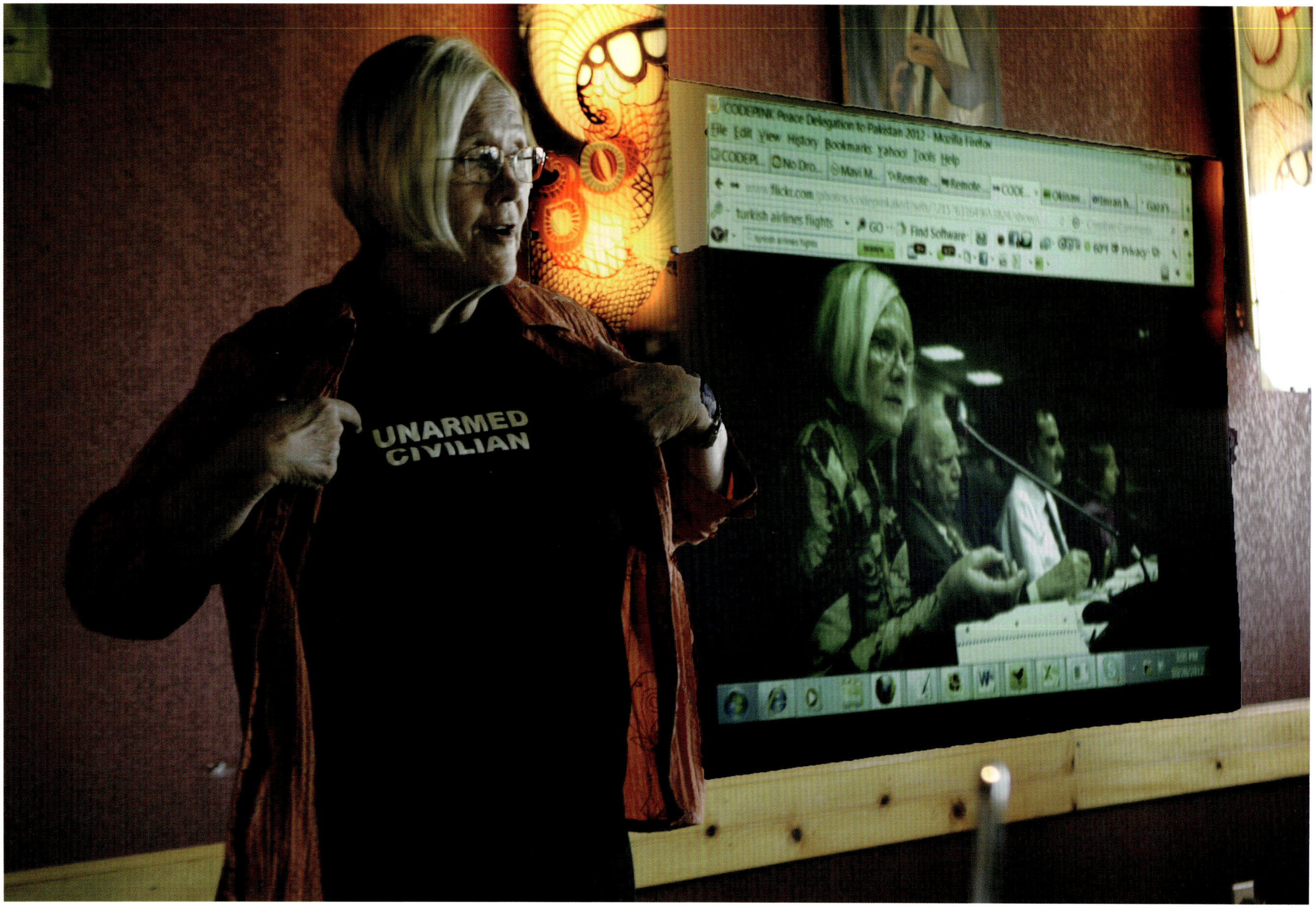

Activist Ann Wright speaks to a group about American drones in Pakistan. The group included a number of Pakistani nationals and Pakistani-Americans. Wright is a retired US Army colonel and sixteen-year veteran of the US Foreign Service. She resigned in 2003 in protest of the American invasion of Iraq, turning her attention to speaking out against drone attacks and on behalf of issues concerning female veterans. She stands next to a screen featuring photos from a recent trip to Pakistan.

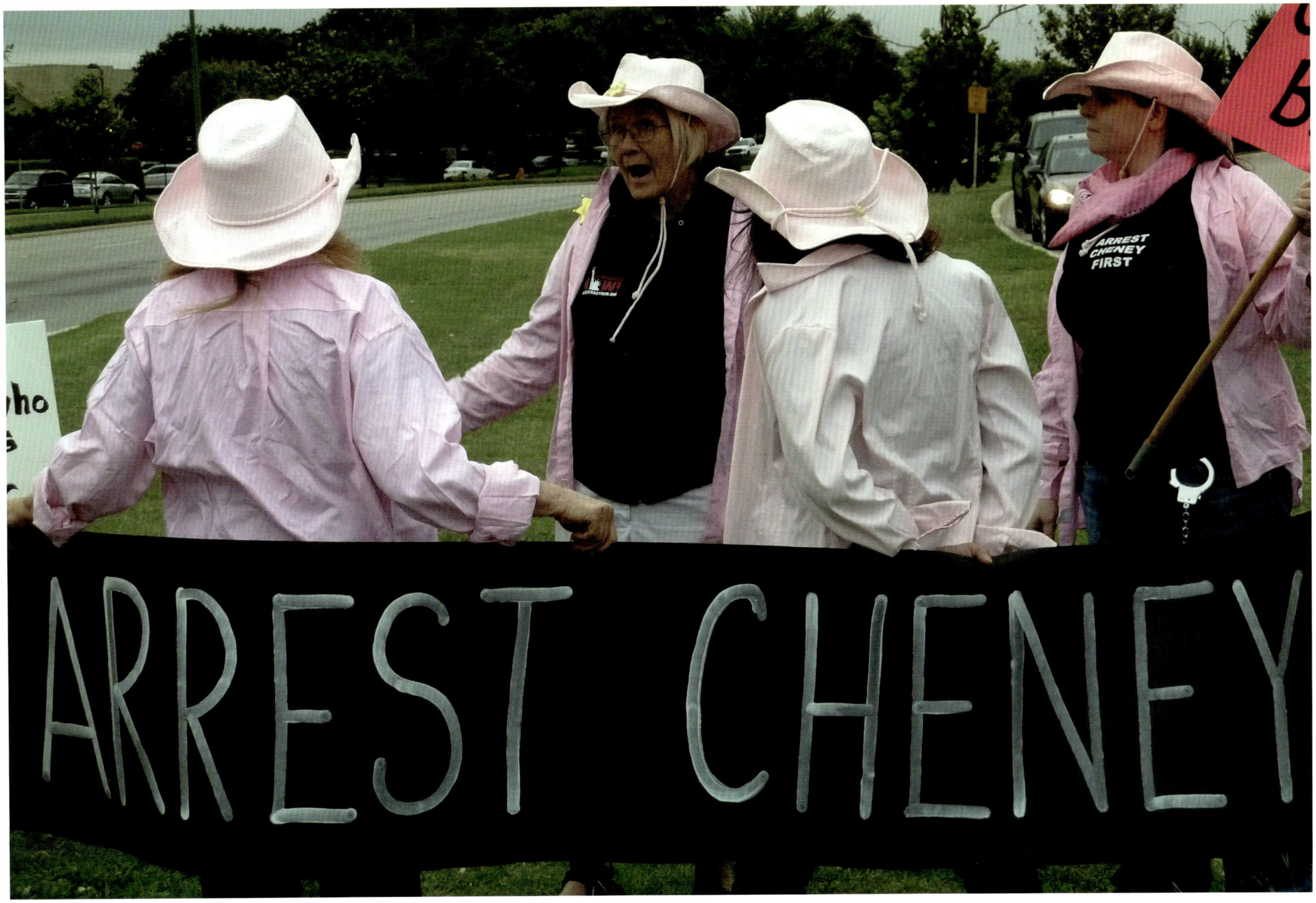

Retired US Army COL Ann Wright speaks with members of Code Pink and Move On, during a protest in Dallas, TX against the presence of former Vice President Dick Cheney and right-wing commentator Glenn Beck, at a fundraising dinner for presidential candidate Mitt Romney.

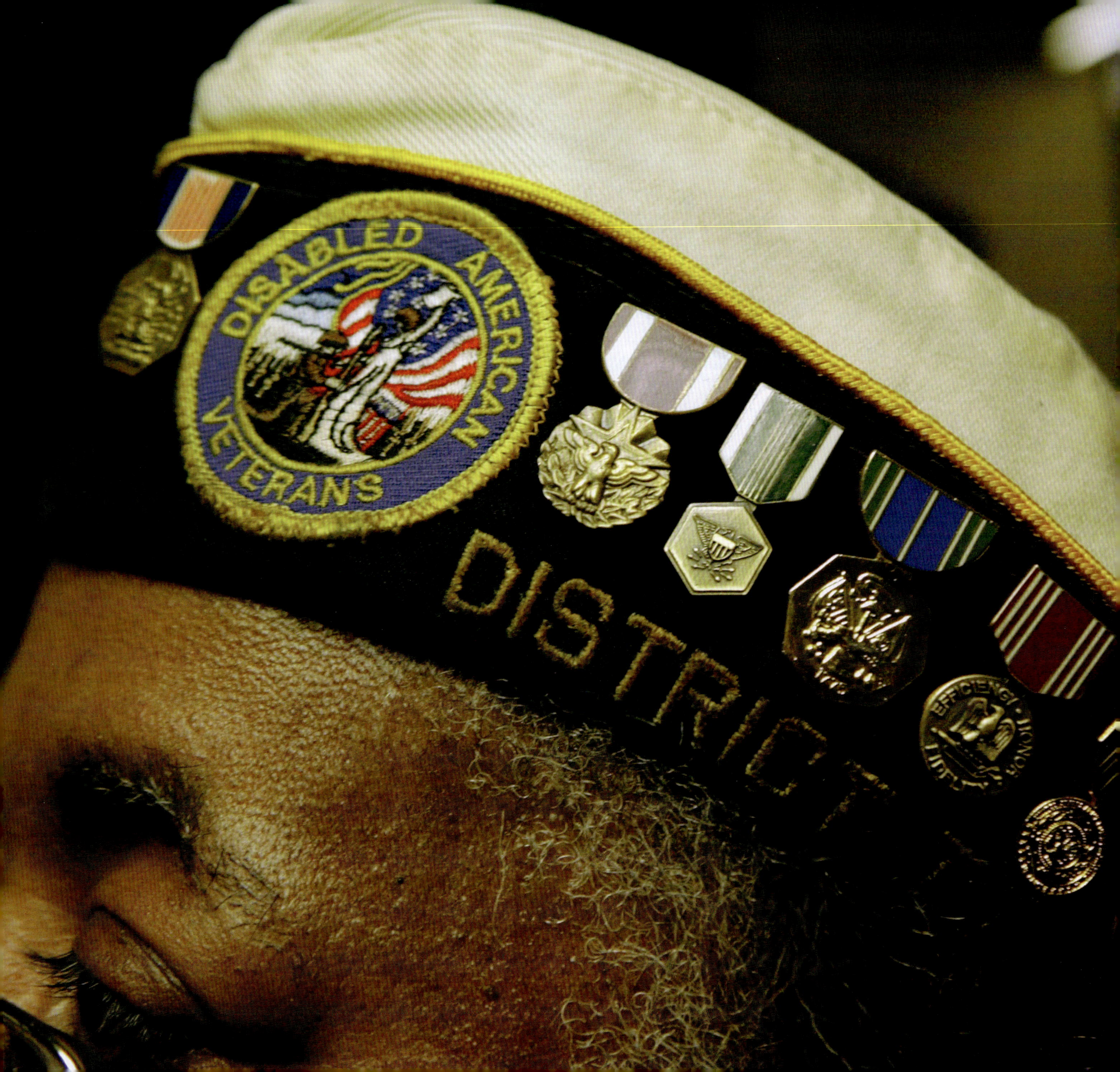
DISABLED AMERICAN VETERANS
DISTRICT
EFFICIENCY HONOR

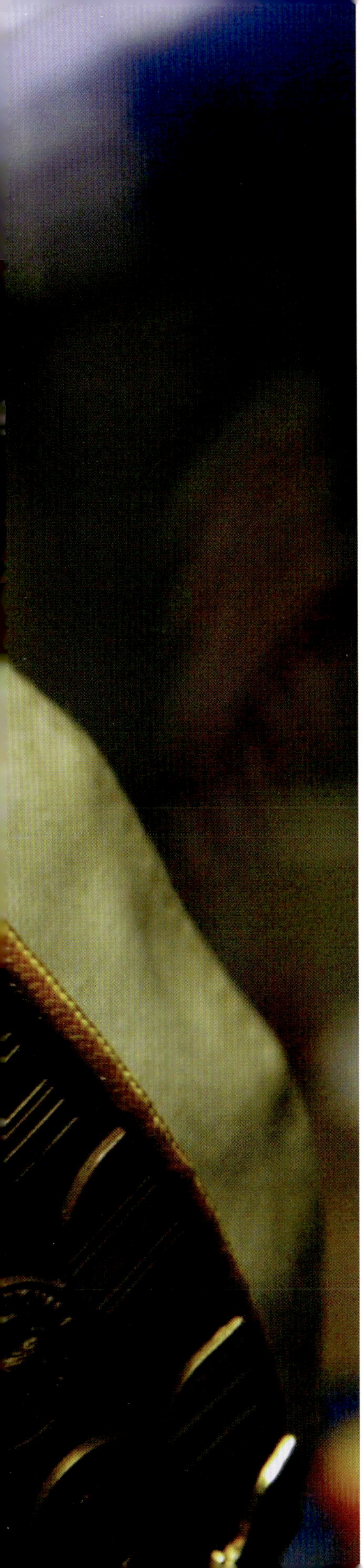

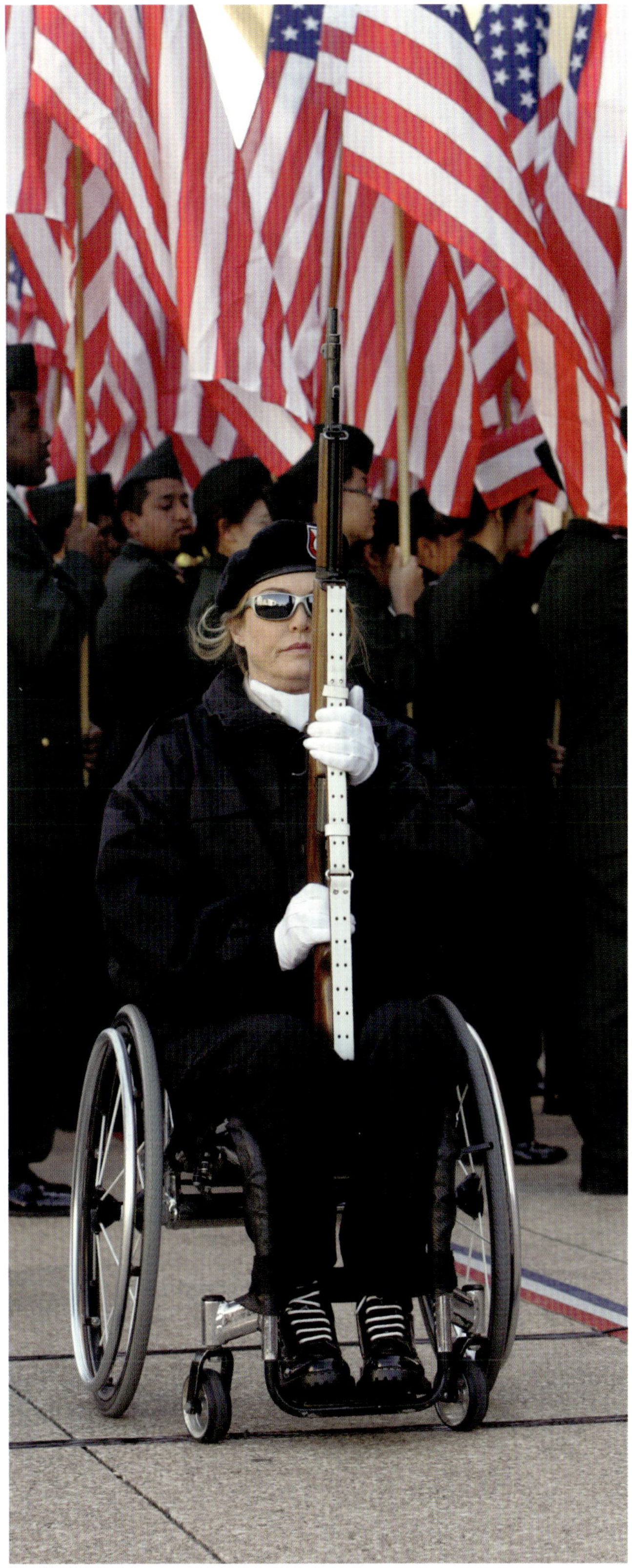

opposite: Details of the hat belonging to retired US Army SG Cynthia Burks. Burks is part of a contingent of official greeters who help welcome home troops as they return from their deployments and arrive at the DFW International Airport.

left: Tricia LaBar, a member of the Lone Star Chapter of the Paralyzed Veterans of America, participates in a rifle salute shoot at the Veteran's Day Parade held in Dallas, TX on November 12, 2012.

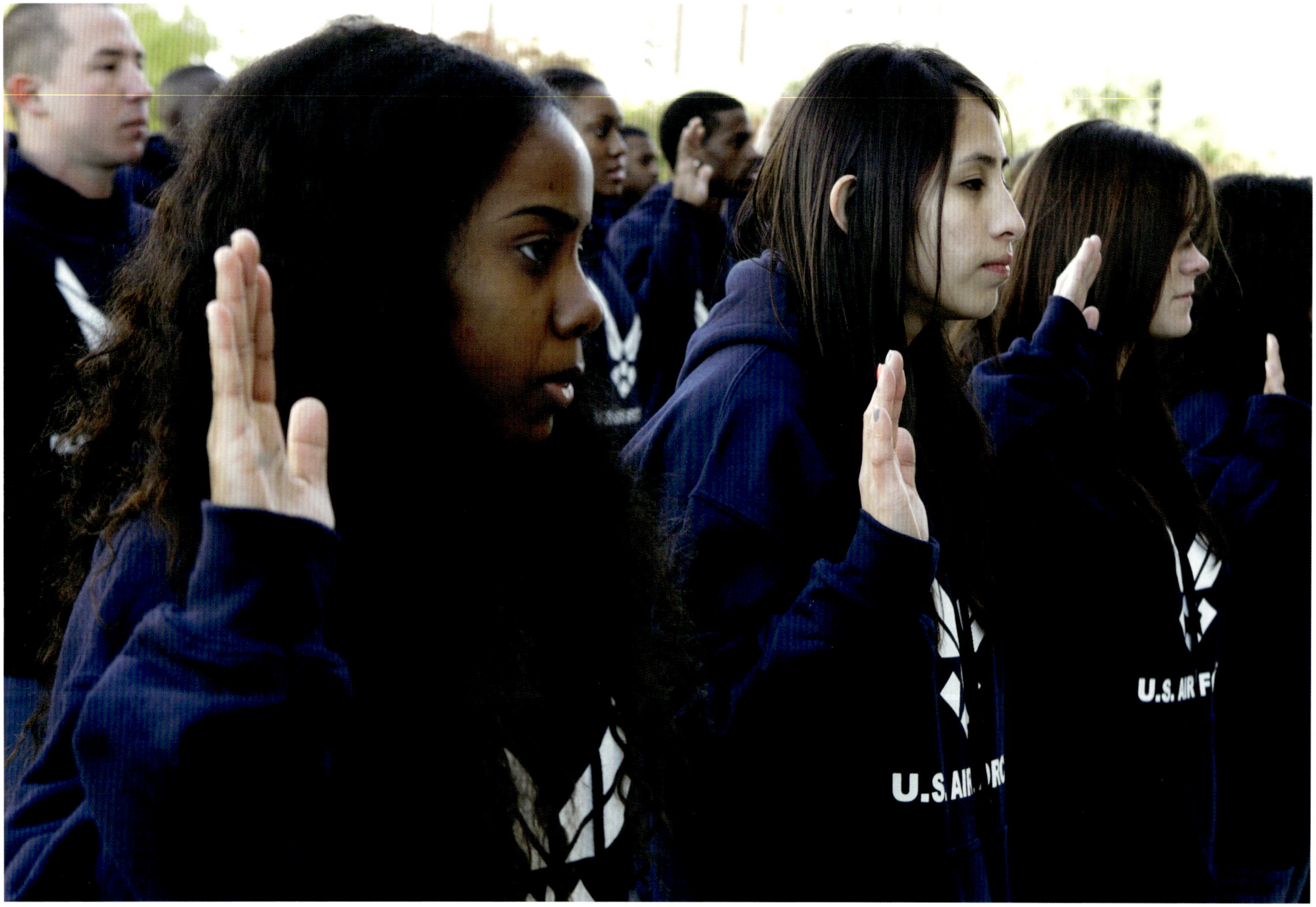

Prior to the Veteran's Day Parade held in Dallas, TX, more than two hundred recruits take the oath required to join American military forces. Typhani Williams, along with two other females, joined the US Air Force on this day.

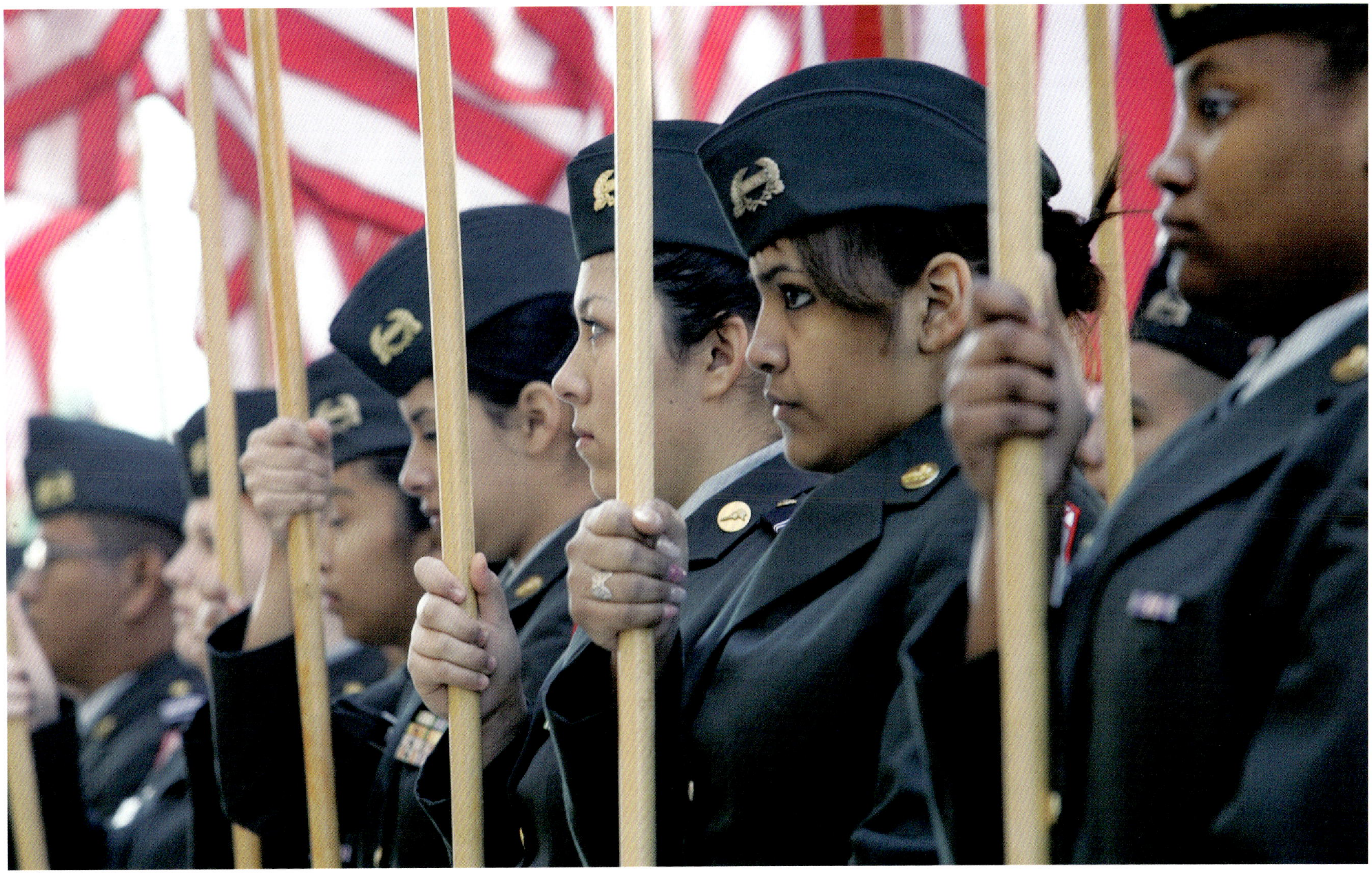

Flag-bearing ROTC cadets stand at attention during the Veteran's Day Parade held in Dallas, TX on November 12, 2012.

With special thanks to the New Mexico National Guard.

Director: Anna Gallegos
Editor: Monika Dziamka
Art and production director: David Skolkin
Designed by David Skolkin
Composition: Set in Bembo and Din
Manufactured in China
10 9 8 7 6 5 4 3 2 1

Library of Congress Control Number: 2023941830
ISBN: 978-089013-681-2

Museum of New Mexico Press
PO Box 2087
Santa Fe, New Mexico
mnmpress.org

page 1: New Mexico National Guard member PFC Jessica Rascon, who practices with a .50-caliber machine gun simulator, undergoes convoy escort practice at the New Mexico National Guard Armory in Santa Fe. The practice took place in a Virtual Convoy Operation Trainer simulator. Inside training goggles and on screen, the simulator displays an animated convoy mission in Iraq. The program includes variables such as IED attacks and small arms attacks. The unit, the 920th Engineers, was about to be deployed to Afghanistan.

pages 2–3: View from the back of a Chinook helicopter over Paktika Province in Afghanistan.

page 4: CPT Ann Savoie monitors the recovery of a young Afghan girl burned in a home accident.